JERUSALEM

KETER BOOKS

This book is compiled from material originally published
in the *Encyclopaedia Judaica*

Copyright © 1973, Keter Publishing House Ltd.
P.O.Box 7145, Jerusalem, Israel

Cat. No. 25067

ISBN 0 7065 1325 8

Printed in Israel

CONTENTS

CONTRIBUTORS

Prof. Michael Avi-Yonah; Professor of Archaeology and of the History of Art, the Hebrew University of Jerusalem.

Prof. Menahem Stern: Professor of Jewish History, the Hebrew University of Jerusalem.

Prof. Haïm Z'ew Hirschberg: Professor of Jewish History, Bar Ilan University, Ramat Gan.

Walter Pinhas Pick: Editor, the Encyclopaedia Hebraica, Jerusalem.

Joshua Kaniel (Mershine); Instructor in Jewish History, Bar Ilan University, Ramat Gan.

Semah Cecil Hyman: Former Minister Plenipotentiary, Ministry for Foreign Affairs, Jerusalem.

Meron Benvenisti: formerly in charge East Jerusalem, Municipality of Jerusalem.

Dr. Elisha Efrat: Senior Lecturer in Geography, Tel Aviv University.

Efraim Orni: Geographer, Jerusalem.

Amihay Mazar: Archaeologist, Jerusalem.

Herrmann M.Z. Meyer (the late): Scholar and Advocate, Berlin, Jerusalem.

Dr. Samuel Abramsky: Senior Lecturer in Jewish History and in Bible, the University of the Negev, Beersheba.

Prof. Joshua O. Leibowitz: Associate Clinical Professor of the History of Medicine, the Hebrew University-Hadassah Medical School, Jerusalem.

Moshe Hallamish: Instructor in Jewish Philosophy, Bar Ilan University, Ramat Gan.

Mrs. Avie Sommer (Goldberg): Staff writer, Encyclopaedia Judaica.

Prof. Hugh Nibley: Professor of History and Religion, Brigham Young University, Provo, Utah.

Gavriel Sivan: Editorial Staff, Encyclopaedia Judaica.

Dr. Bezalel Narkiss: Senior Lecturer in the History of Art, the Hebrew University of Jerusalem.

Dr. Bathja Bayer: Librarian of the Music Department, the Jewish National and University Library, Jerusalem.

Part One

HISTORY

1 INTRODUCTION

LOCATION. Jerusalem is located on the ridge of the Judean Mountains between the mountains of Beth-El in the north and of Hebron in the south. To the west of the city are slopes of the Judean Mountains, and to the east lies the Judean Desert, which descends to the Dead Sea. The geographical position of Jerusalem is linked to the morphological structure of the Judean Mountains, which appear as one solid mass unbreached by valleys, although vales and ravines are found on their western and eastern descents. This unbroken length of mountains turns the city into a fortress dominating a considerable area. Its position at the crossroads leading from north to south and from west to east enhances its importance: only by ascending to its plateau is it possible to cross the mountain. The road through the length of the mountains follows the plateau, and any deviation to east or west meets with steep ravines on one side and deep canyons on the other. This road, connecting Hebron, Bethlehem, Jerusalem, Ramallah, and Nablus (Shechem), is of the utmost consequence, and Jerusalem is located on its axis, at the very point where it crosses the road from the coast to the Jordan Valley. Jerusalem is about 9 to 10 mi. (15 to 17 km.) from the western boundary of the Judean Mountains and only about a mile (2 km.) from their eastern boundary.

NAME. The first mention of the city of Jerusalem is in the Egyptian Execration Texts of the 19th–18th centuries B.C.E. The name is spelled wš mm and was presumably pronounced "rushalimum." In the Tell el-Amarna letters of the 14th century B.C.E., it is written *Urusalim*, and in Assyrian *Ursalimmu* (Sennacherib inscription). In the Bible 3 it is usually .spelled *yrushlm* and sometimes *yrushlym* (pronounced "Yerushalayim"). The city of Salem (Gen. 14:18; Ps. 76:3) is evidently Jerusalem. The Greek *Hierosolyma* reflects the "holiness" (*hieros*, "holy") of the city. It seems that the original name was *Irusalem*, and the meaning of the two words composing it is "to found" (*"yarah"*) and the name of the West Semitic god Shulmanu, or Shalim. The god may have been considered the patron of the city, which had contained a sanctuary in his honor. The popular later midrashic explanation of the name Jerusalem as "foundation of peace (*shalom*)" is associated with the poetic appellations given to the city.

The name Jebus is that of the Jebusite people living in Jerusalem at the time of the conquest of Canaan by the Israelites and the city was so designated until its occupation by King David. The name Zion, whose meaning is not known, at first signified a part of the Jebusite city, probably the king's fortress—the "Stronghold of Zion" (II Sam. 5:7; I Chron. 11:5). King David called this part "David's City" (*"Ir David"*), which at first indicated the fortress (II Sam. 5:9; I Chron. 11:7). With the passage of time, both names became synonyms for the entire city. Jerusalem has many names of admiration and reverence given by the Prophets and later Hebrew poets: "The City," "God's City," the "Holy City," the "City of Justice," the "Faithful City," the "City of Peace," the "Beautiful City," etc.

2 PREHISTORY

The earliest evidence of the existence of man in the area of Jerusalem has been assigned by scholars to the Pleistocene period. Flint implements of the Acheulian and Levalloisian types have been found in the Rephaim Valley. Various prehistoric sites of the Lower Paleolithic period have been found. In the Mesolithic period, which followed, the climate was stabilized in its present form and, due to the prevailing dryness, conditions became much more difficult for prehistoric man in the Jerusalem area. Only two sites are dated to this period. The agricultural revolution of the Neolithic period enabled man to make progress against the desert: 16 sites are indicated for this period. In the Chalcolithic period, settlement contracted somewhat, probably because of the strong attraction of the Jordan Valley and the Negev, which led to a relative decline of the mountain areas.

3 THE CANAANITE PERIOD

It is in the Early Bronze Age that Jerusalem emerges into the full light of history together with a large number of other ancient cities of Canaan. It is one in a line of towns settled on the watershed road from north to south. Its natural advantages were limited; its territory extended only over the basin from Mount Scopus to the Ramat Raḥel ridge, with a westward expansion along the mountain slopes. Jerusalem is mentioned as a Canaanite city-state in the Execration Texts of the 19th–18th centuries B.C.E. In the earlier group of these texts, two kings, spelled *Yqrᶜm* and *Šsᶜn,* are mentioned; one more ruler appears in the later group, but his name is illegible. More information about this period, the age of the Patriarchs, is obtained from the Bible. In Genesis 14:18, Melchizedek, king of Salem, appears as priest of the "Most High"—Hebrew *El Elyon,* a well-known Canaanite deity. Early Jerusalem, in common with many other cities in the Orient, was regarded as the property of a god whose vice-regent on earth was its priest-king. This theocratic dynasty, the members of which bore an individual name combined with *ẓedek,* reappears in the time of Joshua, when Adoni-Zedek was king of Jerusalem (Josh. 10:1).

More information about Jerusalem in the Late Bronze Age is available in the El-Amarna letters. Its ruler at the time was *ARAD Ḥeb/pa;* the latter *(Ḥeb/pa)* is the name of a Horite goddess and the ruler's name was pronounced either *Abdi Ḥeb/pa* or *Puti Ḥip/ba.* In one of his letters to Pharaoh, the king complains bitterly of the Egyptian garrison of Kaši (Cushite?) soldiers in the city and of the growing dangers from the Ḥabiru (Hebrew?) invaders, with whom he and other kings loyal to Pharaoh were struggling. In the book of Joshua (10:1ff.), the king of Jerusalem was the head of the coalition of Amorite kings which fought against Joshua at Gibeon. He was defeated and killed, but his city was not conquered; although the tribe of Judah seems to have taken it temporarily (Judg. 1:8), they could not hold it. The division of Canaan into tribal lots assigned Jerusalem to Benjamin (Josh. 15:8; 18:16) but it remained a Jebusite (not an Amorite) city until the time of David (Judg. 19:11–12), thus cutting the Israelite territory in two and separating the central tribes from the southern ones.

The situation and topography of the Canaanite city have been clarified to a large extent in the course of archaeological research going on in and around Jerusalem for a century. Scholars agree that the earliest city was situated on the eastern slopes of two hills. The only spring in the area, the Gihon, which issued from the eastern slopes of the southern of the two hills, was obviously the deciding factor in the location of the early city. The narrow ridge in the southern part of the hill gave Canaanite Jerusalem a good defensive position; the only weak spot was the narrow northern saddle, and it was here that the city wall was made strongest. Even at a very early stage, arrangements were made to ensure the water supply of Jerusalem in times of siege. A tunnel was dug in the slope, curving and descending by steps in the direction of the spring, for hauling water from within the city. An earlier attempt to sink a shaft directly down to spring level failed because the stone strata proved too hard for the primitive bronze tools. In the course of the excavations at Ophel in 1961, directed by K. M. Kenyon, it was ascertained that the Jebusite wall of Jerusalem passed fairly low down the eastern slope of the city hill and that the mouth of the water tunnel was well within that wall. Canaanite Jerusalem thus had the shape of an elongated oval, apparently with four gates in the four main directions; the western gate was discovered in 1929 by J. W. Crowfoot. In addition to walls, foundations, and water-supply installations, the archaeo-

logical remains of Canaanite Jerusalem include a series
of tomb-caves, dated by their finds (mainly pottery) to the
period from Early Bronze to the Late Bronze Age.

4 DAVID AND FIRST TEMPLE PERIOD

CONQUEST BY DAVID. Recent excavations have thrown new light on the story of David's conquest of Jerusalem (some time after 1,000 B.C.E.) as told in II Samuel 5:6ff. and I Chronicles 11:4ff. Having unified the tribes under his rule, David wanted to eliminate the foreign enclave that divided his own tribe of Judah from the rest of Israel. At the same time, he hoped that by taking Jerusalem—which was practically outside the various tribal areas—he would create a national capital and thus avoid intertribal jealousies. The capture itself was effected with surprising ease through a stratagem involving only "the king and his men," i.e., the standing forces and not the general levy of the Israelites; therefore no one could dispute the royal possession of the conquered city. Opinions differ about both the recorded story of the Jebusites' parading their blind and lame on the walls and the stratagem that led to the conquest. It seems that the parade of the deformed was a magic rite, intended to arouse fear in the enemy. On the other hand, the new excavations strengthen the views of those who regard the *ẓinnor,* or "gutter" (II Sam. 5:8), as the water tunnel of Jerusalem. By getting up this tunnel—which meant scaling in darkness a rock wall several meters high—Joab and his men took the city by surprise, penetrating behind its wall. David did not exterminate the vanquished people; on the contrary, they seemed to have been assigned certain administrative functions. Araunah, who sold David the threshing floor outside the north wall of Jerusalem, where the Temple was to stand, was probably the last king of Jebusite Jerusalem (II Sam. 24:18–25). Having captured the city and defended it successfully

The eastern ridge of Jerusalem, generally agreed to be the site of the Jebusite settlement which became the City of David.
Photo David Eisenberg, Jerusalem.

against the Philistine assaults, David could establish it as "David's City" and the capital of the united monarchy. By transferring the Ark of God there from its temporary abode at Kiriath-Jearim, he transformed Jerusalem from a Canaanite sanctuary into a city sacred to God, the religious, as well as the political, center of Israel, the successor to Shiloh. It was due to this act that Jerusalem became the chief city of the Land of Israel (a position which neither its geographical nor its economic advantages seemed to warrant) and was frequently so throughout the ages. Moreover, in the course of his conquests, David made Jerusalem the center of an empire extending from Egypt to the Euphrates, although it was only in the reign of his successor, Solomon, that full advantage was taken of this fact.

David's buildings in Jerusalem were mainly of a utilitarian nature. He fortified the city, rebuilt the Jebusite citadel called "Zion," and prepared the extension of the city

northward by enlarging the saddle to the north by the

Eastern slope of the city hill (the Ophel), showing the thick "Jebusite wall" at the foot of the ridge (1) and above it the Israelite wall, probably of David's City (2). Photo David Eisenberg, Jerusalem.

Eastern slope, looking north to south, showing the site of the
Jebusite citadel called "Zion," and the terracing believed to be
the Millo ("filling") referred to in I Kings 9:15 and 24. Photo
David Eisenberg, Jerusalem.

"filling" (Millo). The position of the Citadel is disputed: it
may have stood at the northern and most threatened end of
the City of David or at its safest, southern end. David also
built a house for his "mighty men" (his guards), probably
with an armory adjoining, and prepared a dynastic tomb
within the city according to royal custom (all other
inhabitants were buried outside the walls). It has been

claimed that remains discovered in the eastern ridge in 1914 by R. Weill were part of this tomb. David inherited from the Canaanite rulers the "king's vale," a tract of fertile land at the junction of the Kidron and Ben Hinnom Valleys, which was irrigated from the surplus water of the Gihon spring, carried down to its pool (the original Pool of Siloam) by an open-air channel.

UNDER SOLOMON. Under Solomon (965 B.CE.) the economic advantages of Jerusalem as the center of the Israelite empire became evident. Caravans from the Euphrates to Egypt could be directed through the royal capital, while for the Phoenician trade with Elath, the Red Sea, and Ophir a passage through Jerusalem was actually the shortest route possible. Additional factors in the rapid development of the city were the establishment of the royal stores, fed by contributions from the 12 districts into which Israel was divided, as well as of the headquarters of the royal merchants. Moreover, the presence of a chariot force, foreign guards, and a sumptuous court, including a numerous harem, also contributed to its growth. The cosmopolitan character of the city at that period was emphasized by the construction, on a hill outside the city, of sanctuaries to foreign gods, which was later accounted as one of Solomon's sins.

The construction of the First Temple and the adjoining royal palace by Solomon gave Jerusalem a unique character, a combination of a holy city with a royal city. The Temple (erected on the summit of the eastern hill just north of the royal palace), although small in dimensions, was famous for its costly materials and technical perfection. It was included in the circuit of the city walls by an extension northward, which brought Jerusalem on the eastern hill to another saddle. It is possible that at that time the saddle was already fortified by towers, later on known as the Tower of Hammeah and the Tower of Hananel (Neh. 12:39). The royal palace, the largest building in the city, occupied the entire span between the two valleys, north of David's City. Besides the throne room and the House of the Forest of

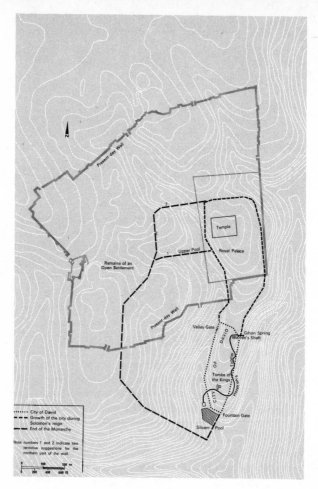

Map 1. Jerusalem at the time of the First Temple. The extension of the city at the end of the Monarchy is the suggestion of N. Avigad in *Israel Exploration Journal,* Vol. 20, 1970, p. 129ff., Figure 3.

Lebanon (guard and chariotry quarters), it had an inner court of women; attached to it was the special palace on the Millo, which housed the princess of Egypt, politically Solomon's most important spouse.

UNDER THE KINGS OF JUDAH. When the united monarchy split in about 930 B.C.E., after Solomon's death, Jerusalem remained the seat of the Davidic dynasty and the capital of the smaller Kingdom of Judah. This territorial decline was accompanied by a corresponding one in economic life. Shishak king of Egypt did not take Jerusalem during his invasion of Judah (c. 925 B.C.E.), but the ransom paid to avoid capture further impoverished the city. Jerusalem derived one advantage from the split between Israel and Judah: many priests and levites, expelled from the Northern Kingdom by Jeroboam, returned to Judah and Jerusalem and "strengthened the Kingdom of Judah" (II Chron. 11:13–17). The situation remained unchanged until the reign of Omri king of Israel (ninth century B.C.E.), when peace was made with the Northern Kingdom and the trade routes opened. Foreign influence followed in the wake of the alliance with Israel; in the days of queen Athaliah, Jerusalem was the center of a revived Baalism. The coup d'état carried out by the high priest Jehoiada (II Kings 11) put an end to such backslidings. In the reign of Amaziah (798–785 B.C.E.), Jerusalem was captured by king Jehoash of Israel, who broke down 400 cubits of its northern wall. Uzziah, who remained true to the alliance with Israel, repaired the breach and strengthened the walls: "And he made in Jerusalem engines, invented by skillful men, to be on the towers and upon the corners wherewith to shoot arrows and great stones" (II Chron. 26:15). It was in the time of Uzziah (8th century B.C.E.) that the voice of the prophet Isaiah was heard in the city, making it the center not only of Temple worship but also of moral and social regeneration (Isa. 1:1).

Uzziah's successor, Ahaz, attempted to curry favor with Assyria by building an altar in the Assyrian fashion and encouraging Babylonian astral cults in Jerusalem. His son

Hezekiah, counseled by Isaiah, prevailed against Assyrian influences. During his reign the Temple was purified and repaired (a prior repair was made under Joash). In anticipation of an Assyrian assault, Hezekiah reinforced the walls of Jerusalem and included in the city part of the western hill, the *Mishneh* (II Kings 22:14) or "second" Jerusalem, which was already settled in his time. Remains of the "other wall" built by him (II Chron. 32:5) have been found recently. He also cut the famous tunnel under David's City, through which the waters of Gihon flowed within the town. The Assyrian army under Sennacherib did indeed besiege Jerusalem in 701 B.C.E., but some kind of disaster in the Assyrian camp forced Sennacherib to agree to a treaty with Hezekiah, which left Jerusalem safe. Hezekiah was the last king buried in the Davidic tomb, in its upper passage. His son Manasseh built, according to II Kings, altars to the "host of Heaven" and the Baalim (21:3–5, 7). The Chronicler adds the story of Manasseh's captivity and repentance, after which he removed all the pagan altars and idols he had set up and "restored the altar of the Lord" (II Chron. 33:15–16). He was then able to add to the walls of Jerusalem and to strengthen them in many directions (II Chron. 33:14). Of the brief reign of Amon, who followed Manasseh, nothing of note for the history of Jerusalem is recorded.

In the reign of Josiah, Jerusalem returned to its historical religious function. After the fall of both the Northern Kingdom of Israel and Assyria, it again became the spiritual focus of the entire remnant of the nation. After Josiah's death in the battle of Megiddo (609 B.C.E.), his weak successors vacillated between Egypt and Babylon. After the brief reign of Jehoahaz, Jehoiakim came to the throne as a tool of Egypt; compelled to submit to the Babylonians, he soon rebelled but did not live to see the subsequent events leading to the surrender of Jerusalem. As early as 597 B.C.E., when Nebuchadnezzar king of Babylon approached Jerusalem, king Jehoiachin, together with his queen, ministers, and servants, came out and surrendered; Nebuchadnezzar crowned Zedekiah king, who was the last king of Judah. Ten years later the Babylonian army laid siege to the city and captured it after several months. The Babylonian captain Nebuzaradan exiled most of the inhabitants: "And he burnt the house of the Lord, and the king's house, and all the houses of Jerusalem, and every great man's house burnt he with fire" (II Kings 25:9). This disaster, of which the prophets Jeremiah and Ezekiel had given ample warning, left Jerusalem desolate for over 50 years.

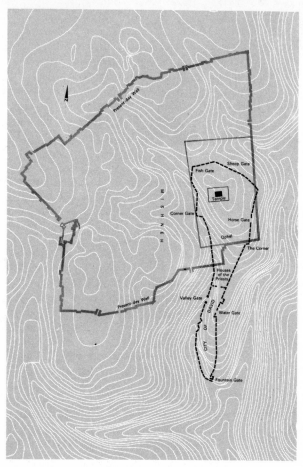

Map 2. Jerusalem at the time of Nehemiah. Based on
M. Avi-Yonah in *Israel Exploration Journal*, vol. 4, 1954.

5   SECOND TEMPLE PERIOD

RETURN TO ZION. The destruction of Jerusalem by the Babylonians (587 B.C.E.) decimated its population and, as described in Lamentations, it remained desolate for five decades. Its ruins represented the decline of Judah. Nevertheless, the Jewish people remained firm in their faith in Jerusalem, which was identified with their common history and their hope for national redemption. Psalms 137:5-6, uttered in Babylonian exile, "If I forget thee, O Jerusalem, Let my right hand forget her cunning . . . ," is a moving expression of this hope.

In 536 B.C.E., after the fall of Babylon, Cyrus, king of Persia, who became the overlord of Judah, issued his famous declaration, which allowed those desiring to return to Zion to do so and to rebuild the Temple on its historic site. The resettlement of the city and the rebuilding of the Temple were effected very gradually, as the surrounding nations were hostile to this activity. Only under Darius I in 515 B.C.E. did Zerubbabel, the governor, and Joshua son of Jehozadak, the high priest, succeed in completing the Second Temple. The city remained almost empty, however; its walls were breached and its gates were burned down. In 445 B.C.E. Nehemiah son of Hacaliah, an important official at the court of King Artaxerxes, moved by reports of the miserable conditions in the Holy City, decided to leave the court and go to Jerusalem. He was appointed governor of Judah and was mainly responsible for the rebuilding of the city. He organized the inhabitants of Judah and took security precautions necessitated by the bitter opposition of its neighbors, especially the Samaritans. First he repaired the wall, following its original course in   19 the period of the monarchy: "They that builded the wall and they that bore burdens laded themselves, every one with one of his hands wrought in the work, and with the other held his weapon" (Neh. 4:11). He then took steps to populate the city by commanding the nobles and one tenth of the rural population of Judah to settle there. He decreed an annual tax of a third of a shekel for the maintenance of the Temple. He suppressed the Tyrian trading market set up outside the city on the Sabbath, erected a strong fortress (the *birah*) north of the Temple, posted guards on the gates, and provided for the security of the city.

It was Ezra the Scribe who was responsible for the restoration of the authority of the Mosaic Law and for making Jerusalem the undisputed religious center of Judaism. The rest of the Persian period is wrapped in obscurity. The many jar-handle inscriptions reading "Jerusalem" or "the city" show that it was an important administrative and fiscal center.

HELLENISTIC PERIOD. Jerusalem submitted peacefully, with the rest of Judah, to Alexander the Great (332 B.C.E.), who confirmed the privileges of the city. The visit of the king as reported by Josephus, however, seems legendary. After the death of Alexander (323 B.C.E.), the city suffered as a result of a series of wars for succession. Ptolemy I, king of Egypt, seized it and deported a part of its population (according to a Greek historian, the conquest was made possible because the Jews would not go out to fight on the Sabbath). With the stabilization of Ptolemaic rule (301 B.C.E.), however, the relationship between Judah and Egypt improved, and a period of prosperity ensued. Judah had broad autonomy in domestic affairs and Jerusalem continued to be its administrative center. At the head of the administration were the high priests, descendants of Joshua son of Jehozadak, and the Council of Elders, which bore the Greek name of *Gerousia*. The high priest was not only the religious head of Jerusalem and Judah but also its political and administrative leader. The *Gerousia*, despite its Greek name, was a direct continuation of the Council of Elders of the Persian times. It was composed not only of Jerusalemites, but also of heads of clans from provincial towns. The Temple was the center of the religious and social life of Jerusalem. Due to its presence, many priests (*kohanim*) lived there and formed a very important social class. A new class, that of the scribes (interpreters of the law), began to develop. In addition to the priestly families and the scribes, a number of noble families came into prominence. Among them was the House of Tobiah, which had extensive land holdings in Transjordan and grew rich from tax farming. These aristocratic families developed close ties with the royal court and the gentile noble families in the empire and thus came under the sway of the Hellenistic way of life.

The Seleucid conquest in 198 B.C.E. was welcomed by the Jews. They helped besiege the Egyptian garrison in the Citadel and were consequently compensated by Antiochus III. A new charter was granted confirming the right of the Jews to live by the "laws of their fathers." The population was exempted from taxes for three years, and the priests and scribes were exempted in perpetuity. In addition, the king forbade the bringing of unclean animals and even the skins thereof into the city. On the surface the situation in Jerusalem seemed to remain as it had been under the Ptolemies as far as its administration, the character of its institutions, and social conditions were concerned. In reality, however, the Hellenization of the upper strata of the society was intensified. The priests and the secular leaders came closer in their thinking and way of life to the corresponding classes among the non-Jews and the Hellenistic influence seeped down to the lower classes. The leaders of the pro-Hellenistic movement who wanted radical changes were the houses of Tobiah and Bilgah. The traditionalists were headed by the high priest, Onias III, but even in his family there was a rent: his brother, Jason, leaned toward the Hellenizers. The struggle became more and more polarized due to the general political situation and the financial crisis that resulted from the defeat of the Seleucid empire by Rome. The king strove to regain his power by aggrandizement of the cities in accordance with the Hellenistic tradition of the polis.

The official in charge of the Temple, Simeon of the house of Bilgah, made an effort to limit the powers of the high priest Onias in the administration of the Temple, as well as in the economic life of the city. When his attempt failed, he turned to the Syrian governor and asked for his intervention. He pointed out that sums of money far beyond that required for ritual sacrifices were known to be in the Temple, and should, by right, be given over to the king's government. Thereupon, the king sent Heliodorus, his chief minister, to investigate. Onias opposed this move vigorously, pointing out that the monies did not belong to the Temple but were sums deposited there for safekeeping, and Heliodorus failed in his mission. Although there is no reason to believe that the king intended to harm the Temple or to intervene in religious affairs, the episode left a sediment of mistrust toward his government. Simeon continued in his attempts. There were riots in the streets of Jerusalem and Onias was compelled to ask the help of the government to maintain order.

In 175 B.C.E., with the ascent to the throne of Antiochus IV Epiphanes, significant changes began to take place. His reign was marked by most energetic steps to Hellenize the empire. Antiochus indicated interest in the affairs of Jerusalem, and Jason seized the opportunity to convince the king to put him in the place of his brother, Onias III, as the high priest. Jason promised the king a considerable increase in taxes, as well as a large tribute, in return for his permission to make changes in the governing of the city. The two major reforms made by Jason, with the full support of the king, were the building of a gymnasium in Jerusalem and the change of the Jewish city into a Hellenistic polis (one of the many in the empire) to be known as Antioch.

The establishment under the Temple fortress of the gymnasium changed the whole spiritual and social atmosphere. It began to rival the Temple as the social center, especially among the young priests and laymen. This was a grievous blow to the traditionalists, particularly as, according to Greek tradition, the gymnasium was under the patronage of the gods Hermes and Hercules. The author of II Maccabees describes with great bitterness how, on a given signal, the priests left the Temple in order to view the games. The conversion of Jerusalem into a polis required a new census, which gave Jason and his supporters the opportunity to make changes in the register of citizens. Jason did not do away with the existing system of administration, and the traditional *Gerousia* continued to function together with the high priest. As the head of Jerusalem and Judah, he followed the line of the house of Tobiah, endeavoring to integrate the city into the general cultural and social life of the empire. Delegates from Antioch-Jerusalem were sent to Tyre to represent the city at the games in honor of Hercules.

Jason did not remain high priest for long; it seems that the king did not consider him sufficiently loyal. Menelaus, an ardent Hellenizer of the house of Bilgah, was appointed in his place. He purchased his position for a high price, and a new chapter began in the relations between the Seleucid empire and Judah. The high priest, who had heretofore represented the interests of the Jews in the king's court, was now made an official of the administration. Menelaus was unable to fulfill his financial obligations to the king and was called to appear before him. His brother Lysimachus was left in charge and immediately availed himself of the opportunity to rob the Temple's treasury. Consequently, a revolt broke out against the rule of Menelaus in which Lysimachus was killed. The three members of the *Gerousia* who were sent to complain to the king against Menelaus were put to death and the latter continued to enjoy the support of Antiochus.

Upon the return of the king from his first war in Egypt in 169 B.C.E., he visited the city and took away with him the golden altar, the lamp, and other gold and silver implements found in the Temple. In the following year, when the 23 king was again at war in Egypt, the rumor spread that Antiochus had died. At this point, the deposed Jason, at the head of a force of 1,000 men, broke into the city and gained control of all but the fortress in which Menelaus and his supporters and the permanent garrison defended themselves. On his way back from Egypt, the king seized Jerusalem, constructed a fortress, the Acra, in a dominant position opposite the Temple, and stationed a garrison there. In 167 B.C.E. Antiochus issued decrees against the Jewish religion that were carried out with special severity in Jerusalem. The Temple was desecrated; its treasures were confiscated. Antiochus converted it into a shrine dedicated to the god Dionysus and ordered the erection of a huge temple of his favorite god, Zeus Olympius. Opponents of Antiochus' policy fled the city, while a Seleucid garrison and the Hellenizers remained in Jerusalem. All around, the countryside rebelled.

HASMONEAN PERIOD. The revolt led by Judah Maccabee aimed at the purification of Jerusalem and the attainment of autonomy. The city was out of reach of the Jewish insurgents; however, they set up a successful blockade around the city and were able to beat back four successive attempts to relieve the Seleucid garrison. After the fourth victory of Judah in battle near Beth-Zur, they were able to reoccupy the Temple Mount, cleanse the Temple of pagan objects, rebuild the altar, and resume the sacrifices in December 164 B.C.E. Since that time Jews have observed the Feast of Dedication, or Ḥanukkah, in memory of this occasion. After the death of Antiochus IV, his successor granted the Jews religious freedom and appointed a new high priest, Eliakim (Alkimos). The Temple walls were breached with the help of traitors, and Judah was forced to leave Jerusalem. After the death of Judah in battle (160 B.C.E.), his brothers, Jonathan and Simeon, had to operate from outside Jerusalem.

Due to the continuous conflicts and intrigues in the Seleucid empire, it became possible for the Hasmoneans to return to Jerusalem several years later. In 152 B.C.E. Jonathan was made high priest and governor of the Jews. He was allowed to reoccupy the city, with the exception of the Acra, which continued to be held by the king's garrison, and all his attempts to gain control of it failed. He therefore built a wall to cut the Acra off from the city and strengthened the wall of Jerusalem. Simeon, Jonathan's brother and successor, finally expelled the garrison and eradicated the Acra of its pagan cults. A triumphal entry into the fallen fortress was made on the 23rd of Iyyar 141 B.C.E., the date which henceforward was celebrated as the day of the final deliverance of Jerusalem.

Early in the reign of John Hyrcanus, Jerusalem was placed by Antiochus Sidetes VII under a heavy siege, which ended in a treaty under which the city wall was breached. From then till 63 B.C.E., for close to six decades, no enemy approached the city. Jerusalem became the capital city of the Hasmonean kingdom, which included the major part of western Palestine as well as Transjordan. It was the center of ever-growing political, economic, and religious activity. The Temple became the ritual and religious center of a large number of people in the Land of Israel who had not previously come under the influence of Judaism. Jews in the Diaspora, converts to Judaism, and sympathizers with Judaism contributed to the wealth of the city by paying half a shekel, and making other contributions. The sages of Jerusalem became renowned throughout Jewry, and their influence was felt wherever Jews resided. Trades and crafts developed in the city.

The "Letter of Aristeas[1]" contains a description of Hasmonean Jerusalem, with its triple wall, its markets, replete with all kinds of wares, its supply of drinking water, and so forth. The Hasmonean palace was built in the former Greek quarter of the city, the Temple towers were strengthened, and a bridge was built to connect the upper city with the Temple Mount. The prosperity of the city is

---

[1]Pseudepigraphic work written in second cent. B.C.E. by unknown Egyptian Jew.

Remains of the Hasmonean city wall at the Citadel show the typical stone dressing of the period, a convex center surrounded by a flat margin. Courtesy Israel Department of Antiquities, Jerusalem.

clearly evident in its remains, such as its new walls, some of which were discovered in the excavations at the Citadel of Jerusalem and around the western hill, which show the typical Hasmonean stone dressing with a boss in the center and margins around; the stones are not large (24 27 in. high). Hasmonean coins and arrowheads were also found in this excavation. To the same period belong some of the splendid monuments in the Kidron Valley, such as the Tomb of the Sons of Hezir (erroneously called the Tomb of St. James), the so-called Tomb of Zechariah, and a newly discovered tomb of Jason (in modern Alfasi St.), which contains one of the earliest drawings of a *menorah* and a picture of a sea fight (this Jason was apparently a retired sea captain).

No external enemy menaced Jerusalem, but it was the scene of violent civil strife in the days of Alexander Yannai. His widow, Salome Alexandra, succeeded in restoring peace to the city, but after her death the conflict

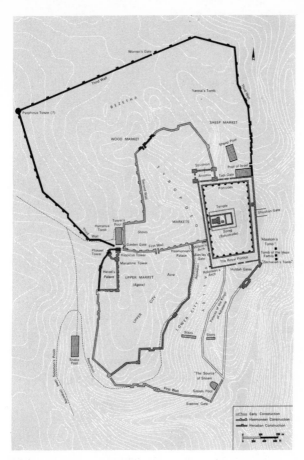

Map 3. Jerusalem at the time of the Second Temple. Based on
D. Bahat, *Jerusalem—Its Epochs,* Jerusalem, 1970.

Tomb of Zechariah, one of the Hasmonean monuments hewn out of the rock in the Kidron Valley. Photo David Eisenberg, Jerusalem.

broke out anew. Hyrcanus II besieged his brother Aristobulus II in the Temple with the aid of the Nabateans, but was forced to retreat. In the end this fratricidal war profited only the Romans. In 64 B.C.E., when Pompey decided in favor of Hyrcanus, the partisans of Aristobulus shut themselves up in the Temple and defied the decision of the Roman general. Pompey was forced to undertake a siege, since the Temple was now defended by a deep fosse on the north. In 63 B.C.E., the Temple wall was breached and the Romans broke into the Temple itself. Pompey entered the Holy of Holies but did not touch the Temple treasuries. He left the government to Hyrcanus and his adviser Antipater the Idumean, the father of Herod. In 40 B.C.E. Jerusalem was seized by the Parthians, who had invaded Judea as allies of Mattathias Antigonus. Three years later, after a prolonged siege, Herod's troops and those of his Roman allies breached the walls of Jerusalem and penetrated the city. There followed great slaughter and looting, until Herod was forced to intervene in order to save the city.

HERODIAN PERIOD. King Herod, who reigned over Judea for 33 years (37–4 B.C.E.), completely transformed the external aspect of Jerusalem. His aim was to make his hold on the city secure, knowing full well how much he was hated by its population; to satisfy his liking for ostentation and splendor; and to placate the populace by providing work. His successful financial ventures and high taxation provided the means. Herod transferred the seat of civil power from the old palace on the ruins of the Acra to a new site in the northwestern corner of the city, on a narrow saddle between the Ben Hinnom Valley and a transversal west-east valley. His palace was protected on the north by three towers: Phasael, Hippicus and Mariamne; the base of Phasael, inserted in the Hasmonean wall, is still standing in the Citadel. Behind the three towers, which formed a fortress, extended Herod's palace, surrounded by a wall with towers, which adjoined the Agora or upper market. Within the wall were extensive gardens and two blocks of buildings, called Caesareum and Agrippeum in honor of Augustus and his general Vipsanius Agrippa, respectively. The palace gardens may have been supplied with water from the Jerusalem aqueduct (see Water Supply, below).

Entrance to the Citadel. The base of the tower is the remnant of Herod's Phasael Tower. Israel Department of Antiquities, Jerusalem.

Herod's other project in Jerusalem concerned the eastern hill of the city. He transformed the old Baris fortress into a much larger structure, with high towers dominating the Temple area, and called it Antonia, in honor of the triumvir Mark Antony. In the Temple area itself, the esplanade was enlarged, especially on its southern side, and it was given the trapezoid shape which is still preserved. The Temple Mount was surrounded by a wall of huge blocks, of which the Western ("Wailing") Wall is but a section. The level of the esplanade was maintained by extensive underpinnings with arches. The Temple Mount was also surrounded by a portico with columns 50 ft. (15 m.) high. The entire south-30 ern side was taken up by a two-story triple hall, the "royal

Herodian south wall of the Temple Mount, with the uncovered portion of the paved street leading to Huldah Gates. Courtesy Israel Exploration Society, Jerusalem, Excavations of the Southern Wall.

basilica." Herod also entirely rebuilt the Temple, doubling its height and richly adorning its exterior.

Extant remains of Herod's building activity include: the walls surrounding the Temple esplanade, which in recent years have been excavated by archaeologists at the south-

Replica of Greek stele from the inner court of Herod's Temple, prohibiting the entry of foreigners and gentiles on pain of death. The stele, discovered by Clermont-Ganneau in 1871, is now in the Istanbul Archaeological Museum. Jerusalem, Rockefeller Museum, Israel Department of Antiquities.

western corner down to the Herodian street; the Herodian addition at the southeastern corner; parts of the Antonia with its pool, the Struthion; Herodian foundations below the present Damascus Gate; the base of the Phasael Tower. Besides these, the tomb of Herod's family (mentioned by Josephus) has been found near the King David Hotel. The so-called Tomb of Absalom in the Kidron Valley is also assigned to his reign; it gives an idea of the rich eclectic ornamentation of Herodian architecture.

UNDER THE ROMAN PROCURATORS. After Herod's death and the banishment of his son Archelaus, Judea was made a province of the Roman Empire (6 C.E.). Jerusalem was ruled by Roman procurators who resided in Caesarea and thus ceased to be the capital of Judea. The procurators, however, would come to Jerusalem from time to time with their troops, especially during the three pilgrim festivals, when it was crowded with pilgrims from all over the country and from abroad. In deference to Jewish religious sensitivity, the troops came to Jerusalem without their standards, which bore idolatrous images. The city government was in the hands of the high priest and the Sanhedrin, which fulfilled the functions of the *Gerousia* in the Hellenistic period, i.e., the municipal council. The last Jewish prince to rule over Jerusalem was Herod Agrippa (41–44), who began to build a new wall on the north side of the city (the Third Wall) but was stopped by order of the Romans. Under the procurators who succeeded him, sporadic riots broke out in the city, usually resulting in clashes with the Roman troops. One of the procurators, Pontius Pilate (26–36), under whose rule the execution of Jesus of Nazareth took place, constructed the first aqueduct which brought water to Jerusalem from the vicinity of Hebron. The small Christian community remained in Jerusalem until 66, when it retired to Pella.

Jerusalem's significance was more than that of the administrative center of a diminished Judea; it was the capital of the Jewish nation. The Temple, the Sanhedrin, and the great houses of study of the Pharisees turned it into a symbol for Jews everywhere. As Philo expressed it in his *Legatio ad Gaium*, Jerusalem was the metropolis not only of Judea, but of many lands because of its colonies. It was renowned even among non-Jews: the elder Pliny wrote that Jerusalem was the most famous among the great cities of the East. A legendary halo surrounded the city. It was the focal point of Jewish unity and attracted Jewish pilgrims and converts (e.g., Queen Helene of Adiabene). Because of the Temple, the main priestly families resided there, as did many important aristocratic families that wished to be close to the center of affairs. Even scions of the House of Herod lived there from time to time, though their kingdoms were some distance away. Jerusalem was the center of spiritual activity. The heads of Bet Hillel[2]—Rabban Gamaliel I

2School of exposition of the Oral Law.

and Rabban Simeon son of Gamaliel—resided in Jerusalem. Houses of learning in the city attracted students from all over the country and from abroad. The city's status helped it to become an important economic center. Its area increased to one square mile and its population was estimated at 120,000.

One of the phenomena of Jerusalem during this period was the presence of many Jews from numerous countries, from Media and Elam in the east to Italy in the west, many of whom settled in the city. These immigrants preserved their different ways of life for long periods and congregated in distinct communities according to their lands of origin. Especially noticeable was the difference between Jews who spoke Hebrew and Aramaic and the Hellenized Jews who came from Egypt, Cyrenaica, and Asia Minor, the latter group having special synagogues of their own. In the last years before the destruction, social tension grew to such an extent that it affected the order and security of the city. In addition to the general enmity toward Roman rule, there were conflicts among the Jews themselves. On the one hand, there was friction among different groups in the priestly oligarchy and on the other, the activities of the extremist fighters for freedom from the Romans (the Sicarii), who used violence and were not averse to killing their opponents. There was also an increase in the activities of visionaries and prophets who spread messianic expectations among the people and the pilgrims.

JERUSALEM AT THE END OF THE SECOND TEMPLE PERIOD. The traveler's first glimpse of Jerusalem was from Mount Scopus (Har ha-Zofim). Crossing the Kidron Valley, he passed the "Tombs of the Kings" (of Adiabene), and reached the Third Wall, which stretched along the Kidron Valley from the Psephinus Tower in the northwest. Entrance to the wall was from an area of gardens and vegetable fields through the Women's Gate. Behind it was the then sparsely populated New City or Bezetha. Approaching the Second Wall, which enclosed the "Mortar," the commercial quarter in the upper Tyropoeon Valley, one could see (outside this wall) the wood and sheep markets, the Pool of Bethesda (or Sheep Pool), and the Pool of the Towers (today called the Pool of Hezekiah). The Second Wall, which ran in a broken line from the vicinity of Herod's Palace to the Antonia fortress, protected the city proper. Outside it were the tombs of Alexander and John Hyrcanus; within it were the various bazaars of the city. From this commercial area one could proceed through the Water Gate or the Garden Gate into the Upper City. The latter, which was the aristocratic quarter, was well laid out in the pattern of a Hellenistic city and covered the whole of the western hill of Jerusalem. Within it stood the palaces of the high priests and of the Hasmoneans. At its northwestern extremity rose the three towers protecting Herod's palace, respectively about 135, 120, and 70 ft. high. A bridge (the remnants of which are now called Wilson's Arch in honor of one of the early archaeologists of Jerusalem) joined the Upper City to the Temple Mount.

The Upper City was protected on the east by another wall facing the Tyropoeon Valley. This valley was a popular quarter with closely set houses and was called the Lower City; it extended to the eastern hill (the so-called Ophel), which was originally the City of David. At its southern extremity was the Gate of the Essenes, and near that was the Pool of Siloam (called by Josephus the "Pool of Solomon") and the issue of Hezekiah's Tunnel, which brought the waters of the Gihon into the city. The mouth of this tunnel was called simply "the spring," since its true origin had been forgotten. Stairs descended from the Upper to the Lower City and rose from the latter to the Temple area.

The esplanade of the sanctuary was protected by a high, massive wall, built of typical Herodian masonry with double margins. It was surrounded by open colonnaded porticoes, of which the southern one, the "royal basilica," was the most splendid. The Temple itself stood within yet another wall; it was very high (about 150 feet) and glittered with gold and white marble "like a snow-covered mountain." The four towers of the Antonia (and especially that at the southeast corner, about 180 feet high) overlooked the esplanade. Outside the walls, and especially to the east and to the south along the valleys of Ben Hinnom and Kidron, stretched the necropolis. Among the great and imposing tombs erected in the first century C.E. were the Tombs of the Judges or of the Sanhedrin in the upper Kidron Valley and the so-called "Tomb of Absalom" and "Tomb of Jehoshaphat" in the central Kidron Valley.

As a fortress, Jerusalem was rendered all the stronger by its topographical position. Situated on the southern slope of a ridge issuing from the watershed line, it was protected on the west, south, and east by the valleys of Ben Hinnom and Kidron, while on the north it had three strongly reinforced walls.

The Siege of Titus. In the autumn of 66 the misrule of the procurators finally provoked the outbreak of a revolt, which soon became a full-scale war. The Roman governor of Syria, Cestius Gallus, advanced with his army to the gates of the Temple in an attempt to quell the uprising, but retreated after a disastrous defeat. For over three years, Jerusalem was free; the silver shekels (the contemporary currency) bearing the legend "Jerusalem the Holy" commemorate this period. However, internecine strife among the insurgents wasted the resources of the city and only when the enemy approached in the spring of 70 did they join forces.

The Temple and the Lower City were defended by John of Giscala, the Upper City by Simeon b. Giora. The attackers were led by Titus, the son and heir of the emperor Vespasian, with an army of four legions at his disposal. After reconnaissance and the establishment of camps in two places around the city, the Romans attacked the Third Wall near Herod's Tower, hoping to penetrate the Upper City and thus end the siege at one stroke. They failed in their plan and had to content themselves with the breaching of the Third Wall and the occupation of Bezetha. Moving his camp to a place called the "Assyrian Camp" (now the

Russian Compound), Titus attacked the Second Wall and scaled it after some bitter fighting in the narrow, winding bazaars. Now the siege began in earnest; attempts were made to attack by the usual methods (siege mounds with movable towers equipped with battering rams). But the besieged defenders fought with great determination, setting fire to the Roman machines of war and undermining the siege mounds reared against the Towers' Pool and the Antonia. Titus thereupon ordered the construction of a siege wall to blockade the city tightly in an attempt to weaken the population through hunger (the quantity of water in the cisterns was apparently sufficient to carry the city through the summer). After this process the attack was renewed. At the beginning of Av (August) the wall of the Antonia was finally stormed, and after a few days the Temple was set aflame (9th of Av). The Romans then spread over the Lower City and the Tyropoeon Valley, but they had to renew their siege operations against the Upper City, which only fell a month later. Most of the people in the city had either been killed or had perished from hunger; the survivors were sold into slavery or executed. The city was destroyed, except for the three towers of Herod, which were spared to protect the camp of the Tenth Legion on the ruins of Jerusalem.

6 THE ROMAN PERIOD

Although the city of Jerusalem remained in ruins for 61 years, a number of the inhabitants (including the Christian community that left for Pella during the siege) returned and settled around the legionary camp. An inscription of an officer of the Tenth Legion, T-Cl. Fatalis, records that he lived there with his freedwoman Ionice, and there were many others like him. Some of the caves and hovels inhabited during that period were recently excavated at the foot of Mount Zion. Later sources state that the returning Jews had as many as seven synagogues in that area. In 130 C.E. the Emperor Hadrian visited Jerusalem and decided to establish a Roman colony on the ruins of the Jewish city. The governor, Tineius Rufus, performed the ceremony of plowing along the line of the projected walls in the name of the emperor and founder. This ceremony is represented on coins of the colony, which received the name of Aelia Capitolina in honor of the family name of the emperor and the Capitoline triad (Jupiter, Juno, and Minerva). Coins found with the Bar Kokhba hoards prove that the colony was functioning before the outbreak of the Bar Kokhba revolt. Its foundation was undoubtedly an important contributing cause of the second Jewish-Roman war. In the course of the revolt, the Roman garrison and civilians were forced to evacuate Jerusalem. It was reoccupied by the Jews, who apparently erected a provisional Temple and resumed sacrifices. This state of affairs lasted for almost three years (132–35). In the last summer of the revolt, Jerusalem was recaptured by the Romans. Hadrian decreed that no circumcised person should be allowed into

Jerusalem and its territory under pain of death; even the

Christian community was forced to change its bishop of Jewish origin for a gentile.

One of the triple arches forming the eastern entrance to Roman Aelia Capitolina, now inside the convent of the Sœurs de Sion at the beginning of the Via Dolorosa. Photo Micha Pan, Jerusalem.

Aelia Capitolina, like other Roman colonies, was built in the shape of a square Roman camp with some divergencies due to local conditions. To this day the Old City of Jerusalem has the shape of a Roman colony. One main road passed from west to east (Jaffa Gate to Lions' Gate), while the other north-south street (which was provided with colonnades) was split in two; one running from the Damascus to Zion Gate, the other following the Tyropoeon to the Dung Gate. The Temple area (called the Quadra or "Square") was left outside the colony plan; the temple of Jupiter was erected on it with an equestrian statue of Hadrian in front. The main city temple, dedicated to the Capitoline triad—the so-called Tricameron—was situated near the forum, the main marketplace; facing it was the temple of Venus, which stood on the present site of the Holy Sepulcher. Other known monuments of Aelia were a tetrapylon (four-arched gate) at the crossing of the main streets, two triumphal arches (one now known as the Ecce Homo arch, the other outside the north (Damascus) gate), and two public baths. Outside the city were steps leading to the nympheum (public fountain) with twelve arches (the Dodekapylon) near the Pool of Siloam. The city was divided into seven wards, which for centuries bore the names of the first headmen or amphodarchs. It did not have the rights of an Italian colony *(jus italicum)* and thus had to pay taxes on its lands. City coins were issued from the time of Hadrian to that of Valerianus (260), but are especially plentiful from the times of Antoninus Pius, Marcus Aurelius, Eleagabalus, and Trajan Decius. The 206 coin types evidence the gods worshiped in Aelia: Sarapis, Tyche, the Dioscuri, Roma, Ares, Nemesis and others are found in addition to the Capitoline triad. The worship of Sarapis is confirmed by a dedicatory inscription; that of the goddess Hygieia is connected with the healing baths near the Bethesda Pool.

Aelia was a quiet provincial city. The great events were imperial visits, such as that of Septimius Severus in 201, which was commemorated by an inscription discovered

Looking through an archway on the Via Dolorosa to a section of the Ecce Homo arch—the eastern entrance to Aelia Capitolina—protruding from the wall of the Sœurs de Sion convent. Photo David Eisenberg, Jerusalem.

near the Western Wall. On this occasion the colony received the honorary title "Commodiana." Toward the end of the third century the Legio X Fretensis (still in Aelia at about 250) was transferred to Elath and replaced by a troop of Moors. In the second and third centuries, the Christian community in Jerusalem developed peacefully; one of its bishops, Narcissus, died a centenarian, after sharing the office with Alexander from Cappadocia. The latter estab-

North gate of Aelia Capitolina beneath the Damascus Gate.
The remnant of an inscription by the city fathers on a stone
above the gate reads: "Co[lonia] Ael[ia] Cap[itolina] D[ecreto]
D[ecuriorum]." Photo David Eisenberg, Jerusalem.

lished a famous library at Aelia. In his time Christian
pilgrimages to the city began. The Jews also profited from a
de facto relaxation of the prohibition against visiting
Jerusalem as pilgrims.

7 BYZANTINE JERUSALEM

The status and appearance of Aelia was completely revolutionized when the Christian emperor Constantine became master of Palestine in 324. At the council of Nicaea, Macarius, the bishop of Aelia, reported to the emperor on the state of the Christian holy sites and persuaded the emperor's mother, Helena, to visit Jerusalem (326). During her visit, the temple of Venus was destroyed and according to Christian tradition the True Cross was found in a crypt beneath it. Constantine decided to erect the Church of the Holy Sepulcher on this spot. The church consisted of a forecourt, a basilica, another court containing the rock of Golgotha (which was cut down to a cube), and the Sepulcher itself, surmounted by a dome supported on columns with silver capitals. The church was built by the architects Zenobius and Eusthatius of Constantinople, and was dedicated in 335. Another church, the Eleona, was built on the slopes of the Mount of Olives. The city then assumed a predominantly Christian character; the prohibition against the entrance of Jews into the city was renewed, with the exception of the 9th of Av, when they were allowed to lament on the Temple Mount.

The growing importance of Jerusalem as a Christian center was temporarily interrupted by the emperor Julian, who reverted to the ancient Greek religion and favored Judaism. In 363 he ordered the reconstruction of the Temple and entrusted the task to his friend Alypius. Work went on until May 27, when an earthquake caused conflagration in the building stores. As the emperor had just started on his Persian Campaign, those responsible for the work suspended it. The death of Julian in Persia and

ENTRANCE TO THE CHURCH OF THE HOLY SEPULCHRE.
Pilgrims buying rosaries and other relics in the forecourt.

From Sir Charles Wilson (ed.), *Picturesque Palestine, Sinai and Egypt,* Vol. I, London, c. 1880. Courtesy A. A. Mendilow, Jerusalem.

the enthronement of the Christian emperor Jovian put an end to this project. During that time the bishop of Jerusalem was the eminent preacher Cyril, who was often exiled but always succeeded in returning (350–86). In his time Christian pilgrims of all countries, from Britain and Gaul in the west to Ethiopia, India, and Persia on the south and east, could be seen in the city.

Cyril's outstanding successor was John (396–417). During his episcopate numerous aristocratic families, led by St. Jerome, fled from Rome to Jerusalem (385–419). Among them were noble and rich women, such as Melania and Poemenia, who erected churches and monasteries (Church of Ascension, 378, Church of Gethsemane, 390). The first hermits established themselves in the vicinity of Jerusalem at that time. The city also served as a place of refuge for fallen grandees, such as the family of the minister Rufinus. In 428 the energetic Juvenal became bishop of Jerusalem. In 438 the empress Eudocia visited Jerusalem for the first time; due to her intervention, Jews were again allowed to live in the city. After her separation from her husband, Theodosius II, she settled permanently in the Holy City (444–60), spending lavishly on churches (including the basilica of St. Stephen north of the city). She also had a new city wall constructed, including Mount Zion within the city (this wall was excavated in 1896). Both Eudocia and Juvenal became involved in the Monophysite controversy. By successful maneuvering, the bishop succeeded in obtaining the status of patriarch and authority over the churches of Palestine and Arabia in 451. He was opposed by the Monophysite monks, however, and had to be reinstated in his see by the Byzantine army.

During the reign of Justinian (527–65), a Samaritan revolt (529) devastated the vicinity of Jerusalem. The churches outside the town were destroyed and had to be rebuilt, and the emperor added a magnificent basilica, the "Nea" (new one), within the city. The structure of Byzantine Jerusalem under Justinian is preserved in the Madaba Mosaic Map. Inside the north gate was a semicircular plaza, with a column in its center, still commemorated in the Arabic name of this gate, Bāb al-ʿAmūd. Two colonnaded streets issued from the plaza leading

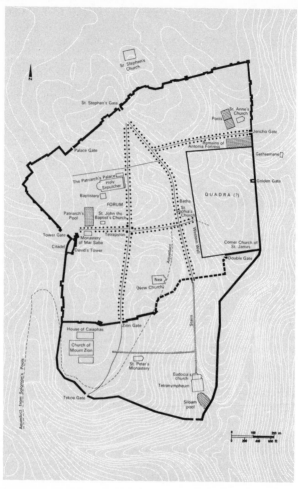

Map 4. Jerusalem in the Byzantine period. Based on D. Bahat, *Jerusalem—Its Epochs,* Jerusalem, 1970.

south. The western one passed the Church of the Holy Sepulcher and continued to the Zion Gate by way of a tetrapylon, passing the churches of St. Sophia and the Nea. On the other side of the Church of the Holy Sepulcher, the forum, the palace of the patriarchs, and the towers and monasteries near Jaffa Gate were visible. The other road (which had an offshoot to the east gate) passed a public bath and ended at another inner gate. The Western Wall was visible east of this street. The Temple area was a wasteland, with one east gate (the Golden Gate) and the Church of St. James at its southeastern corner. In the southern part of the city was the Church of Mount Zion, with its Diakonikon (deacon's church) and the baths at the Siloam Pool. The Probatike (Sheep Pool) bath and church filled the northeastern corner of the city. In the time of Justinian, two Church councils were held in Jerusalem (536 and 553), mainly concerning the Origenist disputes. The patriarch Eustachius had to be installed by the army.

In the course of the last Byzantine-Persian war, the Persian army of Chosroes II approached Jerusalem in 614 and besieged it with the help of its Jewish allies. The city wall was breached, many inhabitants were slain, and the patriarch Zacharias and the "True Cross" were taken into exile. The Persians handed the city over to the Jews, who ruled it under a leader known only by his symbolic name, Nehemiah. The Persian conquest led to the destruction of most of the churches in Jerusalem. After some time, however, the Persians handed the city back to the Christians, who began to rebuild their holy sites under Modestus. The victories of the emperor Heraclius led to a return of the Byzantines; on March 21, 629, he made a triumphal entry into Jerusalem, bringing back the "True Cross" relic, and the Jews were again banished from there. When the Muslim forces invaded Palestine, Jerusalem was besieged from 637 onward. As there seemed to be little hope of rescue following the decisive battle of Yarmuk (636), the patriarch Sophronius, successor to Modestus, surrendered the city to the Muslim caliph Omar in March/April 638. **47**

8 ARAB PERIOD

From the time Jerusalem was conquered by the Arabs in the year 638, it remained a provincial town and never became the seat of rich princes who had chroniclers at their court. Consequently, Arabic historiography on Jerusalem consists of only one work, *al-Uns al Jalīl fī Ta'rīkh al-Quds wa al-Khalīl* ("The honorable company on the history of Jerusalem and Hebron"), which was written by Mujīr al-Dīn al-ʿUlaymī at the end of the 15th century. The modern historian must therefore combine accounts gathered from manifold sources.

After the Arabs invaded Ereẓ Israel in the year 634, four years elapsed until they finally took Jerusalem. In those years the city, somehow isolated from its hinterland, suffered greatly, as is demonstrated by the sermons delivered by the patriarch Sophronius. The accounts of the conquest of Jerusalem differ considerably; according to the most probable version, the caliph Omar, then at the headquarters at al-Jābiya in the Hauran, sent a subaltern officer to occupy the town. Some historians relate that the town surrendered under certain conditions, among which was the continued nonadmission of Jews, who had not been allowed to live there under Byzantine rule. The inhabitants probably submitted under the usual conditions—that their persons, churches, and buildings should be safe as long as they paid the poll tax *(jizya)*.

Omar's visit to Jerusalem shortly after the surrender has been the subject of divergent and clearly tendentious accounts. The Christian Arabic historian Eutychius, who wrote in Egypt at the beginning of the tenth century, says that Omar refused to pray in the Church of the Holy

Sepulcher, whereupon Sophronius showed him the site of the Holy Rock identified with the talmudic Even ha-Shetiyyah, the site of the Temple Holy of Holies, on which the world was believed to be founded. Muslim writers, on the other hand, relate how the Christians attempted to deceive the caliph when he asked about the site of the Rock by bringing him to the Church of the Holy Sepulcher and to Mount Zion instead. Other sources relate that the Jewish convert Ka'b al-Aḥbār proposed to Omar that the Muslims should pray to the north of the Rock (so as to include the Rock in the *qibla* (direction of prayer) to Mecca), but that his proposal was turned down by the caliph. It is clear from the nature of the tales that the account transmitted by Eutychius was meant to safeguard the Church of the Holy Sepulcher, whereas the story about Ka'b's failure discloses an anti-Jewish tendency. Apparently the attempt in this instance was to show that Omar refused to turn when praying to the Holy of Holies (the Temple sanctuary) of the Jews and to the Ka'ba at the same time. From these tales it may be assumed that Omar ordered the Temple area to be cleaned and a place for Muslim worship established there.

Various accounts confirm that Omar had Jews in his retinue who were his advisers and that he entrusted them with keeping the area in good order. Although Omar did not accept Ka'b's suggestion, quite rightly seeing in it a Judaizing tendency, Jewish traditions and beliefs influenced early Islam's attitude toward the holiness of the Temple Mount and its surroundings. These influences can therefore be seen as explaining why Omar did not pay attention to Sophronius' misleading information. Jewish tradition can also be recognized as the major factor in the ascription to Jerusalem of all events connected in Islam with the last judgment. In turn Muslim descriptions influenced later Jewish Midrashim which show an intimate knowledge of the Temple Mount, the Gates of the Ḥaram (the walled area of the Muslim sanctuaries), the Mount of Olives (see below), Mount Zion, and their surroundings. All these descriptions show that Jews lived in Jerusalem in the early Arab period. The prevailing opinion, which is based on Christian sources, that the Jews were not allowed to live in the Holy City or its surroundings during the whole Byzantine period is not confirmed by any non-Christian source. One suspects that these reports are biased in order to glorify the victory of the Church, as there is extant literary and archaeological evidence that there was a synagogue on the so-called Mt. Zion where the Cenaculum now stands. Hebrew and Greek inscriptions near the gates to the north and the south of the Ḥaram area are from the late Byzantine or the early Muslim period. There are also extant *piyyutim* from the same time. In any event there is no doubt that during the Persian conquest (614–28) Jews lived in Jerusalem. It seems that even after the recapture of the city by Heraclius many of them remained in its vicinity. This may have caused Sophronius' request that no Jews should be allowed to stay in Jerusalem.

A document (in Judeo-Arabic) found in the Cairo *Genizah* reveals that the Jews asked Omar for permission for 200 families to settle in the town. As the patriarch opposed the action strongly, Omar fixed the number of the Jewish settlers at 70 families. The Jews were assigned the quarter southwest of the Temple area, where they lived from that time. As is evidenced by various surviving texts, they could also pray in the neighborhood of the Temple area. A late source, R. Abraham b. Ḥiyya (12th century), mentions that they had even been allowed to build a synagogue and a *midrash* (college) on that area.

Although many Arabs came to live in Jerusalem, the great majority of the inhabitants was still Christian. The information culled from *Genizah* fragments and other Rabbanite and Karaite sources concerning the earliest Jewish inhabitants of Jerusalem during the Umayyad period is insufficient for even a general description of historical events and the daily life of the Jewish community during Umayyad rule and the first hundred years of the Abbasid dynasty. Even the date of such a major event as the transfer to Jerusalem of the talmudic academy from its seat in Tiberias during the late Byzantine and earliest Muslim periods is unknown.

UMAYYAD RULE. The Umayyad caliphs, who resided in Damascus and in other towns and townlets of Syria and Erez Israel, showed a keen interest in Jerusalem, the holy city which was so near to their residence. Mu'āwiya, the founder of the dynasty, was proclaimed caliph in Jerusalem (660), and he probably erected the first primitive building on the place where the mosque known as al-Aqṣā (the further mosque, i.e., the furthest place reached by Muhammad on his Night Journey) was built. The Frankish bishop Arculf, who visited Jerusalem in 670, describes this mosque as a rather ugly building whose walls consisted of simple planks, but which was able to hold 3,000 men. The mosque may have been built on the site of the Byzantine Church of Mary, which had been destroyed by the Persians in 614, and partly superseded it. Above the Holy Rock the great Umayyad caliph 'Abd al-Malik built a splendid cupola, Qubbat al-Ṣakhra (the Dome of the Rock). Its construction was finished in 72 A.H. (691), as can be seen from the inscription on it. The Muslims believe that Muhammad placed his feet on the Rock on his Night Journey and therefore consider it holy. Both medieval Arabic writers and modern scholars have expressed the view that 'Abd al-Malik's purpose was to divert the pilgrimage from Mecca, where the counter-caliph Abdallah ibn al-Zubayr resided. The Umayyad caliph intended to build a magnificent Muslim house of worship in Jerusalem which would surpass the numerous churches there. A well-informed Arabic geographer explicitly says that the Dome of the Rock should be seen as a counterpart to the Church of the Holy Sepulcher.

A fact characteristic both of the tolerance of the Umayyads and of the role the Jews then played in Jerusalem is that 'Abd al-Malik appointed some Jewish families as guardians of the Ḥaram and decreed that they should be exempt from the poll tax. 'Abd al-Malik also had 51 a government palace built in Jerusalem and the town's walls repaired. Sulaymān, one of his sons and successors, planned to make Jerusalem his residence but changed his mind and resided in Ramleh, which he had founded. From that time, Ramleh was the capital of southern Erez Israel, and Jerusalem, which began to decline in importance, was neither the seat of a provincial administration nor the residence of a strong garrison which could provide work for craftsmen. The trade routes did not reach it, and the only product which could be exported from the surrounding area was olive oil. The last years of Umayyad rule were unhappy ones for the town, for other reasons as well: after a revolt against the last Umayyad caliph Marwān II, he had the town walls razed, and shortly thereafter an earthquake wrought havoc on the Dome of the Rock.

ABBASID RULE. The reign of the Abbasid caliphs, who came to power in 750, brought a long period of slow but progressive decay to Jerusalem. Erez Israel was no longer at the center of the Muslim empire and the caliphs residing in Baghdad did not show much interest in the town. The first Abbasids continued to visit Jerusalem—al-Manṣūr in 758 and 771 and al-Mahdī in 780—and had the al-Aqṣā mosque repaired. Al-Ma'mūn (813–33) never came to Jerusalem, although he spent some time in Syria and Egypt, but he allotted certain sums for repairing the buildings on the Temple area. The later Abbasids showed no interest at all in the holy town. During the reign of al-Muʿtaṣim (833–42) a great disaster befell the city when the peasants all over Erez Israel rose under the leadership of a certain Abu Ḥarb, besieged Jerusalem, and sacked all its quarters, mosques, and churches; again many inhabitants fled. On the other hand, it seems that in this period the non-Muslims still enjoyed tolerance, especially the Christians, on behalf of whom Charlemagne successfully intervened with the caliph.

A new period in the history of Jerusalem began in 878, when it was annexed, with the rest of Erez Israel, to the Egyptian kingdom of Aḥmad ibn Ṭūlūn. From that date the town remained under the dominion of the rulers of Cairo,

The Temple Mount, with the Dome of the Rock in the center.
Photo Werner Braun, Jerusalem.

53

with interruptions during the Crusades (see below) until the Ottoman conquest (1516). After the downfall of the Ṭūlūnids in 905, governors appointed by the Abbasids again took over; in 941 Ereẓ Israel fell to an Egyptian dynasty, the Ikhshidids. Jerusalem itself is rarely mentioned in the chronicles of this period, because it did not play a role in the political life of the Near East. The Arabic historians do not mention the town, aside from relating that the rulers of Cairo were brought to Jerusalem after their death to be buried there, a new custom which became current in this period. Christian authors, on the other hand, dwell on the harassment and persecution of their coreligionists by the Muslims: it seems that fanaticism grew greatly in the course of the tenth century. The hatred between the various religious communities increased, as is borne out by a letter of complaint against the Jews which was sent in 932 by the Christians of Jerusalem to the Holy Roman Emperor Henry I. In 938 and once more in 966 the Muslims attacked the Christians and sacked and burnt the Church of the Holy Sepulcher and other churches. On the latter occasion, when the Muslims were joined by the Jews, the patriarch was murdered and his corpse burnt.

According to *Genizah* sources, living conditions, for the most part, were difficult for Jews in Jerusalem. Aside from the tension and strife between Muslims, Christians, and Jews, the burden of various taxes and duties imposed upon the poor Jewish inhabitants was very heavy. A North African Jew describes the economic situation of the population in a letter (mid-11th century) as follows: "Meat is scarce and their cotton garments are worn out." Solomon b. Judah served for a time as *ḥazzan* of the community, which persuaded him to accept its offer because he was a man capable of being satisfied with a small livelihood: "I accepted it and spent my time sometimes for better and sometimes for worse until this day; ... but the Jerusalemites did not give me anything worth a *perutah*, because they do not have anything." The documents show

that the majority of the community had to draw its

livelihood from gifts sent from the Diaspora or offered during the pilgrimages to Jerusalem. The Karaite Daniel b. Moses al-Qūmisī (see below) proposed a practical scheme to maintain a strong Karaite community in Jerusalem: each town (in the Diaspora) should delegate five people to dwell in the Holy City and should provide for their maintenance. Clearly, some inhabitants were also busy as merchants and in trades and handicrafts, and it seems that copying of manuscripts for the Diaspora was one of the main sources of income.

Religious Life. As mentioned, the exact date when the talmudic academy was moved from Tiberias to Jerusalem is not known. It seems that arrangements were made for the academy's head and most of its important members to divide their time between Ramleh, the Arab seat of government, and Jerusalem. A part of the western slopes of the Mount of Olives served as the main gathering place for Jewish pilgrims, and the celebrations on the festivals were held there. Among the *Genizah* fragments at Cambridge, there was found a guide to Jerusalem written in Arabic by a contemporary Jew. The extant portion gives Hebrew and Arabic topographical names, describes archaeological sites, Jewish, Christian, and Muslim alike, and supplies a religious-historical background by references to the Bible and the Talmud. As the Jewish prayers inside the town, in the neighborhood of the Temple area, and at the Gates were gradually restricted, a place on the Mount of Olives was bought by the community for that purpose. On Hoshana Rabba, the seventh day of Sukkot, the gathering on the Mount of Olives was especially large, as the head of the academy, his deputy, or special messenger was accustomed to pronounce the fixing of the festival calendar for the following year and also to interdict the Karaite adversaries (see below). That interdiction sometimes caused incidents and even brawls between the two parts of the community. The Karaites used their influence to get the authorities to intervene on their behalf and to make the head of the academy responsible for peaceful celebrations. 55

Many pilgrims were accustomed to offer large sums of money for the maintenance of the academy and the payment of the many onerous taxes and duties imposed on the poor Jerusalem community.

The Karaites probably began to settle in Jerusalem during the second third of the ninth century. The report, related by a later Karaite source, that Anan, the founder of this sect, immigrated with many followers to Jerusalem deserves no credence. *Genizah* sources confirm the information given by the Karaite Salmon b. Jeroham (first half of the tenth century) that in the preceding century the Karaites began to build up a center in Jerusalem. They occupied a special quarter which was known as "the quarter of the Easterns," since most of its inhabitants were from Iraq and Persia. They called themselves Avelei Zion ("the mourners for Zion"), as well as Shoshannim (lilies). The Karaite missionary propaganda and especially the appeals of Daniel al-Qūmisī succeeded in moving many of his fellow Karaites to spend their life in the Holy City. Sahl b. Maẓli'aḥ (a younger contemporary and colleague of Salmon) gives interesting information about life in Jerusalem. Rabbanite disciples followed many of the doctrines of Karaism, and an important Karaite center began to develop in Jerusalem.

This missionary propaganda inevitably caused friction between the two parts of the Jewish population, and it has been assumed that Karaite activities influenced the old Rabbanite community to strengthen its position in Jerusalem. The Rabbanites also moved their academy (or a part of it) to Jerusalem in an effort to diminish the power of the Karaite *nasi* ("prince," descendant of David's stock) and the head of the Karaite academy in Jerusalem (*rosh yeshivat* Ge'on Ya'akov). Aaron Ben Meir (first half of the tenth century), the famous opponent of Saadiah Gaon and head of the Rabbanite academy, describes the clashes between the two opposite parties and mentions that one of his ancestors was killed on the Temple Mount area by the Karaites and an attempt was made to kill others. By personal intervention at the caliph's court in Baghdad and with the help of influential coreligionists in Iraq, he was successful in his endeavor to diminish the power of the Karaites, who for thirty years presided over the Jewish community in Jerusalem and represented it before the Muslim authorities. Nevertheless, even after Ben Meir's successful intervention, the spiritual power of the Karaites in Jerusalem did not decline, and they could muster an array of authors, scholars, and religious leaders like Salmon b. Jeroham, Sahl b. Maẓli'aḥ, Japheth b. Ali, Ibn Zuta, Joseph ibn Nūḥ, Ali b. Suleiman, and many others. They did important research into the Hebrew language, and wrote commentaries on the Bible and the precepts, which influenced all the Karaite communities in the Diaspora. During the leadership of Solomon b. Judah and especially his successor Daniel b. Azariah (1051–62), both of whom resided in Jerusalem and Ramleh alternately, the relations between the Rabbanites and Karaites improved. Indeed, the general situation in Ereẓ Israel was so bad that there was no place for internal strife.

General Description. The descriptions of the Arabic geographers and other writers make it possible to conceive of what Jerusalem was like in that period. It appears that the town—called at first by the Roman name Aelia, later Bayt al-Maqdis (the Holy House, or the Temple), and from the tenth century al-Quds (the Holy)—was larger in the first four centuries of Muslim rule than at a later time. In addition to the strong town walls, which had eight gates, it also had a moat on some sides. The Persian traveler Nasir-i-Khusrau, who visited the city in 1047, says that it had high, well-built, and clean bazaars and that all the streets were paved with stone slabs. Most Arabic authors dwell on the descriptions of the al-Aqṣā mosque and the Dome of the Rock. Besides these buildings and the Citadel, there was the so-called mosque of Omar, built within the precincts of the Church of the Holy Sepulcher in 936. The town was still predominantly non-Muslim and had a great number of splendid churches. The Jews had two quarters, one southwest of the Temple area and one north of it, near the gate of the cave (of Zedekiah). A letter written in the late 11th century mentions Ḥārat al-Yahūd (the Jewish Quarter) near a church (Gottheil-Worrell, Fragments p. 120 1. 30). At the end of the tenth century the Christians apparently were still the strongest element in the town. The Arabic geographer al-Maqdisī (end of the tenth century), who was a Jerusalemite, complained that there were no Muslim theologians in the town and that nobody was interested in Islamic sciences, whereas the Christians and the Jews were numerous. He also said that it was difficult to make a living. In addition, he emphasized that there were always many strangers in the city, most of whom were surely pilgrims—Christians, Jews, and Muslims—but others also came to live in it permanently, such as members of dissident Islamic sects or adepts of Muslim mysticism. The Karrāmiyya, a Muslim sect from Persia, was strongly represented, as were various currents of Sufism. Some of the founders and leaders of the Sufis came to Jerusalem, among them Bāyazīd al-Bisṭāmī, Ibrāhīm ibn Adham, Bishr al-Ḥāfī, and in the 11th century al-Ghazālī. The information about the political situation of the Jews in Jerusalem in the tenth century is varied. According to Salmon b. Jeroham the Muslims and the Christians persecuted the Jews and tried to diminish their rights. Al-Maqdisī's assertion seems to be an exaggeration, at least in relation to the Jews.

FATIMID RULE. The Fatimid conquest, following that of Egypt in 969, at first brought some relief to the Jewish population but ushered in a period of troubles. Whereas Egypt under the first Fatimids enjoyed security and economic prosperity, Erez Israel suffered greatly from the wars between the Fatimids and their enemies, first the Qarmatians and later the Banū Jarrāḥ, chieftains of the great Bedouin tribe of Ṭayy' who for 70 years tried to overthrow Fatimid rule. The coastal towns of Erez Israel probably took a commensurate part in the revival of international trade in the eastern Mediterranean, but Jerusalem remained far from the trade routes. The plight of the Christians and the Jews in Jerusalem in the

11th century was especially precarious. The deranged Fatimid caliph al-Ḥākim persecuted the non-Muslims and in 1009 had the churches destroyed, among them the Church of the Holy Sepulcher. The latter was rebuilt, but once more was destroyed by an earthquake in 1034 and remained in ruins until the Byzantine emperor paid for its restoration in 1048. Only the Church of the Resurrection was rebuilt, however, and the basilica of Constantine was never restored.

The town apparently changed a great deal in those days. The decline of the old settled population—Jews, Christians, and Muslims—was only one of the changes. In 1033 the town walls were repaired, but the area within them was diminished, the entire area of Mount Zion remaining outside the walls. The decline of Ramleh in the middle of the 11th century and the increase of Christian pilgrims from European countries gave sorely afflicted Jerusalem another chance, but then in the last third of the century it became a bone of contention between various political powers. In 1071 Jerusalem was taken by the Seljuk general Atsiz and annexed to the great empire of the sultans of Iraq and Persia. Five years later the inhabitants revolted against Atsiz, who had left to fight a war against the Fatimids, and when he returned and took the town once more, it was severely punished. Some years afterward the Seljuks appointed the Turkoman officer, Urtuq, prince of Jerusalem. In 1091 Urtuq left the town to his sons Suqmān and Ilghāzī, whose rule lasted no more than five years. In 1098 Jerusalem fell for a second time to the Fatimids, who held it against an attempt of the Seljuk prince Riḍwān. In 1099 Jerusalem was conquered by the crusaders.

9 CRUSADER PERIOD

The crusaders besieged Jerusalem for five weeks, from June 6 to July 15, 1099. When several attempts to seize the city by direct attack failed, they constructed siege towers and concentrated their forces on two weak spots: the first between the Damascus Gate and the tower in the eastern section of the northern wall, and the second in the area of Mount Zion. The attack began on the night of Thursday, July 14 and was concluded the next morning. The troops of Flanders and of northern France, led by Godfrey de Bouillon, scaled the walls in the north-eastern sector, which was defended by both Muslims and Jews, the latter fighting to protect their own quarter nearby. At the same time, the Provençal force, led by Raymond of St. Gilles, surmounted the wall adjoining Mount Zion, while the Normans from Sicily, headed by Tancred, entered the northwest corner of the city in the vicinity of the tower (subsequently called the Tancred Tower).

The population, Muslims and Jews alike, was massacred. Many Jews perished in the synagogues that were set on fire by the conquerors; others were taken prisoner and sold into slavery in Europe, where they were later redeemed by the Jewish communities. Some Jewish prisoners were taken to Ashkelon (still in Muslim hands) along with the Egyptian commander of the city's fortress, who had surrendered; they were ransomed by the Jewish communities of Egypt and brought there. As a result of the massacre, the city was largely depopulated and the first period of the crusaders' rule were years of insecurity and economic difficulties. During the second decade of their rule, in order to repopulate the city, the crusaders transferred Christian

Arab tribes from Transjordan and settled them in the former Jewish quarter, between the Damascus and Lions' Gates. In order to encourage people to settle there, the duty on food was reduced. As a matter of course, Jerusalem became the capital of the crusaders' kingdom, which was called the Kingdom of Jerusalem *(Regnum Hierusalem)*, or Jerusalemite Kingdom *(Regnum Hieroso-lymitanorum)*, or even Kingdom of David *(Regnum David)*. Jerusalem was chosen to be the capital despite economic, administrative, and security problems due to its location in the crusaders' southernmost territories.

Jerusalem developed and flourished in the middle of the 12th century because of the concentration of all the government and Church bodies there. The king's court, his administration, and the centers of the ecclesiastical institutions, as well as of the various monastic and military orders, were located there, providing a livelihood for a considerable number of permanent inhabitants. The most important factor in the development of Jerusalem at that period, however, was the stream of pilgrims from all countries of Christian Europe (there are records of pilgrims coming from as far as Russia, Scandinavia, and Portugal). Tens of thousands of pilgrims visited Jerusalem every year. These pilgrimages were not only an important source of income but also added to the city's population, since a number of pilgrims remained there. Owing to its geographical position, however, it remained a consumer city, as in earlier and later periods.

THE CITY AND ITS INSTITUTIONS. Jerusalem during the crusader period was located within the walls of the previous Arab city. The basic pattern of the city remained the same, although there seems to have been an increase in the number of inhabitants. A period of construction began, the likes of which had not been seen since the time of Herod. Many of the buildings that had remained intact were used for the same purposes. First and foremost was the Citadel by the western gate (Jaffa Gate), which the crusaders called Turris David (David's Tower). It housed

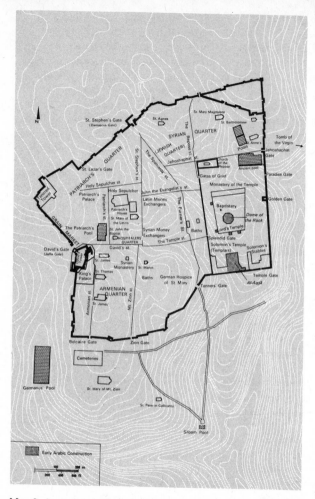

Map 5. Jerusalem in the crusader period. Based on D. Bahat, *Jerusalem—Its Epochs,* Jerusalem, 1970.

the king's garrison, the food warehouses for the army and probably for the entire city, and the customs administration for imports, which were directed through this gate. Adjoining the Citadel was the king's palace, on the site of Herod's palace and the administrative center during the Roman and Byzantine periods.

At first the king and his court had their residence in the al-Aqṣā Mosque and vicinity, but when this area was given to the Templars, the king moved to the vicinity of the Citadel, which was traditionally associated with the rule over the city. Just as the Citadel and the palace signified the secular power, the Holy Sepulcher and its environs signified the rule of the Church and its religious ritual. Near the Holy Sepulcher stood the palace of the patriarch of Jerusalem, and opposite its southern entrance were the monasteries of the Benedictines and the area of the Order of St. John, the Hospitalers (now the New Market). The Templars were situated in the al-Aqṣā Mosque, which the crusaders called the Temple of Solomon *(Templum Solomonis)* and which is known in Jewish tradition as *Midrash Shelomo* (Solomon's House of Study). The German-speaking order of knights, a branch of the Hospitalers, was located near the Temple Mount (in what is now the Jewish quarter); the Order of St. Lazarus, the Leper Knights, was outside the city wall, near the present New Gate.

The establishment of the crusaders' rule invigorated Christian religious life. Throughout the 12th century many Christian traditions associated with Jerusalem and its vicinity were established, particularly those pertaining to the life of Jesus. Thus the tradition of Via Dolorosa was defined. The crystallization of these traditions stimulated an unusual amount of building in the city. Many Muslim shrines were turned into churches, as, for example the Dome of the Rock ("Mosque of Omar") called by the crusaders the Lord's Temple *(Templum Domini)*. New churches were also built, among them the new Church of the Holy Sepulcher, the most important architectural endeavor of the 63

Sculptured frieze from the Holy Sepulcher, crusader period. Scenes from the life of Jesus: right, the Last Supper; left, largely obliterated, the entry into Jerusalem. Jerusalem, Rockefeller Museum, Israel Department of Antiquities.

64

crusaders in Jerusalem, which was dedicated in 1149, 50 years after the conquest. The crusaders concentrated a number of churches under one roof. Some were built in the Byzantine period, including the Anastasis (Church of the Resurrection), which is the traditional site of the tomb of Jesus, the Martyrion, and the chapel of Queen Helena (Church of the Holy Cross). The ancient buildings did not blend well with the new structure, and there was a lack of symmetry among the component parts: a Byzantine church in the west, a Romanesque church in the middle. The southern gates (there was only a small gate in the west) are the best examples of crusader art in architecture and sculpture of that period. Among the outstanding churches built were the Church of St. Anne, in fine Romanesque style; the renovated "Tomb of Mary" church in the Valley of Jehoshaphat; and the churches of Mount Zion.

POPULATION OF THE CITY. Most of the inhabitants of 12th century Jerusalem were of European origin, except for the Eastern Christians—the Syrians (Suriani), the Jacobites, and the Copts, who lived in the northeastern corner of the

The "Tomb of Mary" in the Valley of Jehoshaphat.
The Romanesque façade leads to a Greek-Orthodox church.
Photo David Eisenberg, Jerusalem.

city near the church of Santa Maria Magdalena. There were also Georgians from Caucasia (Georgiani), whose center was the Monastery of the Cross outside the walls of the city. The majority of the population was of French descent. French was the main language (official documents were written in Latin in the 12th century and in French in the 13th). The others congregated in ethnic or linguistic communities, such as the German knights mentioned above, the Spaniards, who settled near Damascus Gate, the Provençals, near the Zion Gate, and the Hungarians near the New Gate. These communities had their own churches and later often hostels for pilgrims from their countries of origin. Muslims and Jews were not permitted to reside in the city; however, the Muslims came into the city for business purposes and some Jews settled near the Citadel. The 12th-century traveler Benjamin of Tudela tells of a few Jewish dyers whom he met while visiting Jerusalem.

THE FALL OF CRUSADER JERUSALEM. After the Battle of Hattin (July 1187) the army of Saladin besieged Jerusalem. The patriarch of Jerusalem and the secular commanders soon agreed to surrender on condition that they would be allowed to ransom themselves from captivity and take their possessions with them. The city surrendered in November 1187 and remained in Muslim hands until 1229. All Christians, except for the Easterners, were forbidden to reside in Jerusalem. The Easterners were allowed to take care of the Holy Sepulcher and some of the other churches. Most of the churches were either restored as Muslim shrines and mosques, like the Dome of the Rock and the al-Aqṣā Mosque, or converted into Muslim charitable or religious institutions. The Church of St. Anne became a madrasa (religious college). The Jewish community was renewed as a result of the initiative of Saladin. Jews came into the city from other towns in the country, for example, Ashkelon, which was destroyed on Saladin's orders. Prominent among these was a group of Yemenites. Others came as immigrants from the Maghreb (North Africa) and Europe. A particularly important group of immigrants were those rabbis who came from France and England (1209–11). In 1218 Al-Harizi reported that Saladin invited the Jews to settle in Jerusalem. It seems that the Jews lived in separate communities according to their country or town of origin.

In the third decade of the 13th century, Jerusalem suffered from a systematic destruction of its fortifications by the Muslims as in other cities which seemed likely to serve as strong points for a renewed effort of settlement by the crusaders. The attempts by the Third Crusade to capture Jerusalem failed, even though the army got very close to the city. What they did not achieve by military action, however, they succeeded in obtaining by diplomatic negotiations. According to an agreement between al-Malik al-Kāmil, the ruler of Egypt, and Frederick II, Holy Roman Emperor and the king of Germany, a corridor to Jaffa through Ramleh was agreed upon, and Jerusalem was divided between Christians and Muslims (Tell ʿAjjūl, 1229). The Muslims received the area of the Temple Mount and freedom of worship therein; the Christians received the rest of the city and Frederick had himself crowned King of Jerusalem in the Church of the Holy Sepulcher. During this second period of occupancy (1229–44), the crusaders tried to resettle the city, but the results were in no way comparable with their achievements during the 12th century, either in population or in economic life. In 1240 the rulers of Egypt, who were competing with Damascus for ascendancy in the area, asked for help from the hordes of the Khwarizm Turks, who attacked Jerusalem in 1244, sacked the city, massacred the Christians, and devastated the Church of the Holy Sepulcher. Only a few Christian inhabitants of the city succeeded in escaping to Jaffa. Naḥmanides mentions in his letter (written 1267) that he found only two Jewish dyers in Jerusalem, because during the Tartar (=Khwarizim) conquest some Jews had been killed but others escaped from the city. It seems that these found shelter in Nablus, because Naḥmanides remarks that the Torah scroll which they took with them was brought back to Jerusalem, when he succeeded in establishing a synagogue (restored soon after 1967). The city suffered greatly and did not recover until the overthrow of the Ayyubids in Egypt by the Mamluks in 1250. Jerusalem became part of the Mamluk kingdom and remained so for over 260 years.

10 MAMLUK PERIOD

Following the death of al-Malik al-Ṣāliḥ Ayyūb, the sultan of Egypt, in 1249, Jerusalem was incorporated for a time into the kingdom of al-Malik al-Nāṣir Yūsuf, ruler of Aleppo and Damascus. While this Syrian Ayyubid was waging war with the Mamluks—who had taken over in Egypt—the Mongols invaded the Near East and penetrated into Ereẓ Israel at the beginning of 1260. The inhabitants of Jerusalem fled panic-stricken when the Mongol hordes swept over the country sacking the townlets and villages. When the Mamluks succeeded in September 1260 in defeating the Mongols at ʿAyn Jālūt (En-Harod), Jerusalem, with all Ereẓ Israel, was annexed to their kingdom and remained under their rule until the Ottomans conquered Syria and Egypt in 1516/17. The situation of Jerusalem in the years after the retreat of the Mongols was very depressed. Naḥmanides reported in 1267 that only a part of the inhabitants had returned to the city and there were no more than 2,000 living there, among them 300 Christians. He persuaded some Jews who had found shelter in the villages to return and reconstitute the Jewish community.

The Mamluks did not care to fortify Jerusalem and repopulate it. Under their long rule Jerusalem became a town of theologians whose life focused on the mosques and madrasas (Muslim theological colleges). Until the last quarter of the 14th century it belonged to the province of Damascus and was administered by a low-ranking Mamluk appointed by the nāʾib (deputy of the sultan) of Damascus. In 1376 al-Malik al-Ashraf Shaʿbān made Jerusalem a separate province and henceforth its head was appointed by the sultan himself. The new administrative entity was a   69

Façade of the 13th-century Ibrahim Tushtumur Mausoleum,
a typical example of Mamluk architecture. Courtesy Israel
Department of Antiquities, Jerusalem.

small one, comprising the Judean hill country with Hebron,
although at times Ramleh and Nablus (Shechem) were
annexed to it. The promotion of its head to a higher rank,
however, did not signify a great change in its status. The

post was often sold to the highest bidder, who later did his best to extort from the townspeople what he had paid. The complaints of the inhabitants sometimes brought about the dismissal of the *nā'ib,* but for the most part they had to submit to his tyranny. Another very important post in the administration of Jerusalem was that of the "superintendent of the Holy Places" *(nāẓir al-ḥaramayn),* who was in charge of the sanctuaries of Jerusalem and Hebron. He administered the endowments and supervised the activities of the staff. Sometimes this post was also held by the deputy of the sultan himself. It seems that the administration was not very efficient, even in the field in which the Mamluks were really interested, i.e., security. Letters of Italian Jews who settled in Jerusalem during the 15th century (see below) contain reports about the lack of security in the town's surroundings, where Bedouin were roaming.

In this period Jerusalem produced soap, manufactured from the olive oil which was supplied by the villages of central Ereẓ Israel, but the Mamluk authorities encroached upon this industrial activity, e.g., by the establishment of monopolies and the forced purchase of large quantities of the raw material at high prices. The Arabic historian Mujīr al-Dīn (d. 1521) dwells on the catastrophic consequences of these measures and one reads in the reports of Jews who settled in the town in the 15th century about the great difficulty of making a living. Even the frequent visits by groups of pilgrims could not change the economic situation. The pilgrims only made short visits and did their utmost to escape the extortions of the authorities as soon as possible. Consequently, Jerusalem remained a very poor town. The population did not increase considerably and Western pilgrims reported that many houses were empty or had fallen into ruins. At the end of the 15th century Jerusalem probably had no more than 10,000 inhabitants. The Dominican Felix Fabri, who was in Jerusalem in 1483, says that there were 1,000 Christians. The Jewish community numbered 100–150 families.

Whereas the Mamluks did nothing for the development

of Jerusalem's economy, they continued the policy and trends of the Muslims since the Crusades in underlining the religious importance of Jerusalem for Islam. Religious propaganda had found expression in the building of madrasas and *zawiyas* (convents—Ar. *zāwiya*, pl. *zawāyā*) for Sufis, and guidebooks for visits to the Holy Places especially in Jerusalem and in Hebron. The Mamluk rulers generously endowed religious establishments, such as mosques and colleges. These activities corresponded well with the efforts they made to appear as the champions of orthodox Islam. The sultan Baybars had the Dome of the Rock repaired in 1261 and in 1263 he founded a hospice for

The Ramban Synagogue, believed to be the one originally built by Naḥmanides in 1267 C.E. The synagogue has been restored several times over the centuries, and the present floor divides the upper third of the building from the lower two-thirds, still unexcavated. From *Qadmoniot*, Vol. 1, Jerusalem, 1968.

pilgrims not far from the western gate of the town. Qalā'ūn (1279–90) repaired the roof of the al-Aqṣā mosque and founded another hospice. The sultans Katbughā (1294–96) and al-Malik al-Nāṣir Muhammad (d. 1341) restored the wall of the Ḥaram, and the latter also repaired the gilding of the roofs of the al-Aqṣā Mosque and the Dome of the Rock. Barsbāy (1422–38) made endowments for the upkeep of al-Aqṣā, and Jaqmaq (1438–53) repaired the roof of the Dome of the Rock once more. Tengiz, viceroy of Syria under the reign of al-Malik al-Nāṣir Muhammad, built a great madrasa in Jerusalem. Other colleges were founded in the 14th century by the emirs Ṭushtumur and Arghūn, and in 1482 by the sultan Qā'itbāy. The Mamluks also spent large sums on the restoration of the water conduits which supplied the town (or more correctly the Ḥaram), among them Tengiz in 1338 and the sultans Khushqadam and Qā'itbāy in the second half of the century. Princes from Persia and Turkey also founded madrasas and hospices for pilgrims in Jerusalem in that period. Thus, these numerous endowments resulted in the construction of numerous religious buildings, which became the striking feature of Jerusalem. (The travelogues of Western pilgrims and other sources give one a clear picture of Jerusalem in the later Middle Ages.)

The contradictory statements as to the existence of town walls point to the fact that Jerusalem was only partly enclosed by walls. Apparently the walls were not completely razed in 1219 and parts were rebuilt in 1229. The walled-in area probably included Mount Zion in the 14th century, whereas in 15th-century descriptions it appears as being outside of the walls, thus indicating changes in the area of the city. On the other hand, there were no suburbs outside the walls. Mujīr al-Dīn mentions some small groups of houses west and northwest of the town; north and east of it there were some *zawiyas* and churches. On the southern outskirts there were also *zawiyas* and a group of houses named after the sheikh Abu Thawr, who participated in the siege of Jerusalem in 1187. The ancient Byzantine town plan 73 had disappeared, although "David Street" (Ṭarīq Dā'ud)—the street connecting Jaffa Gate and Bāb al-Silsila, the main entrance of the Ḥaram—remained the main artery of the town. The area north and west of the al-Aqṣā Mosque was occupied by many colleges and convents of Sufi mystics: Mujīr al-Dīn mentions 44 madrasas and about 20 *zawiyas*. The palace of the *nā'ib* was also located northwest of the Ḥaram. The area which the Christians held in the town was reduced, and Saladin had established a convent of Sufis in the former palace of the patriarch, north of the Church of the Holy Sepulcher. The church of the Hospitalers had become a Muslim hospital, a part of the hospital itself was also handed over to Sufis, and south of the Church of the Holy Sepulcher a mosque was built.

Since the number of the madrasas had increased so markedly, Jerusalem became a center of Islamic studies in the later Middle Ages. The most important schools were al-Ṣalāḥiyya al-Tengiziyya, al-Muʿazzamiyya, and al-ʿUthmāniyya, but other madrasas had students from other towns in Ereẓ Israel, and even from other countries. The theologians who taught at the madrasas were the most distinguished group in the town's population. Among them there were families which for a number of generations had held certain prominent posts in the clerical hierarchy, such as the Ibn Jamāʿa, Ibn Ghānim, al-Qarqashandī, and al-Dayrī. Some of the teachers at the madrasas of Jerusalem were well known in the Muslim world, e.g., Ibn al-Ḥā'im (d. 1412) and Kamāl al-Dīn ibn Abī Sharīf (d. 1500), both of whom were prolific writers in various branches of Islamic theology.

In view of the fact that the Muslim theologians played so great a role in the town, one can easily understand that persecutions of the non-Muslims were frequent. The atmosphere was charged with fanaticism and the interventions of Christian princes who tried to protect their coreligionists were not always successful. For the most part, the outbreaks of Muslim fanaticism were directed against the Latin Friars (Franciscans) who had established a monastery on Mount Zion in 1334. Several times the Friars were imprisoned and sent to Damascus or Cairo. The possession of some sites on Mount Zion, which were coveted by Christians and Muslims, and sometimes even by Jews, became a point of contention. Time and again the chapel situated above David's supposed tomb passed from the Christians to the Muslims and vice versa. When the Christians built a church on Mount Zion in 1452 on the site where Mary is believed to have lived for a long time, it was immediately pulled down by Muslim fanatics. At times the Muslims penetrated into the Church of the Holy Sepulcher and other churches, devastated them, and destroyed some parts completely. In 1489 the Franciscans obtained permission once again to build a church on the site where Mary had lived, but in 1490 it was pulled down.

The role of the Jews in Jerusalem was very modest. Until the end of the 15th century their number was apparently quite small. In about the middle of the 14th century there was a yeshivah in the town whose head was a rabbi named Isaac ha-Levi Asir ha-Tikvah. At the beginning of the 15th century immigration of Jews from European countries began, but the attempt of German Jews to acquire the room above the supposed tomb of David almost brought it to a stop. The Christians applied to the pope, who asked the Italian merchant republics to stop taking Jews on board their ships sailing for Erez Israel; this happened in 1428. The Mamluk government also harassed the Jews, and in about 1440 it imposed a heavy tax on them to be paid yearly. Most Jews were craftsmen or petty merchants who could not afford to pay the tax and many left the town. Details on the economic situation of the Jews are given in a letter of R. Elijah of Ferrara, who settled in Jerusalem in 1438 and became rabbi of the community. R. Isaac b. Meir Latif (c. 1470) states that there were 150 Jewish families in the town, whereas Meshullam of Volterra, who visited Jerusalem in 1481, spoke of about 250, but this was probably an exaggerated figure. Even in that period the Jews suffered greatly from heavy taxation and Muslim intolerance. In 1474 the Muslims destroyed an old synagogue, but the sultan intervened and after a long lawsuit had it returned and rebuilt. R. Obadiah of Bertinoro, who went to Jerusalem in 1488 and became the spiritual head of the community, complained about its poverty and oppression, which caused Nathan Sholal to move from Jerusalem to Cairo, where he became *nagid* (leader) of Egyptian Jewry. Obadiah found no more than 70 Jewish families and many widows in Jerusalem, but shortly afterward a change took place. On the one hand, the government abolished the heavy tax and the Italian republics once more allowed Jews to travel on their ships to Erez Israel, and on the other hand, the immigration of the Spanish exiles began. A pupil of R. Obadiah related in a letter written in 1495 that about 200 Jewish families were living in Jerusalem.

In the beginning of the 16th century there were scholars in Jerusalem who took part in the controversy which arose over the fixing of the dates of the sabbatical (*shemittah*) years. Scholars in Safed also took part in the dispute, not missing the opportunity to underline their reverence for the Jerusalemites. The celebrated scholar R. Isaac Sholal (d. 1524), who was the *nagid* of Jewry in Mamluk lands and resided in Cairo, moved to Jerusalem at the end of Mamluk rule and published ordinances (*takkanot*) for the welfare and good order of the community; they are quoted in R. Moses Basola's travel book.

11 UNDER OTTOMAN RULE
   (1517–1917)

SULEIMAN THE MAGNIFICENT AND HIS WORK. The present wall around the Old City of Jerusalem was built by the sultan Suleiman I (1520–66), who was called al-Qānūnī ("the Lawgiver"), and in the West, the Magnificent. According to contemporary evidence, most of the wall was in ruins at the end of the Mamluk period and Suleiman, known for his widespread activities in the building of numerous mosques and public buildings in the empire, ordered that Jerusalem be surrounded by a wall in order to protect its inhabitants against marauding Bedouins.

The following statement was made by an anonymous contemporary "Jewish" inhabitant of Jerusalem or Hebron: "Jerusalem the Holy City has been destroyed through our sins. Nothing is left of the old structure except for a little of the foundation of the walls. Now in 1537 they have begun to build the walls around the city by order of the king, Sultan Suleiman. They have also put a great fountain in the Temple ..." The sources show that the building of the wall made a great impression on the Jewish world and Joseph ha-Kohen recorded it in his chronicle: "In that year 1540 [an insignificant error], God aroused the spirit of Suleiman king of Greece (= Rumelia) and Persia and he set out to build the walls of Jerusalem the holy city in the land of Judah. And he sent officials who built its walls and set up its gates as in former times and its towers as in bygone days. And his fame spread throughout the land for he wrought a great deed. And they did also extend the tunnel into the town lest the people thirst for water. May God remember him favorably" (*Sefer Divrei ha-Yamim le-Malkhei Zarefat u-Malkhei Beit Ottoman*, Sabionetta, 1554, 261b–262a). As is stated in the former source, the wall was rebuilt on top of its former remains, some of which dated to the Second Temple times. In certain places the planner-engineer deviated from the ancient pattern, e.g., by leaving part of present-day Mount Zion outside the wall. According to tradition he was executed for this.

The construction of the wall lasted from 1537 to 1541, as is recounted in the 11 original inscriptions inserted in various parts of the wall, especially near the gates. Thus, for instance, the inscription near the Jaffa Gate (Bāb al-Khalīl, the Gate of Hebron) contains the date 945 A.H. (1538–39). The southern wall contains the Zion Gate (Bāb al-Nabī Dā'ud, i.e., Gate of the "Prophet" David, since it is near "David's Tomb" which is on Mount Zion). Next is the Dung Gate (Bāb al-Maghāriba, or Moor Gate, because of its proximity to the quarter of the Maghreb Muslims). On a tablet nearby is the date 947 A.H. (1540–41). Further east along the southern wall are three gates which are closed off, dating to pre-Ottoman times: the Double Gate, the Triple Gate, and the Single Gate. Northward along the eastern wall is the Mercy Gate (which the Muslims call by the same name, Bāb al-Raḥma, or al-Dahriyya, i.e., Eternal, and the Christians call the Golden Gate). There are several legendary reasons for its being closed. Inside the area of the Temple Mount this gate has been divided into two since the early Middle Ages, one being called the Gate of Repentance (Bāb al-Tawba). In the east is the Lions' Gate (Bāb Sitt Maryam, the Gate of the Lady Mary, because of its proximity to the traditional birthplace of Mary, Jesus' mother; the Christians call it St. Stephen's Gate). On the northern side is Herod's or the Flower Gate (Bāb al-Zahra, a corruption of Sāhira since it leads to the plain of Sāhira (Sura 79:14) on which the Muslims believe all creatures will congregate on the day of the resurrection of the dead). The most magnificent and the most ornate of the gates is the Damascus Gate (Bāb al-'Amūd, Gate of the Pillar or Column). The seventh gate is the New Gate in the

wall near the Christian Quarter (opposite the Hospice of

The Jaffa Gate, so called because it was the terminal of the highway from the coast. The moat between the gate and the Citadel, of which the tower on the right forms part, was filled up in 1898. Photo David Eisenberg, Jerusalem.

Inscription set in the wall by the Jaffa Gate, stating that the gate was built by command of Sultan Suleiman in 1538–39. Photo Zev Radovan, Jerusalem.

The Dung Gate in the south wall, dating from 1540–41, is the one closest to the Temple Mount and leads to the Kidron Valley. Photo Zev Radovan, Jerusalem.

Notre Dame), which was opened at the time of the sultan Abdul Hamid II (1876–1908) and for this reason was first called the Sultan's Gate; it was to facilitate the connection between the Christian Quarter and New Jerusalem.

The Zion Gate on Mount Zion in the south wall. The plaque on the right commemorates the reopening of the gate by the Israel Defense Forces Engineers after the Six-Day War. Courtesy J.N.F., Jerusalem. Photo Dafni.

Suleiman also introduced changes in the buildings on the Temple Mount. He ordered that the mosaics covering the walls of the Dome of the Rock be removed and replaced by beautiful marble tablets and facings, which adorned the

The blocked-up, pre-Ottoman Triple Gate in the south wall.
Photo David Eisenberg, Jerusalem.

building until the 1950s and were in part replaced during
the repairs conducted by the Jordanian government.
During Suleiman's reign four *sabīls* (public fountains) were
set up in the city, and one outside it near the Sultan's Pool,
in order to provide water for passersby. The most beautiful
of these is opposite the Chain Gate (Bāb al-Silsila) in the
wall surrounding the Temple Mount. The two Jewish
sources mentioned above emphasize the special attention
devoted to one of the age-old problems of Jerusalem, the
city's water supply, especially for the Temple Mount area.
The conduits bringing water from the vicinity of Solomon's

Pools (near Bethlehem) were repaired and widened by order of

Suleiman and his wife Roxelana, and in 1536 the Sultan's Pool was constructed on the foundations of an ancient pool. Its water was collected by means of the dam in the Hinnom Valley (on what is the present-day road to Mt. Zion) and on it is also the fifth *sabīl*.

The blocked-up pre-Ottoman Single Gate leading to the under ground structure in the Temple Mount area known as "Solomon's Stables." Photo David Eisenberg, Jerusalem.

Junction of the southern wall and the wall of the Temple
Mount. In the corner, below the al-Aqṣā dome, can be seen
part of a decorated frieze above a sealed gateway called the
Double Gate. Photo David Eisenberg, Jerusalem.

The Mercy Gate seen from inside the wall. Photo Zev
Radovan, Jerusalem.

The post-Byzantine Mercy Gate (Golden Gate) in the eastern wall above the Valley of Jehoshaphat, facing the Mount of Olives. Courtesy J.N.F., Jerusalem. Photo Albert.

The Lions' Gate in the east wall, leading to the Via Dolorosa, 1538–39. Courtesy J.N.F., Jerusalem. Photo Zev Radovan, Jerusalem.

Detail of lions above the Lions' Gate. According to tradition, they were placed there by Sultan Suleiman to perpetuate his dream that he would be devoured by lions unless he built a wall around Jerusalem. Photo Zev Radovan, Jerusalem.

Herod's Gate in the north wall, near the Rockefeller Museum.
Courtesy Israel Department of Antiquities, Jerusalem.

The New Gate near the northwestern corner of the wall,
constructed in 1889 by permission of Sultan Abdul Hamid II.
Photo David Eisenberg, Jerusalem.

The Damascus Gate, the most magnificent and busiest of the gates, opposite the Nablus road. At its base on the left can be seen the remnants of the Roman gate uncovered in 1937. Courtesy Government Press Office, Tel Aviv.

In order to maintain the madrasas (Muslim theological colleges) and shelters for the Sufis *(zāwiya, khanqa, tekke)* which were established in former times, many properties *(waqf)* such as lands, shops, and flour mills were dedicated, bringing a flow of money to Muslim Jerusalem. Roxelana also established a khan (inn), and especially an ʿimāret (a soup kitchen providing free meals for students of the madrasas, dervishes, and other poor Muslims). These institutions were supported by taxes levied on numerous villages throughout the country. Repairs, which were ordered by the sultan, were made on the fortress near David's Tower (Turk. *Qishla,* winter barracks for the soldiers). A Turkish aga encamped at this fortress together with an escort of a troop of janissaries.

88

FOUNTAIN OF THE GATE OF THE CHAIN—BAB ES SILSILEH.
Supplied with water from Solomon's Pools.

From Sir Charles Wilson (ed.), *Picturesque Palestine, Sinai and Egypt*, Vol. I, London, c. 1880. Courtesy A. A. Mendilow, Jerusalem.

The *sabil* or public fountain near the Sultan's Pool at the foot of Mt. Zion, built by Sultan Suleiman in 1536. Photo David Eisenberg, Jerusalem.

THE DECLINE OF JERUSALEM. After this period of construction, however, the development of Jerusalem was halted. The authorities did nothing to preserve the show pieces of Muslim architecture and prevent their destruction through the agency of time and of man. Administratively, Jerusalem was the seat of the governor of the district or sanjak (Ar. *liwā'*; Turk. *sanjaq*, both meaning "standard"). However, the *mīr liwā'* or *sanjaq bey* (i.e., the governor) was usually of a lower status than the other local regional rulers (Safed, Nablus, Gaza), since the central authorities regarded Jerusalem as no more than a town bordering on the land of the Bedouin *(Arabistan)*. Jerusalem's governor was subordinate to the general governor (Turkish wali) of the province *(eyālet)*, usually that of Damascus, but sometimes to the wali of Sidon (and Acre), and had no direct contact with the central authorities in Constantinople. In 1756/1169 A.H., however, Jerusalem was raised for a short time to the status of an independent provincial unit *(eyālet)*, ruled by a governor *(mutaṣarrif)* bearing the standard of two *tughs* ("horsetails")—though only in the second half of the 19th century did it become an independent *mutaṣarriflik* ruled by a "two-tail" pasha—directly subordinate to the Sublime Porte in Constantinople (see below). In the city of Jerusalem the immediate control of all municipal matters was in the hands of the qadi. He was also the authority over all non-Muslims.

The Ottomans introduced no changes in the composition of the Muslim population of Jerusalem. During their 400-year reign only a few Turks settled in the country. The Turkish language did not take the place of Arabic, although a number of Turkish words were incorporated into the spoken Arabic. This absence of a permanently settled Turkish class facilitated the establishment of a kind of local nobility in Jerusalem, composed of the distinguished Arab families which derived their power and influence from farming taxes and duties *(iltizām)* and from their control of hereditary religious functions, and at the end of the Ottoman period exercised administrative functions. These were the *a'yān* (the notables, "eyes" of the community), the effendi (masters), e.g., the families of Khatīb, Dajjānī, Anṣārī, Khālidī, 'Alamī, and later Nashāshībī and Ḥusaynī. Several of Jerusalem's Christian families were also well-known: Salāmeh, Tanūs, 'Aṭallah, and Katan.

One reason for the Ottoman rulers' disparaging attitude toward Jerusalem may have been its insignificance from a strategic and political point of view when there was no longer a danger of renewed Crusades. At the Ottoman conquest of Ereẓ Israel (1516) even the exact date of Jerusalem's capture was not noted. Because of its insignificance the rebels and invaders did not attempt to conquer it. The same situation existed at the time of Ẓāhir al-Omar, who in 1773 controlled the whole country except for Jerusalem. Similarly, Napoleon did not consider it necessary to conquer Jerusalem and was satisfied with the towns of the coastal strip and the plain. Another reason was the city's economic insignificance. According to the Ottoman records of land registration from the 16th century, the inhabitants of the district of Jerusalem were much fewer in number than those of Gaza, Nablus, and Safed. Accordingly, the income of Jerusalem's governor was smaller than that of the other governors. Apart from soap and Christian religious objects, almost nothing was manufactured in Jerusalem which could be exported to other districts or abroad. Nor did local trade play an important role in the city, since industry and craft did not develop in Jerusalem, which had no fertile rural areas surrounding it. Jewish, Muslim, and Christian sources were therefore justified in repeatedly emphasizing that most of the city's inhabitants were extremely impoverished. During the Ottoman Empire's period of abundance, the sultans regarded it as a duty to exempt the city's inhabitants from various taxes, and even sent yearly contributions for distribution among the poor.

JEWISH JERUSALEM. Even before the Ottoman conquest there were many indications that Jewish Jerusalem was awakening from its lethargy. At the beginning of the 16th century it attracted the kabbalists who were awaiting the imminent redemption, such as Abraham b. Eliezer ha-Levi. Isaac Sholal, the *nagid* of Egypt, also settled in the city. After the conquest, and especially in light of the sympathetic attitude of Sultan Suleiman, which aroused such a positive response on the part of the Jews, it appears as if there existed the political and social conditions which could enable Jerusalem to reassert its function as the spiritual and religious center of Judaism. Levi b. Ḥabib, who settled in the city and was one of the greatest scholars of his time, attacked Jacob Berab for wanting to reestablish ordination (*semikhah*) in Safed and succeeded in foiling that plan. David ibn Abi Zimra and, later, Bezalel Ashkenazi taught in Jerusalem. However, the overwhelming poverty of the scholars and all the Jewish inhabitants placed the city at a disadvantage, and Safed, which attracted in the 16th century the greatest scholars and most of the immigrants, superseded Jerusalem for a time in importance as a center.

However, the communities of Egypt and Syria (especially Damascus) aided the Jerusalem community, as is attested by Moses Trani (De Trani): "All the holy communities which send contributions to Jerusalem know that in addition to what is distributed among the scholars and the poor, they are also used for all the fines and penalties levied on the community, for the inhabitants of Jerusalem can pay only the *kharāj* (poll tax) . . . and the remaining burdens . . . have to be met from outside contributions; for if they did not do thus, no one would want to settle in the city." The situation of the scholars and yeshivot was especially difficult and there are recurring and repeated complaints about this in the literature of the period.

Apparently the local rulers hindered the consolidation of the city's Jewish population. According to official censuses in 1525, 1533–39, and 1553, the number of Jews in the town ranged between approximately 1,000 and 1,500. They lived in three quarters, Sharaf, al-Maslakh ("Slaughterhouse"), and Rīsha, which are coextensive with the present-day Jewish Quarter. David ibn Abi Zimra conveys in his responsa the interesting information that the Jewish Quarter is called the "City of Zion" by the Jews, and Ṣahyūn by the Arabs. He explains that in the laws pertaining to the holiness of Jerusalem a distinction is to be made between that part to which these laws pertain, called by the Arabs *Quds* (=Jerusalem), and the other part ("Zion") which is considered outside of Jerusalem. In 1586 the authorities deprived the community of the synagogue named after Naḥmanides (restored only after the Six-Day War).

After Safed's decline at the end of the 16th century Jerusalem was built up. A major role in this rebuilding was played by Bezalel Ashkenazi, who had come from Egypt.

He was not content merely to act as *dayyan* but also lent his help in the organization of material assistance and even went on a mission to organize aid and save the synagogue which had been confiscated. He died in the early 1590s, however—shortly after his immigration—and was unable to carry out his activities. His initiative persisted after his death and Jewish Jerusalem continued to recover. The stream of immigrants from Turkey, North Africa, Italy, and Western Europe soon turned to Jerusalem. One of the most distinguished and famous among them was R. Isaiah Horowitz (immigrated in 1622), author of *Shenei Luḥot ha-Berit,* whose influence was of great spiritual importance for the community. He found a population in Jerusalem composed of Sephardim, Ashkenazim, and Italians (who were considered one community), Maghrebis, and Mustaʿrabs (Moriscos). There was also a small Karaite community. Shortly after his arrival the community suffered severely from the persecution of the governor Muhammad ibn Farruk (1625), which is described in the pamphlet *Horvot Yerushalayim* (published anonymously in Venice, 1636). This governor, however, was removed from his post a short while later and the community recovered.

In general, the situation improved in Jerusalem, but the tax burden and other impositions were not eased. There are various extant sources from this period, including several interesting diaries and travel descriptions—among them that of R. Moses Poryat of Prague (1650)—which make it possible to achieve a faithful reconstruction of the situation. There are also descriptions from the end of the 17th century which render an exact description of the situation in Jerusalem. There were then about 300 Jewish families, with nearly 1,200 persons. This number exceeded the quota established by the Ottoman authorities for the Jews in the city, and they therefore had to be bribed so that they would not expel the "extra" ones. The extortion of monies resulting from the increased numbers of Jews caused some of the people within the community to seek to limit the number of new settlers and make them go elsewhere.

The only possibility for the economic consolidation of the community was to send emissaries abroad to seek aid. Among the Jerusalem emissaries was the pseudo-messiah Shabbetai Zevi, who only arrived in the city in 1662 but made such a strong personal impression that he was entrusted with collecting contributions in Egypt. He did, in fact, succeed in raising considerable sums but he used them for disseminating propaganda for his movement. The sages of Jerusalem, who were not convinced by his messianic claims, excommunicated him and compelled him to leave Jerusalem. This, however, led to conflict and some of the Jerusalem emissaries who went abroad engaged in Shabbatean propaganda, caused friction within the Jerusalem community, and even undermined it economically and caused its breakdown, since they hindered an effective organization of aid to the community. Spiritually, in contrast, Jerusalem flourished during the 17th century. The city inherited Safed's place in the study of the Kabbalah. R. Jacob Zemah settled there in the late 1630s and edited the writings of R. Hayyim Vital with the help of the latter's son Samuel. He himself wrote a series of books and commentaries explaining the teachings of R. Isaac Luria and Vital. Other mystics also settled in the city and from then on Jerusalem became the center of the kabbalists.

An important contribution to the development of the city's spiritual life was made by Jacob Hagiz, who came from the Maghreb (Fez) by way of Italy, as did most of the North African immigrants of that time. With the financial assistance of an Italian family of philanthropists he established the *bet midrash* Beit Ya'akov (1658) in which leading contemporary scholars taught talented disciples.

At the end of the 17th century the Jewish community numbered approximately 1,000 persons. According to the record of poll taxes there were around 180 payers of the *kharāj*. A quarter of them were scholars and rabbis; the remainder were craftsmen and small businessmen. Neither group belonged to the wealthy classes who paid the highest tax *(a'lā)*, only a quarter paid the intermediate *(awsaṭ)*, and the great majority the lower tax *(adnā)*.

Although the Shabbatean movement failed and seemed to abate at the end of the 17th century, the ferment it had aroused did not cease. A group, 500 strong, headed by Judah b. Samuel he-Ḥasid and Ḥayyim Malakh, which contained extreme and moderate Shabbatean trends came to Jerusalem from Poland in 1700 and settled in the courtyard which was later the site of the Ḥurvah Synagogue. Before their arrival the population was around 1,200, about a sixth of whom were Ashkenazim. The group broke up quickly, however, since their behavior led to quarrels within the community, until the veteran inhabitants had to turn to Poland and Western Europe and request assistance in their battle against the newcomers. In addition the burden of debts owed by the Ashkenazim to the Muslims became so heavy that they no longer could bear them or maneuver with the creditors. Due to disruptions on the roads in Europe financial help did not arrive from there. On Nov. 8, 1720, the Arabs broke into the Ashkenazi synagogue and burned the Scrolls of the Law. They also seized the plot and held it until the migration of *Perushim* to Jerusalem approximately 100 years later (1816). For some time no Ashkenazi Jew could show himself in the streets of Jerusalem unless he disguised himself in Eastern dress. One of the first Ashkenazim who decided to return to Jerusalem was R. Abraham Gershon of Kutow, brother-in-law of the Baal Shem Tov, the founder of Ḥasidism (c. 1750).

During that period of depression, the community of Constantinople had to take the Jews of Jerusalem under its wing. A "council of officials" was established in the capital of the Ottoman Empire which undertook the responsibility for clearing up the community's debts and arranging its financial affairs. The officials from Constantinople also instituted ordinances and special arrangements in order to prevent a recurrence of those events which had brought about the community's economic downfall. A special *parnas* was sent from Constantinople to supervise public affairs. Knowledge about the economic improvements resulting from these efforts became widespread and numerous immigrants again began to settle in Jerusalem, especially scholars. A special impression was made by the immigration of R. Ḥayyim b. Moses Attar of Salé who went with disciples from Italy and established a prominent yeshivah (1742) in a building which is still standing. According to the rule "competition among scholars increases wisdom," more yeshivot were established in Jerusalem and the sounds of study echoed in its alleys. Wealthy Jews from all parts of the Diaspora contributed to the establishment and maintenance of these yeshivot. This activity also led to the increase in written works, especially of responsa, which were published in Constantinople, Izmir, Salonika, and the towns of Italy.

At the end of the 18th century, however, there was another decline in Jerusalem's Jewish population. According to a possibly somewhat exaggerated estimate approximately 10,000 Jews lived there in the middle of the century, but as a result of the insecurity in the southern part of the country, the decline in influence of the central authority in Constantinople, and also epidemics and natural disasters, the population at the end of the century was estimated at half that number or even less.

CHRISTIAN JERUSALEM. According to the Ottoman *defters* (lists of taxpayers) in Jerusalem, the number of Christian households increased from 119 to 303 between 1525 and 1533; if monks, clergymen, and bachelors are added, the increase was from 600 to 1,800 persons. In the villages surrounding Jerusalem—Bethlehem, Beit Jalla, Beit Sāḥūr—there were also Christian families. Most of them were permanent resident Syrian Christians, but all spoke Arabic. They were called *"Christiani dela centura,"* i.e., the girdled Christians, referring to the *zunnār* which was their special mark of difference from the Muslims. In the course of time the sign was forgotten but the name remained. In their way of life the Christians were no different from the Muslims; their women covered their faces in the streets like the Muslim women and would not

97

go among men. Several travelers point out that drunkenness and prostitution were widespread among the Christians: in particular, the last night of the Easter celebrations, when permission was granted to all the Christian inhabitants to congregate in the Church of the Holy Sepulcher, was believed to have been occasion for wanton immorality.

The Muslims despised the Christians and in official documents they are sometimes called "infidels." They were usually subject to all the restrictions applying to the "People of the Book" in relation to the erection and maintenance of churches and other religious institutions. The authorities delayed permission for repairs, and when any attempt was made to introduce something which had not existed previously, they were forced to remove the addition. In the words of R. Gedaliah of Siemiatycze (beginning of the 18th century): "The idol-worshipers are also in exile here—like the Jews," their number in Jerusalem exceeding the number of the Ishmaelites (Turks and Arabs). They were not allowed to marry without obtaining permission from the governor, for which they had to pay the *rusūm* tax, and the appointment of their religious leaders had to be approved by the governor or the qadi of Jerusalem.

From a religious point of view the *"Christiani dela centura"* were not a single entity but were divided into the various Eastern sects and churches, the Latins, i.e., the Catholics, being a negligible minority. Christian visitors usually counted seven to nine religious communities with an established claim to the Church of the Holy Sepulcher: Franciscans, i.e., Latin Friars of the order of St. Francis, called the "Little Brothers"; Greeks, the Orthodox Melchites, members of the Byzantine Church; Georgians; Armenians; Abyssinians, also called "Indish"; Jacobites; Syrians; Nestorians; and Copts. Each community held a certain part of the Church, to which, as well as to various honorific ceremonial functions, it claimed a prescriptive right. There were frequent conflicts among the clergy, therefore, over real or imagined encroachments and the

Muslim authorities often had to mediate and decide between the combatants (during the Ottoman period, the British Mandate, and later, the keys of the Holy Sepulcher were in the hands of a Jerusalem Muslim family). The Franciscan Friars, "Custodia Terrae Sanctae," were responsible for the Christian pilgrims who came to worship at the holy places. They would transfer to the authorities the taxes levied on the pilgrims at the gates of the city near the Church of the Holy Sepulcher, which the Muslims deprecatingly called *al-Qumāma* ("a heap of rubbish") instead of *al-Qiyāma* ("the Church of the Resurrection"). Probably only a few of the pilgrims knew that the tax collected from them was for the Muslims in the city. Conflicts periodically broke out among the Franciscans and clergymen of the other communities.

ATTITUDE OF THE EUROPEAN POWERS. No less surprising than the coolness of the Ottoman authorities toward Jerusalem (see Decline of Jerusalem, above) was the attitude of the countries of Christian Europe—first and foremost among them France, the first European power to enter into a capitulations agreement with the Ottoman Empire. Francis I, king of France and "the most Christian of Christians," saw himself as the defender of the Christian holy places and in 1528 complained about the confiscation of the church in Jerusalem, which was made into a mosque by the Muslims. This probably referred to the Cenaculum, the Church of the Last Supper on Mount Zion. The sultan made no response to the complaint but promised that the other places in the vicinity of the mosque would remain under Christian control and would not be harmed by the Muslims.

In 1535 a capitulations agreement was reached between Francis and Suleiman the Magnificent. It contained a clause which stated explicitly that the pope could join the agreement and enjoy all its benefits. From that time on the Christian states, especially the pope, began to appeal to the French kings to protect the interests of the Christians and Christianity in Palestine. The capitulations were intended to regulate the activities of France in key places in Palestine, especially in Jerusalem. It was reasonable to expect that a permanent French representative in Jerusalem would also be responsible for the maintenance of Christian and pilgrim holy places. However, it was only about 100 years after the first capitulation agreement and about 80 after the appointment of a French consul in Tripoli, Syria (1544), that the first French consul in Jerusalem was appointed.

The following are excerpts from the writings of the Frenchman E. Roger, who visited Palestine in 1631, as he recorded in *La Terre Sainte* (1664; 461–4):

"The third consulate is that of Jerusalem which our king, the most Christian of Christians, St. Louis [the 13th, 1610–43], blessed be his memory, established in 1621 for the protection of our monks that by means of its influence they might establish and consolidate themselves in those places and overcome the insults and injustices inflicted on them by that barbaric people."

After describing the consul's duties toward the merchants, he continues: "The fourth and fifth clauses [of the capitulations] deal only with the holy places and the monks inhabiting them, the pilgrims who also come to visit them, and other Christian passersby who are under the protection of that consul. They need him on every occasion in order to receive assistance and support in all their dealings with the Turks; he uses his influence to convince the Turks to maintain the capitulations and to practice according to the agreements. Nevertheless, the Turks do not refrain from perpetrating their tyrannical deeds both on the monks and the Catholic Christians who are not monks. These deeds would have been a thousandfold more difficult to bear were they not curtailed by that French consul whom the king has appointed for this purpose. A constant cause for praising and blessing our king is that in all the towns in which there is a consul or vice-consul a chapel is permitted in which he usually maintains two or three of our monks from the Jerusalem community, who celebrate a holy mass daily for our king in the presence of the consul and the merchants, both those living in the towns and those at anchorage or from the ports ... The reason that the attitude of the Turkish authorities to the monks and the Christian Catholics in Jerusalem is worse than in any other part of the sultan's kingdom is that there is no consul there. For the Turks, seeing that M. Jean Lempereur, whom the king sent as consul, prevents their carrying out their usual tyrannies toward the monks, made false accusations against him to the pasha in Damascus and he was taken there by a troop of Turks. However, he proved his innocence and went to Constantinople. The pashas and qadis, who have since been in Jerusalem, do everything in their power to prevent his return, since he would hinder them from filling their pockets as they do in the absence of a consul. They daily invent new means, under the pretext of administrative action, of gradually destroying us. And when we have just escaped from one matter, they raise up another, a worse one in its stead. They do this not only during our lifetime but also after our death. For it is forbidden to bring a monk or a Catholic Christian for burial unless the guardian priest has first obtained the permission of the qadi who demands 12 dinars for it, although the contents of the permit, which I wish to include here in order to show the contempt in which they hold us, reads as follows: 'I Abu Suleiman, qadi of Jerusalem, permit the guardian of the Franjis to bury the cursed monk, so-and-so . . .'"

The attempts to appoint a consul to succeed Lempereur were futile, but in 1699 a French consul was again appointed in Jerusalem. However, he fled to Bethlehem several months later because of the pasha's oppression. Another consul, the third in line, went to Jerusalem in 1713, but he too was only able to hold out for a short while. From then until 1843 no French consul was appointed in Jerusalem; the consul in Sidon would come during Easter to the Holy Sepulcher in order to maintain the splendor of the Latin ceremonies.

The most important topic which interested the European public—or at least those broad sections of the public having no direct connection with commercial dealings—in connection with the Holy Land was without doubt the assurance of the rights of the Christian faith and the protection of its holy places, especially in Jerusalem, and of its faithful who came to worship at these places. Nevertheless, no other country besides France attempted to establish a consulate or at least a consular agency in Jerusalem. All their efforts were directed toward the maintenance of representatives in the commercial centers. The Franciscan order retained the function of looking after West European pilgrims, without regard for differences in religious ritual, i.e., including

Protestants, Calvinists, etc. The problem of Orthodox pilgrims coming from outside the borders of the Ottoman Empire arose only during the 19th century; until that time pilgrims from Russia were not a significant component of the general stream. The faithful of the other Eastern Churches were subjects of the Ottoman sultan.

One characteristic feature in the lives of the Christian communities of Palestine should be pointed out: their spiritual rulers and religious institutions were outside the borders of Palestine. The Latin Church had an historical and dogmatic justification for this attitude, since Rome was its cradle and focus, but this was not the case with the Eastern Churches in general and the Orthodox Church in particular. Nevertheless, the Orthodox patriarch of Jerusalem, whose Church claimed priority in Christianity and thus greater rights to the Church of the Holy Sepulcher, the Church of the Nativity (in Bethlehem), and other holy places, had his seat in Constantinople. Moreover, no Church concerned itself with the establishment in Palestine of an institution of higher learning and education for its priests and monks. All the Christian travelers and tourists in Palestine reported the ignorance of all the lower clergy, both those included in the monastic orders and the "secular," i.e., those outside the orders who were scattered among the smaller communities and villages. The few clergymen on a higher level sent from Rome, Athos (the important center of Greek clergy), or Constantinople were involved in controversies over prestige, real or imagined, and in intercommunal conflicts, and had no time free for study or teaching.

THE CHANGE IN THE 19TH CENTURY. Beginning with the end of the 18th century there was an increase in the interest of the European powers, primarily France and England, in the Middle East, especially from an economic point of view. The Christian powers generally began to display great interest in the Christian holy places, to be concerned for their protection and welfare, and to support their traditional administrators: the Eastern and Western Christian

Churches, the Orthodox and Latin orders, and the new monasteries which had sprung up. This necessitated the prolongation of the capitulations agreements and the effective protection of European citizens and stateless persons under the protection of the foreign consuls, and even the sultan's non-Muslim subjects. It is clear, however, that the international powers which now made an appearance in Jerusalem—France, Russia, England, Austria, and Prussia—did not regard religious matters as the major and principal motive for their activities. The true intentions of the European powers became manifest when they intervened in 1840 to put an end to Muhammad Ali's revolt against Ottoman rule.

In 1835 Ibrahim Pasha, who ruled Ereẓ Israel and Syria on behalf of Muhammad Ali, gave the Jewish community of Jerusalem permission to "repair" its four ancient synagogues, which were in a state of disrepair, after all previous requests to the Ottoman authorities had been rejected. They now began some basic projects which were tantamount to reconstruction. It was necessary to break down weak parts of the foundations, to replace the wooden ceiling in one of the synagogues, which had been covered with mats, by a stone dome, etc. There was a danger, when these demolition works were begun, that the permission could be cancelled under pressure from Muslim circles—since this actually was new construction, which was not permitted by Muslim religious law. Furthermore, there were not sufficient funds to complete the "repairs" quickly so that they could be pointed to as a fait accompli. A special emissary was sent in order to collect contributions for these urgent needs to the "towns of the inner west" (i.e., Morocco). Nevertheless, the community incurred numerous debts. A. M. Luncz states in *Jerusalem* (1894; p. 211 n. 3), "The community's debts increased as a result of the repairs and expansion of the R. Johanan b. Zakkai and Istambuli synagogues undertaken by the sages and rabbis of the community during the rule of Ibrahim Pasha. The former had been very small and they expanded and 103

The *bimah* and the women's gallery in the Istambuli Synagogue, one of a complex of four built by the Sephardi community in the early 16th century. This, like all the other synagogues in the Old City, was destroyed after the capture of the Jewish Quarter in 1948. Courtesy Ministry of Education, Jerusalem. Y. Pinkerfeld Collection.

The Johanan ben Zakkai Synagogue, another of the Sephardi
complex, looking beyond the *bimah* to the two Arks of the Law,
in Late-Gothic style. Courtesy J.N.F., Jerusalem. Photo Schweig.

improved it. The latter had been covered with mats for a
long time and only then did they cover it with a stone
ceiling."

In the emissary's letter to Morocco five synagogues were
mentioned which were suffering the ravages of time and

were in need of repair, including the synagogue of R. Judah he-Ḥasid, which had become a *ḥurvah* (ruin) since the "Shiknāz," i.e., immigrants from Eastern Europe, had been forbidden to settle in Jerusalem. Great efforts were made to have this harsh decree by the Ottoman rulers abolished. In 1836 Muhammad Ali published a firman which laid down the conditions for a legal arrangement for the resumption of immigration to Jerusalem from Eastern Europe. The firman was decreed with the active support of the European powers which aimed at increasing their influence among the Jewish population of East European immigrants. The few *Perushim,* the disciples of R. Elijah the Gaon of Vilna, who were tolerated in Jerusalem, immediately seized the opportunity and started to clean out the "Ḥurvah" and erect a synagogue, called Menaḥem Ẓiyyon, which was dedicated several days after the earthquake in Safed (24th of Tevet, 1837). During the tribulations which befell Safed several times in the fourth decade, many people began to leave the town and move to Jerusalem where conditions for settlement had improved; Jerusalem became the center of the *Perushim,* who influenced the Ashkenazi community.

Establishment of Consulates in Jerusalem and Increased Christian Activity. As the policy of supporting the Ottoman Empire against the rule of Muhammad Ali and his son Ibrahim Pasha came to be adopted by most of the European states, they began to pay attention to strengthening their position in the country. Thus, already in 1838 Britain made overtures toward opening a consulate in Jerusalem, the first in the city after the abolition of the French consulate more than 100 years previously. It was headed by a vice-consul (1838) and later (1841) a consul (initially W. T. Young). Even before this the British consul general (whose headquarters was in Beirut) was represented in Safed and Acre by a consular agent, Moses Abraham Finzi, member of a distinguished Italian Jewish family, who was officially appointed to his position in May 1837. Since the Anglicans did not yet have their own churches in
Jerusalem and no English Christians lived there, it was the

British vice-consul's declared function to protect the Jews—as was the function of the agent in Safed. Thus it was stated explicitly in the instructions of Foreign Secretary Palmerston to Young on Jan. 31, 1839: "Viscount Palmerston has instructed me to signify that part of your function as British vice-consul in Jerusalem will be to offer protection to the Jews in general . . ." He also had to take care of pilgrims and tourists from England.

Russia opened its own consulate in Jaffa in 1812 in order to assist Orthodox pilgrims who were beginning to come from Russia. It is learned from the reports made by Young during his first year of office that there was a Jewish agent in Jerusalem who represented the Russian consul and whose duty it was to take care of 40 Russian-Jewish immigrant families in Jerusalem. He maintained that the Russian consul removed one agent and appointed another in his stead, who was an Austrian subject, not a Russian.

Young also obtained possession of a letter from C. M. Basily to R. Isaiah Bardaki. Basily had been appointed a short while previously (1839) as Russian consul for Syria and Palestine. His permanent seat was in Beirut, but in the course of time he moved to Jerusalem. Basily found it necessary to explain that Bardaki's appointment as consul of Russia had been made by his predecessor, Graf Alexander Medem. The style of the letter reflects an energetic man who already at the beginning of his career in the Middle East could control the situation. He was appointed consul general in 1844 and held important functions in guiding his country's policies in the Middle East. He had a broad range of knowledge and wrote an important work on contemporary events in Palestine and Syria.

Isaiah Bardaki, son-in-law of Israel b. Samuel of Shklov, author of *Pe'at ha-Shulhan*, played an important role in Jewish Jerusalem. After two or three years he became the consul of Russia and Austria and bravely combated missionary activities. Of special significance was his widespread activity in the internal matters of the *kolel* of the *Perushim*. Young expressed the fear that Isaiah Bardaki 107 would attempt to take care of all the European Jews. As a reaction to this report, he was immediately instructed by the Foreign Office in London to appoint a *wakīl* (officer-in-charge) for the English Jews in the same way that the Russian agent had been appointed. Young offered this position to David Herschell, son of Solomon Herschell, Ashkenazi chief rabbi of England, but he refused to accept the post, as he wanted to keep out of the controversies among his brethren in Jerusalem. Another reason for his refusal, it appears, was the suspicion that the British intended to use him for purposes of intelligence.

Perhaps Herschell was also apprised of the intentions of religious circles in England to initiate missionary activities in Palestine; in fact, in 1840 an agreement was signed between Queen Victoria and Frederick William, king of Prussia, establishing an Anglican episcopacy in Jerusalem which would also supervise missionary activity in Palestine. The bishop would always be a member of the Anglican Church and would be appointed alternately by the archbishop of Canterbury and the king of Prussia, while both countries would cover the costs. The first bishop who arrived in Jerusalem in 1841 was the apostate Michael Solomon Alexander, who had formerly been a *ḥazzan* in Dublin. Four years later permission was received from Constantinople for the establishment of a Protestant church in Jerusalem. Alexander immediately began his missionary activities, which were not in fact viewed with favor in the British foreign service since they raised many difficulties. James Finn (1845–62), the British consul in Jerusalem who succeeded Young, was also accused of missionary intentions and was finally compelled to leave his post.

Cyril II, the Greek Orthodox patriarch for Jerusalem from 1845 to 1872, was a distinguished and, in many ways, a progressive person. He moved his abode from Constantinople, which had been used by his predecessors as the center for their activities, to Jerusalem, the official seat of the patriarchate. In 1849 he established a printing press near the Holy Sepulcher for his community's needs.

In 1843 France reopened its consulate in Jerusalem after a lapse of 130 years. This did not please the Franciscans and they were especially disturbed by the fact that Pope Pius IX established a Latin patriarchate in Jerusalem (1847), one of whose functions was to check the increasing influence of the Orthodox and the Protestants. The Protestant clergy—Anglican, Prussian, and American—did in fact develop widespread missionary activities among the local population. Since activity among the Muslims was prohibited by the law of the land and could arouse the anger of the authorities, the missions conducted their activities among the Eastern Christian and Jewish communities. This led to the establishment of Protestant communities among the Christian Arabs of Palestine and Syria. A few Jews also converted for financial gain. There were also cases of Christians who converted to Judaism, well-known among them being the U.S. consul, Warder Cresson, and David Classen, owner of an estate near Jaffa.

APPOINTMENT OF ḤAKHAM BASHI FOR JERUSALEM. In view of the rivalry for the support of the "alien" Jews of Palestine, the sultan was finally compelled to do something for his Jewish subjects, particularly in Palestine. The firman of the beginning of Ramadan 1256 A.H. (end of October 1840), achieved by Montefiore, Crémieux, and Munk—after the blood libels in Damascus and Rhodes—for the protection of the Jews, was considered a kind of bill of rights for them, since it stated explicitly that the rights granted to all the subjects of the sultan in the Khaṭṭi sherif decree of Gülhane (dating from 1839) applied to the Jews as well. The firman was particularly relied on by the Jews of Jerusalem in defending themselves before Muhammad Pasha, the governor of the pashalik, against the blood libel which was propagated at the beginning of March 1847 by the Greeks in Jerusalem, with the support of their patriarch.

One direct result of the changes in the status of Jerusalem was the appointment of a *ḥakham bashi* (chief rabbi) of Palestine, whose seat was in Jerusalem. In his *Jerusalem* (1892) Luncz points out the reasons for this appointment: **109**

"In the year 1840 [!] the government saw fit to elevate the holy city Jerusalem to the status of a district town and to place in it a pasha who in the course of his duties would govern its inhabitants and the inhabitants of the towns surrounding it, and by means of this elevation in its political status the Jews gained the right to appoint a chief rabbi authorized by the government as a *ḥakham bashi* . . . The leaders and elders of the community then realized that for the welfare and peace of their community, which had began to spread and increase, it was necessary that the rabbi heading it should be authorized by the exalted government, so that he might be capable of standing in the breach and legally defending the rights of his community. And through the efforts of the minister Abraham di Camondo of blessed memory, who knew the aforementioned rabbi [Abraham Hayyim Gagin] and esteemed him greatly, this aim was realized, and shortly after his appointment he received the statement (firman) of the king confirming him for the position, and he was the first *ḥakham bashi* of Palestine" (p. 210).

The imperial authorization of appointment (*berāt humāyūn*, at the beginning and in the body of the document), which was issued in Constantinople in 1841, was of vital significance for the Jewish community of Jerusalem and Palestine. Of special significance were the rights indirectly guaranteed the community, since they indicated a legal breakthrough in the restrictions concerning the synagogues and *battei midrash*. In all versions of the *berāts* it was established that the reading of the law—i.e., reading from the *Sefer Torah*—in the house of the *ḥakham* or in other Jewish houses was in accordance with the Jewish religion, and that it was permitted to hang up curtains over the arks of the law and lamps, i.e., to set up permanent places of worship. In these *berāts* there is a certain shrewdness which permits the Covenant of Omar—which prohibits the establishment of new synagogues and *battei midrash*—to be overlooked, and permission is given to hold public worship everywhere without running the risk of disturbances and oppression.

The synagogues and their properties are protected—they may not be harmed or seized in collection of debts, which formerly occurred frequently. Each *berāt* delineated the rights and obligations of the *ḥakham bashi* and the community, and it was renewed with each new appointment to the position by the imperial authorities.

CAPITULATIONS IN THE 19TH CENTURY. The European states probably did not rely on the written promise of the *Khaṭṭi humāyūn* (i.e., the order whose beginning was written by the sultan's own hand), which was given (1856) to the sultan's subjects but not their own, and they took care to safeguard the physical and property rights of those under their protection, as well as caring for the holy places. Britain and France also sought to ease restrictions on economic expansion, to gain a liberal law which would enable their subjects to buy land, etc. Opposing them, the sultan maintained that he could not both recognize the special status of alien subjects on the basis of the capitulations and grant them complete equality with his own. If Britain and France wished to obtain economic rights for their subjects, they would have to give up their protection according to the capitulations.

Jerusalem, however, did not remain only an attraction for pilgrims. The scope of the activity of the foreign consuls widened because of the intrigues between them and the agencies and institutions for special functions which were connected with them. Jerusalem became the residence of the various delegations, religious and secular, which were devoted to a wide range of activities in education, missionary work, medicine, and charity. The Jews were the first of the city's inhabitants to foresee this development, which involved a transformation in the status and importance of Jerusalem. The founders of the Naḥalat Shivah quarter, who left the Old City, were the pioneers and builders not only of the new Jewish Jerusalem, but of Greater Jerusalem with all its communities and nationalities.

THE DEVELOPMENT OF JERUSALEM, 1840–1917. Muhammad Ali's successful uprising against the central authorities in Constantinople, which had only been terminated under pressure from the European powers, had demonstrated the weakness of Ottoman rule. The growing interference of foreign powers in Turkish affairs was particularly perceptible in Jerusalem, which was no longer off the beaten track. Improved communications with Europe, as the result of the use of steamships on regular sea routes, facilitated an increased flow of visitors and pilgrims. The Turks tried to improve their administration and the relative security that ensued encouraged an increase in immigration, which brought about a revolution in the composition of the population of Jerusalem within less than 40 years.

The opening of the British consulate in Jerusalem was followed within a few years by the inauguration of Russian, Prussian, Austro-Hungarian, Sardinian, Spanish, and United States consulates. In 1848 the first "bank" was opened by the Valero family. In the absence of Turkish postal services, the Austrians opened a post office in the same year, followed by France, Prussia, and Italy. The press of the (Latin) Custodianship of the Holy Land was opened in 1847, followed in 1848 by the Armenian press and five years later by that of the Greek Orthodox patriarchate. The status of the Holy Places determined in a Turkish decree of 1757 was confirmed in 1852 (the "Status quo").

These were preceded, however, by the Hebrew press of Israel Bak, which had been transferred from Safed after the 1837 earthquake and in about 1841 published the first book printed in Jerusalem, H.J.D. Azulai's *Avodat ha-Kodesh*. Apart from religious works, polemical tracts, and, later, newspapers were also printed by this press. Despite the fact that in the unanimous opinion of the visitors the Jews were the most abject and lowly of the population, changes were introduced in their lives as well. In order to free them from dependence on the missionaries, Montefiore established a clinic in Jerusalem in the early 1840s, to which he sent medications periodically and which functioned for

וה"ל"צ"י"ב

סדר

עבודת הקודש

פעולת מ"ק לחיים הרב
הגאון התפו'**חיד"א** זצ"ל
ע"י הרב המדפים מו"הרר

ישראל נ"ק סי"ו

נדפס פה

פה"ק **ירושלים** תוב"ב

סנת **תר"א** לפ"ק

Title page of *Avodat ha-Kodesh* by Ḥayyim Joseph David
Azulai (Ḥida), the first book printed in Jerusalem, 1841. The
printer was Israel Bak. Jerusalem, J.N.U.L.

20 years. He also subsidized the services of a physician, Dr.
Frankel, who came in 1843. The number of Jerusalem's   113

inhabitants in 1845 has been estimated at 15,000, including 7,100 Jews.

The Crimean War, which was partly caused by struggle for control over the Holy Places, again demonstrated the weakness of Turkey vis-à-vis the European powers, whose representatives in Jerusalem became increasingly more influential—even defeated Russia increased its influence in the city. The great prestige of France was attested by the fact that in 1856 the sultan Abdul-Mejid gave the Ṣallāḥiyya building (the ancient Church of St. Anne) as a gift to Napoleon III. It was renovated by its new owners and became the most impressive remnant of crusader architecture in Palestine. Bells were installed for the first time in the Monastery of the Cross in the same year and in 1867 in the Holy Sepulcher; church bells became an integral part of the sounds of the city. In 1858–59 the Austrian hospice (now the Government Hospital on Via Dolorosa) and the hospice of the German Johanniter Order were built. Crowds gathered to gaze at the two-wheeled vehicles—surplus from the Crimean War—used in the building, for they were the first vehicles seen in the city. The filth in the city was still so great, however, that a "cleanliness society" was established under the auspices of the pasha, but to no avail. As late as the 1860s tourists were complaining about animal carcasses lying in the city's gates and streets. These carcasses, often of animals which had died during the frequent droughts, were devoured by the stray dogs depicted in many pictures of the period.

The 18-bed Rothschild Hospital was opened in 1854 and a small "rival" institution, which later became the Bikkur Holim Hospital, was opened at about the same time by the *Perushim.* In 1856 a school named after the Austrian Jewish nobleman Laemel was opened due to the efforts of L. A. Frankl; it was the first modern school for boys in Jerusalem.

In the summer of 1859, through the initiative of the
Ashkenazi community and with the aid of the "Hod"

East aisle of the 12th-century Church of St. Anne.

(= Holland Deutschland) *kolel,* a plot of land was bought near Mt. Zion, and by 1861 the first of the *"battei mahaseh"* (shelter houses) were built on it. Sir Moses Montefiore, who again visited Jerusalem in 1855 and 1857, contributed more than any other single man of his generation to changing the city's face in general. In 1855 he used funds from the legacy of the American philanthropist Judah Touro to acquire a plot of land west of the walls, despite many legal difficulties, to house Jews who were living in the dark cellars of the Old City. On the plot which he had bought, he also built a windmill, which became one of the land-marks of the city and was its first "industrial" structure. Building this quarter raised difficulties, since it was supposedly too close to the Citadel, and Montefiore was only permitted to continue building after the Russians had begun building outside the city. Montefiore got the authorities to move the municipal slaughterhouse *(maslakh)* from the end of the street of the Jews, near the Zion Gate—where it had been since the Mamluk period—outside the walls. He also planned a railroad from Jaffa, the paving of interurban roads, and even afforestation, but without any practical outcome. The city's population in 1856 was estimated at 18,000.

The year 1860 marked the beginning of the growth of the "new" city, and the relative decline of the Old City. Jerusalem began to emerge from behind the walls and construction started on an impressive series of buildings (inns, a cathedral, and hospitals) in the present-day Russian Compound. The buildings were erected in the Maydan area, which until then had served as a parade ground for the Turkish army and an encampment for tourists. At the same time, the building of Mishkenot Sha'ananim, the first Jewish quarter outside the walls, was completed by Monte-fiore (the Yemin Moshe quarter was added to it in 1894). At the same time, further northwest, the German Protestant priest Ludwig Schneller built the Syrian orphanage for orphans from the massacres of Christians in Syria. This institution expanded and became the pride of the German

The Mishkenot Sha'ananim apartments, the first Jewish settlement outside the city walls, built between the years 1855 and 1860 on the initiative of Sir Moses Montefiore. Photo David Eisenberg, Jerusalem.

Yemin Moshe, the quarter named after Sir Moses Montefiore. Photo David Eisenberg, Jerusalem.

residents of Palestine. It burnt down in 1910 but was rebuilt. More Jewish quarters were founded: Maḥaneh Yisrael, built by oriental Jews in 1868 and Naḥalat Shivah (1869) on the main road to Jaffa. The establishment of these quarters resulted several years later in the opening of the city gates (which had been closed at night and during the Muslim midday prayers on Fridays) 24 hours a day and this greatly contributed to the security outside the city. Communication between the new quarters and the Old City was by paths through stony fields, which soon became

Roofs of Naḥalat Shivah, which takes its name from the seven inhabitants of the Old City who, in 1869, established it as the third Jewish quarter outside the wall. Photo David Eisenberg, Jerusalem.

roads and some of them (starting with Jaffa Road) even
paved streets, although in 1917 there were still no tarred
streets in the city. In the 1870s cabs and carts began to make
their appearance in the streets of new Jerusalem and on his
last visit in 1875 Montefiore drove from Jaffa in a carriage.
False rumors regarding a visit by the sultan in 1864 resulted
in practical attempts to level the alleys of the Old City. The
water supply was very poor, despite several attempts by the
administration and the waqf (in 1812, in the 1850s, and
1860s) to repair the ancient conduit from ʿAyn ʿArrūb and
Solomon's Pools; the stone pipes were regularly sabotaged
by the fellahin.

During the frequent drought years, water was brought by
animals and carriers in filthy animal-skin bags from En

Seal of the Moses and Judith Montefiore Foundation, 1886. On
the left of the windmill are the Mishkenot Sha'ananim buildings,
on the right, the Kerem Moshe area on which the Yemin Moshe
quarter was built. Jerusalem, H. Feuchtwanger Collection.

Rogel (Bi'r Ayyūb) and the Gihon Spring (Umm al-Daraj), through the Dung Gate and sold at high prices. However, the water supply mainly depended on the cisterns near the houses in which rainwater collected; in the 1860s there were almost a thousand of them. This water was only fit for drinking as long as it was not contaminated by sewage water (there was no sewage system) and the pollution of the drinking water brought about a severe plague in 1864, which claimed hundreds of victims, and led to the city being placed in quarantine for four months. Sir Moses Montefiore came again in 1866 to help the inhabitants, Jews and non-Jews, and contributed money for improving the water supply. By 1863 two newspapers, *Ha-Levanon*, published by the *Perushim*, who set up a new press for the purpose, and *Havazzelet*, published by Israel Bak and the Hasidim, appeared in the city, competing against each other until they were closed down by the authorities. *Havazzelet* reappeared in 1870, followed by numerous short-lived journals. In 1868 a Jew opened the first modern bakery—a small but notable improvement in a city where many of the inhabitants had to bake their own bread. By 1865 the city was linked to the Coastal Plain by the Turkish telegraph, which contributed to security, trade, and convenience. In 1866 negotiations began for the paving of a "carriage route" to Jaffa, which was completed in 1868; it had to be repaired in preparation for a visit from the Austrian emperor Franz Josef, who was returning from the opening ceremony of the Suez Canal. Another visitor of that year was the heir to the Prussian throne (later Emperor Frederick III), who received the eastern Muristan area as a gift from the sultan in order to build a church. In the 1850s and 1860s Jerusalem attracted noted archaeologists and students of the Bible and the Ancient East, including C. Warren, W. R. Wilson, C. Schick, M. de Vogüé, F. de Saulcy, and other well-known scholars (see below: Archaeology).

In 1867 the German hospital was built for lepers, who until that time used to dwell near the city wall at the end of the street of the Jews. In 1868 the Germans built on a prominent site outside the city (now King George Avenue) the Talita Kumi school for Arab girls; there was already a school for Jewish girls. In the same year the magnificent building of the Latin patriarchate was built within the walls northwest of the Jaffa Gate. The French Soeurs de Sion convent was built on the Via Dolorosa. The Jewish community too was not inactive. In 1864 the first Jewish school for girls, named after Evelina de Rothschild, opened despite the vociferous protests of the religious zealots. In the same year the magnificent Beit Ya'akov Ashkenazi synagogue was completed in the courtyard of the Ḥurvah of R. Judah he-Ḥasid. It had taken seven years to build, and shortly after its dedication, construction began on the Tiferet Yisrael (Nisan Bak) synagogue, which was completed in 1872.

In the 1860s the Jewish population in the holy city steadily grew, because of increased immigration and the reduced death rate. In the middle years of the decade the Jews became a majority in the city for the first time in 1,800 years. The British consul reported in 1865 that there were approximately 18,000 residents in the city (as in 1856), of whom 8–9,000 were Jews. From that time the Jewish community continually gained in strength.

The development of Jerusalem continued in the 1870s, as testified by the establishment of a "municipal council" (majlis baladiyya) in 1877. The German Quarter was founded by the Templers in 1873 and a road was built to reach it, which also served the Mishkenot Sha'ananim quarter and the eye hospital built by the Order of St. John in 1876. From this road developed the paved road to Bethlehem and Hebron. There were already two hotels in the city: one near the Damascus Gate and the other in the Christian Quarter near the Pool of Hezekiah. However, the pilgrims preferred the inns of their communities and wealthy tourists still set up encampments outside the walls.

Near the road to Bethlehem the Arab Abu Tor (Ṭūr) quarter began to develop, apparently in the 1870s. Unlike

The *bimah* and Ark of the Law in the "Ḥurvah" Synagogue.
Courtesy Central Zionist Archives, Jerusalem.

View across the Jewish Quarter to the dome of the Rabbi
Judah he-Ḥasid Synagogue, known as the "Ḥurvah." This most
magnificent of all Ashkenazi synagogues in the Old City was built
between 1857 and 1864 on the ruins of one started by Judah
he-Ḥasid, c. 1701. Courtesy Keren Hayesod, United Israel
Appeal, Jerusalem.

The Tiferet Israel Synagogue in the Old City, dedicated in 1865 and universally known by the name of Nisan Bak. Courtesy Keren Hayesod, United Israel Appeal, Jerusalem.

the Jewish quarters, which were built as uniform blocks, usually as closed courtyards (for security reasons), the Arab and Christian quarters grew organically and slowly. Among them was Katamon which gradually grew near Saint Simon, the summer residence of the Greek patriarch. In north Jerusalem there were also signs of settlement and Arab houses were built in Karm al-Sheikh (near the present-day Rockefeller Museum), west of it (near the present-day Herod's Gate, or Bāb al-Zahra), and to the north in Wadi Joz (Jawz). Due to this expansion, Herod's Gate was opened in 1875. 125

HEZEKIAH'S POOL, FROM THE SOUTH
SIDE.

The swallows flying towards the turbid water,
the man dipping his jar into it from a balcony,
and the smokers in the foreground, are all
characteristic of the spot at the end of the
summer, when good water is scarce.

Hezekiah's Pool, which used to exist inside the Jaffa Gate, with
the domes of the Holy Sepulcher in the background and buildings of the Christian Quarter on the right. From Sir Charles
Wilson (ed.), *Picturesque Palestine, Sinai and Egypt,* Vol. I,
London, 1880. Courtesy A. A. Mendilow, Jerusalem.

Near the Damascus Gate, apparently at that time,
the Musrarah quarter was built. A first scientific demographic survey at that time counted 20,500 inhabitants
in Jerusalem, including 10,500 Jews.

In 1871 the mosque of the Mughrabis was built in the Old City. In the Via Dolorosa the rebuilding of the Church of St. John was completed (1874), followed two years later by the monastery of the White Fathers (Pères Blancs). In the course of the work many archaeological remains were discovered. Other excavations resulted in the discovery of Bethesda. Outside the city French Jewish apostates built the Ratisbonne monastery (1874). The city's expansion toward the northwest and the north was entirely due to the activities of the Jews. The Me'ah She'arim quarter was established in 1874; Even Yisrael in 1875; and shortly thereafter (1877) the Beit Ya'akov quarter, which was later assimilated into the neighboring Maḥaneh Yehudah (1887). In 1876 the traditional tomb of Simeon the Just near the road to Nablus was bought, one of the few holy sites to come into the possession of the Jews. The Tombs of the Kings

The market in the Orthodox Me'ah She'arim quarter, with a notice requiring women to be dressed modestly, 1959. Courtesy Government Press Office, Tel Aviv.

located nearby were acquired in 1878 by French Jews, who transferred them to the French government several years later (1885). The Ḥabad synagogue (Keneset Eliyahu) was dedicated in 1879.

In the 1880s Jerusalem gradually began to acquire the character of a "Western" city. Road links were established with Nablus to the north and Jericho to the east. A regular carriage service was established with Jaffa (the carriages usually left in the afternoon and, after spending the night at Sha'ar ha-Gai (Bab al-Wād), arrived in Jaffa at noontime the following day). The first modern shops were opened, as well as banking agencies. To cater for the increased tourism, workshops were opened for woodwork, mother-of-pearl, and embroidery. Jerusalem's cosmopolitan character was recognized by the Turks, and from 1887 it became the capital of an independent sanjak, ruled by a governor holding the title of *mutaṣarrif*, who was directly responsible to Constantinople. He was advised by a *majlis idāra* (district council), as distinct from the *majlis baladiyya* headed by the mayor. Latin Orthodox, Armenians, Protestants, and Jews participated in both bodies. The Turkish garrison consisted of an entire battalion.

In 1881 the American Colony was built north of the Old City and many Swedes settled in it. On the way from the Damascus Gate to the American Colony the British general Charles Gordon claimed to identify, in 1883, the tomb of Jesus. The place, which was named the "Garden Tomb," was bought by Protestants in 1895.

Considerable construction was carried on by the foreign powers, especially the French. In 1880 they built the convent of the Soeurs du Sainte Rosaire on Mamilla (now Agron) Street, in 1884 the convent of St. Claire (in the southern part of the city), in 1886 the monastery St. Vincent de Paul (on Mamilla Street), in 1888 the convent of the Soeurs de Reparatrice (near the New Gate), and in 1889 the St. Louis hospital. In 1881, with the aid of the French, the Armenian Catholics built the Church of Our Lady of the

Spasm in the Via Dolorosa. In 1886 the Germans built (on present-day Hillel Street) the Catholic Hospice and Schmidt College. In 1887 they dedicated the Leper Hospital (in Talbiyyeh). In the same year they separated themselves from their Anglican partners (since 1841) and established a separate Lutheran community, headed by an independent clergyman who built his house in the present-day Shivtei Yisrael Street. In 1888 the Russian royal court built the Church of Gethsemane, with the five onion-shaped towers, on the slopes of the Mt. of Olives.

In 1883 the Ohel Moshe and Mazkeret Moshe quarters (in present-day Agrippas Street) were built. At about that time the Battei Ungarn (Hungarian Houses) were constructed opposite Me'ah She'arim. In 1884 the Diskin orphanage was established. In the 1880s (apparently in 1889) Yemenite

The onion-domed Russian Church of Gethsemane, built in 1888. Photo David Eisenberg, Jerusalem.

Jews settled in the village of Silwān (Kefar ha-Shilo'aḥ)—an unusual area in the history of Jewish settlement in Jerusalem (the place was abandoned by Jews in the

The Maḥaneh Yehudah market, established in the late 1880s. Photo Zev Radovan, Jerusalem.

Nineteenth-century lithograph of a group of Jerusalem seamstresses. Cecil Roth Collection.

The Wailing Wall
c. 1880.

131

19th-century Jewish cotton-cleaner separating seeds from cotton by the ancient process of bowing it. From Sir Charles Wilson (ed.), *Picturesque Palestine, Sinai and Egypt,* Vol. I, London, c. 1880. Courtesy A. A. Mendilow, Jerusalem.

disturbances of 1936–39). In 1887 the Maḥaneh Yehudah quarter was established with its large market and two years later the Sha'arei Ẓedek quarter (Abu Baẓal) was built west of it. The number of Jerusalem's residents at the end of the decade was 43,000, including 28,000 Jews, 7,000 Muslims, 2,000 Latins (Catholics), 150 Greek Catholics, 50 Armenian Catholics, 4,000 Greek Orthodox, 510 Armenians, 100 Copts, 75 Abyssinians, 15 Syrians (Jacobites and Malkites), and 300 Protestants.

From the early 1890s and for many years the French hostel of Notre-Dame de France was prominent northwest of the Old City. Its construction, claimed to be on the

19th-century Jewish shoemaker's shop, Jerusalem. From Sir Charles Wilson (ed.), *Picturesque Palestine, Sinai and Egypt*, Vol. I, London, c. 1880. Courtesy A. A. Mendilow, Jerusalem.

biblical Garev hill, began in 1887. Two other French institutions were established north of the Damascus Gate after 1892: the school of the "Frères" and the Church of St. Etienne of the well-known biblical institute (École Biblique; established 1890). The same year was marked by another important event: the completion of the railroad from Jaffa to Jerusalem, also a French enterprise. The French company bought the construction rights that had previously been granted by the sultan to a Jerusalem resident, Joseph Navon. The width of the rails was one meter and its equipment was bought from surpluses of the Panama Canal company, which had gone bankrupt. The scheduled travel

Façade of the Monastery of Notre-Dame de France, established 1887. Photo David Eisenberg, Jerusalem.

time (seldom attained) on the train, which left once a day, was two and one-half hours from Jerusalem to Jaffa and three hours from Jaffa to Jerusalem. The company had to struggle against numerous financial difficulties in the absence of extensive freight traffic.

In the fall of 1898 Jerusalem was placed in a turmoil by the impending visit of the German kaiser William II and his wife. In order to enable the visitors to enter the Old City by vehicle, the Turks filled up the moat of the Citadel and made a gap in the wall near the Jaffa Gate. The emperor's purpose was to dedicate the Erloeser Kirche in the

Muristan (on lands given to his father in 1869). The Turks gave the visitor another gift: a plot of land on Mt. Zion on which the Dormition Abbey was built. While in Jerusalem, the emperor granted an interview to Theodor Herzl.

In the meantime the building of Jewish quarters continued: in the north the Simeon ha-Zaddik quarter (1891), Bet Yisrael (1894), and the Bukharan quarter (also called Reḥovot; 1892).

At the turn of the 20th century the population was estimated at 45,600, including 28,200 Jews (15,200 Ashkenazim), 8,760 Christians, and 8,600 Muslims. Evidently the number of inhabitants did not increase greatly, perhaps because of the difficulties raised for Jewish immigration. Despite this, the city continued to develop in every direction except (for geographical reasons) eastward, though the crest of the Mt. of Olives began to be covered with buildings, mainly churches and religious institutions and a few private homes such as in the al-Ṭūr village. In 1900 the city comprised about 60 separate Jewish quarters, the spaces between which gradually became filled by new buildings and quarters. Paths became roads and later streets. Jaffa Road, near the city wall, acquired a distinctly urban character. Most of the changes in the city from now on occurred outside the Old City walls. Ha-Nevi'im (Prophets) Street became a main artery. Along it were the English Hospital, the German Hospital, the French St. Joseph monastery, the Rothschild Hospital, and the Italian Hospital (built in a medieval Florentine style). North of it the Ethiopians built their church. The German Catholic Hospice of St. Paul was completed opposite the Damascus Gate. On the road northward the Anglican Church of St. George was built. Within the walls, the Muristan market was completed (1905). Near the southern wall the Dormition Abbey was built in 1906. The round building was constructed on the model of German castles. The Augusta Victoria convalescent home and hostel on Mt. Scopus was dedicated in grand style in 1910. In 1900 the American School of Oriental Research was established in Jerusalem.

Mount Zion, looking east toward the Dormition Abbey, built above the spot where Mary, mother of Jesus, is believed to have fallen into eternal sleep. Just behind, on the right, are the traditional tomb of King David, and the Cenacle, the hall of the Last Supper. Photo David Eisenberg, Jerusalem.

The Augusta Victoria Hospital on Mount Scopus, opened in 1910, which served as the first residence of the British high commissioner. Courtesy State Archives, Jerusalem.

The area in front of the Jaffa Gate, c. 1913. Courtesy New York State Board of Education.

Before the outbreak of World War I the Jewish quarters of Zikhron Moshe (1905), Sha'arei Ḥesed, Aḥavah, Even Yehoshu'a, Battei Varsha (Warsaw Houses), and Ruḥamah (all c. 1908) were built and Givat Sha'ul began to grow in the extreme west (1910). In 1906 Boris Schatz established the Bezalel Art School. The number of inhabitants in 1912 was estimated at more than 70,000, including 10,000 Muslims, 25,000 Christians (half of them Greek Orthodox), and 45,000 Jews. The number of Jews had increased by some 17,000 in the course of a dozen years, most of them settling in the new city, to which the center of gravity shifted. The area of the city reached about 5 sq. mi. (13 sq. km.) and the map of Jerusalem in 1914 already foreshadowed the development of the city (at least the western part) during the subsequent 50–60 years.

There are no authoritative statistics about the city's population at the beginning of World War I, but it was estimated at 80,000, including temporary residents. The development of the city came to a halt after Turkey's entry into the war at the end of 1914, and the only large building to be completed was, apparently, Zion Hall, serving from 1916 for movie shows and theatrical performances.

The consuls of the Entente countries left Jerusalem during World War I, the U.S. and Spanish consuls remaining as neutral representatives to observe the action of the Turks. Epidemics, famine, arrests, and expulsions wreaked havoc among the inhabitants, whose number at the end of the war was estimated at only 55,000. Toward the end of 1917, as the British approached, the Turks had to abandon the city, and it was surrendered to the British. On Dec. 11, 1917, General Allenby, commander-in-chief of the British forces, entered it accompanied by French and Italian representatives.

SOCIO-INTELLECTUAL DEVELOPMENTS IN THE 19TH CENTURY. Although the Ashkenazi population of Jerusalem ceased to exist as a distinct community in 1721, the Ashkenazim continued to appear in the city either as residents or as tourists. In 1812 an epidemic broke out in Safed and some of its Jews, including the leaders of the community, R. Israel of Shklov and R. Menahem Mendel of Shklov, fled to Jerusalem. The latter decided to settle permanently in the

Holy City and revive its Ashkenazi community. In 1816 he established his home in the city and around him was formed a small nucleus of about a dozen disciples of Elijah of Vilna, who quickly set up a center for learning and prayer in the yeshivah of Ḥayyim b. Moshe Attar, which was placed at their disposal by the Sephardi community. The latter, which was well established, took the handful of Ashkenazim under its protection since officially its leaders served as the legitimate representatives of the Jews vis-à-vis the ruling authorities. The Ashkenazim were still persecuted by the Muslim residents, who regarded them as the inheritors of the debts from 100 years previously. Even now the Ashkenazim were compelled to don Sephardi dress so that their origin would not be recognized. Contemporary evidence shows that the Ashkenazim, and their head Menahem Mendel prayed in the Sephardi synagogue and even had to use a Sephardi to complete their own *minyan*. This situation continued until the 1830s, when the numerous calamities suffered by Safed—epidemics, robberies, and above all the earthquake of 1837—forced its Jews to flee to Jerusalem and the spiritual leadership and the major center of the Ashkenazi community in Ereẓ Israel was transferred from Galilee to the Holy City.

From this period on the social, spiritual, and economic life of the Jerusalem Jewish community began to be more firmly based. The dominant figure of the Ashkenazi community of the 1860s was R. Isaiah Bardaki (see above). On the other hand the rabbi of the Sephardi community secured official recognition from the authorities in 1840, in the form of the title *ḥakham bashi* (see above). The situation of the Ashkenazi community was also eased. Its efforts and diligence bore fruit, and Muhammad Ali announced that the debts of its ancestors to the Arab creditors were void. The homogeneity of the first settlers was thus destroyed and a meaningful pluralism began. While the first nucleus was composed mainly of *Perushim*, disciples of the Vilna Gaon, the immigration to Palestine now brought additional elements, such as the members of "Hod" (Holland- 139

Deutschland) and "Ohavei Zion" (lovers of Zion) some of whom adhered to the spirit of European culture. This immigration brought scholars, entrepreneurs, and educators such as R. Yehosef Schwarz, Eliezer Bergman, and Isaac Prag. From 1840 the ḥasidic community began to consolidate itself in the city. Its leaders were Israel Bak and his son Nisan, who were opposed to the leadership of the *Perushim*. This pluralism led to the emergence of separate social groups, which originated from a particular district or town and maintained independent *kolelim* that competed for independent *ḥalukkah.*

With the increasing strength of the Ashkenazim, there was growing friction between them and the Sephardim. Apart from linguistic, historical, cultural, and halakhic differences between the communities, economic and political bases of contention were added, and a fierce struggle for positions of strength within the community developed. With the aid of the foreign consuls who were interested in strengthening the position of the Ashkenazim and had them under their protection, and with the assistance of European Jewry, the Ashkenazim were released from Sephardi suzerainty. The custom of transferring heirless legacies to the treasury of the Sephardi community was abolished; the Ashkenazim set up a separate cemetery and even established independent *sheḥitah;* and they reached regular agreements with the Sephardim regarding arrangements for collecting *ḥalukkah* funds. Thus the Sephardi community lost a considerable income, although they incurred many debts as representatives of the Jewish community vis-à-vis the authorities, being responsible for handing over various taxes and other unofficial expenditures connected with the right of passage to the Western Wall, maintenance of Rachel's Tomb, etc.

However, in day-to-day life social and cultural relationships were formed between the various communities. It cannot be said that there were breakthroughs in the communal boundaries, but personal contact made its impact. This was especially the case among the younger generation, to whom the world of the East was not as strange and foreign as it was to their fathers, and some of them even tried to mingle. In the course of time mixed marriages between Ashkenazim and Sephardim began to occur. There were also reciprocal influences in language, customs, and folklore. Ashkenazim would pray in Sephardi synagogues and even wore oriental clothing when there was no longer any need for this. Though these manifestations were not very common, they were significant in light of the deep differences between the communities.

It would be incorrect to assume, however, that the Sephardi community was entirely homogeneous. There were bitter struggles within it against attempts to break off and create separate communities. Especially well-known is the struggle of the Mughrebis. Among the other communities the Georgians and later the Bukharans should be mentioned. In general, the power of the *hakham bashi* was decisive, and the authorities granted legal validity to his judgments. The *bet din* was composed of nine *hakhamim*. Even judgments of corporal punishment are known to have been handed down. The Ashkenazim had a separate *bet din,* which is first mentioned after the arrival of R. Samuel Salant in Jerusalem in 1841. From that time and for many decades onward he led the community, R. Meir Auerbach serving together with him as *av bet din* and rabbi of the community.

One of the major problems concerning the population of Jerusalem was that of education. The children and youth received their education at the *heder* and the *talmud torah,* which were modeled on Eastern European institutions, or in the *kuttāb* (Ar. boys' schools), the oriental counterpart. The older members of the community studied regularly in the *battei midrash* of their *kolelim.* The purpose of those who came to settle in the Holy City was "to worship God on His holy mountain," to be free of all material concerns, and to devote themselves to purely spiritual matters. However, with the increase in the number of Jews and the growth of a young generation which had been born in Jerusalem, it was difficult for large numbers to maintain this ideal. A number of institutions and individuals—mainly outside the *yishuv*—took up the question of productivization. Efforts were made to teach young people handicrafts and even a modicum of general secular knowledge. For this purpose Montefiore, Frankl, the Alliance Israélite Universelle, and others tried to establish boys' and girls' schools in Jerusalem, but their attempts were received with violent hostility and fierce opposition. Those who opposed these plans feared that their religious aims would be frustrated, basing their opposition on the experiences of the Haskalah in Europe.

The old *yishuv*, however, did not stagnate. With the increase in immigration and the maturing of the second generation of settlers, a new type of leader arose, public workers, scholars, and publicists such as Yosef Rivlin, Israel Dov Frumkin, and Abraham Moses Luncz, who were more responsive to contemporary problems. A local press was established, including *Ḥavaẓẓelet, Ha-Levanon, Yehudah vi-Yrushalayim,* and *Sha'arei Ẓiyyon,* which was considered the organ of the Sephardi community. The establishment of new neighborhoods outside the walls prepared the ground for new initiatives. Attention was given to the solution of economic problems. Mutual aid programs, which were highly developed among Jerusalem's inhabitants in the form of dozens of charitable institutions, began in certain instances to assume a character other than that of mere material assistance. Attempts were made to engage in social and cultural activities. A typical example was the Tiferet Yerushalayim company founded by Ḥasidim.

The Jewish population of Jerusalem toward the end of the 19th century could be divided into three principal groups: one promoting extreme adherence to the old way of life without changing anything; the second, the moderates, practical people, tradesmen, and the like, who were devoted to religious tradition but willing to absorb new ideas; and the third, a more limited group of *maskilim* who had been educated in Palestine or abroad, or new settlers such as

142 Eliezer Ben-Yehuda, who advocated revolutionary ideas.

12 UNDER BRITISH RULE
(1917–1948)

In December 1917, the Turkish troops and officials began to evacuate the city. On December 9, the mayor, a member of the Husseini family, walked with a white

The surrender of Jerusalem by the Turks, December 9, 1917. The surrender was offered to two British soldiers by the mayor (with walking stick) and the chief of police (far left). Courtesy State Archives, Jerusalem.

flag to the hill overlooking Liftā (Mei-Neftoah) to surrender it to the British, but found only two privates
who were looking for water. The surrender of the city
was formally effected only on December 11, after a
last battle with the retreating Turks near Sheikh Jarrāḥ,
when General Allenby, commander-in-chief of the Egyptian Expeditionary Force, made his official entry. He
entered the Old City on foot through the Jaffa Gate, and his
proclamation, which made no mention of the Balfour

General Allenby entering the Old City on foot through the Jaffa
Gate, December 11, 1917. Courtesy Imperial War Museum,
London.

Soldiers of the Jewish Legion at a *seder* in Jerusalem, 1918.
Courtesy Jerusalem Municipality Historical Archives, Photo
Ben Dov, Jerusalem.

Declaration[3], was read from the steps of the Citadel in
English, French, Italian, Arabic, and Hebrew.

In the conditions of war, especially with the normal wheat
supplies from Transjordan and overseas cut off, Jerusalem
was plagued by starvation, which the British military
authorities tried to ameliorate by food rationing. The first
military governor of Jerusalem was Ronald Storrs, until
then oriental secretary to the British residency in Cairo. No
sanitary arrangements whatsoever existed in the Old City
and hardly any in the newer quarters outside the walls. A
British architect was brought in to report on the condition
of the buildings in the Temple area, which the Turks and
Muslim authorities had allowed to fall into neglect. On July
1, 1920, the military administration, officially called the
Occupied Enemy Territory Administration, was replaced
by a civil administration under a high commissioner who
resided in Jerusalem. The first to hold office was Sir Herbert
Samuel, whose term lasted until 1925.

[3] Declaration made by British government in 1917 expressing agreement to
establishment of a Jewish national home in Palestine.

Jerusalem was a conglomerate of districts and neighborhoods each with its own character. The Old City, within the walls, contained the holy places—the Temple area with the Dome of the Rock and al-Aqṣā Mosque, the Church of the Holy Sepulcher and the Via Dolorosa, and the Western Wall. To the west new quarters had developed in the later Ottoman period along Jaffa Road to Maḥaneh Yehudah, spreading north to religious quarters around Me'ah She'arim and south to the railway station and the German (Templer) Colony. To the east were various Christian establishments and the site of the Hebrew University on Mount Scopus; and, dotted around, various newer quarters—some Jewish, some Christian, some Muslim, and some mixed, such as Bak'a, the Greek Colony, and the Armenian Colony. The city was slowly recovering from the setback caused by World War I. The 1922 census showed a population of only 62,578, of whom 33,971 were Jews, 14,699 were Christians, 13,413 Muslims, and 495 others. The Jewish population of Jerusalem, estimated in 1910 at about 45,000 (over one-half of the Jews in Ereẓ Israel), had been reduced by the end of the war, through expulsions, disease, and maladministration, to 26,600.

The civil government soon set up administrative institutions in Jerusalem, including a Supreme Court (composed of a British chief justice, one other British judge, and four Palestinian judges). Storrs founded the Pro-Jerusalem Society (later dissolved) for the preservation and embellishment of the city and a school of music (later presented to the Jewish community). In 1922 a British-French arbitration tribunal fixed the sum payable by the Palestine government for the Jaffa-Jerusalem Railway, owned by a French concessionary, at 565,000 Egyptian pounds. In the same year houses and buildings that had been taken over by the government were restored to their previous owners. The Hebrew University on Mt. Scopus was formally opened by Lord Balfour in 1925. In 1928 the concession for the supply of electricity (within a radius of 12 mi. (20 km.) of the city) was taken over by the Jerusalem Electric and Public Services Corporation Ltd. (with British and Jewish capital).

One of the first acts of the British administration was to appoint a new municipal council consisting of two Muslims, one of whom acted as mayor, two Christians, and two Jews, one of whom, Yizḥak Eliachar, was deputy mayor. In 1924 a new council, with three members from each community, was appointed. When the municipal council was elected for the first time, it had four members from each community. In 1934, under the Municipal Councils Ordinance of that year, the city was divided into twelve constituencies, each electing one councillor. Six of the constituencies were Arab and six Jewish, although 75% of the taxpayers were Jews. The government always appointed a Muslim as mayor, despite the Jewish majority, on grounds of precedent, with one Christian Arab and one Jewish deputy. There was also a community council, *Va'ad ha-Kehillah*, representing both Ashkenazim and Sephardim, to look after specifically Jewish affairs, especially in the religious sphere. It was first elected in 1918 on the initiative of the Zionist Organization's Palestine Office. From 1932 it was elected under regulations issued by Keneset Israel, the representative body of the *yishuv*.

The progress of the country, due partly to the ordered administration and mainly to Jewish immigration and development, was shared by Jerusalem. This was reflected in the 1931 census figures, which showed a population, of 90,503, including 51,222 Jews, 19,894 Muslims, 19,335 Christians, and 52 others. The economy of Jerusalem, however, remained based on the city's being an administrative, religious, political, and educational center, industry continuing only on a small scale. Jerusalem was the seat of the Zionist Executive (later the Executive of the Jewish Agency), the Keren Hayesod and the Jewish National Fund, the Va'ad Le'ummi (national council of the *yishuv*), the Chief Rabbinate, the Supreme Muslim Council (established in 1921), and the Arab Higher Committee (1936). The residence of the high commissioner for Palestine (which included Transjordan) was in the Augusta Victoria hospital   147 building on Mt. Scopus until it was severely damaged by the 1927 earthquake. The Russian Compound in the center of the city became an important administrative area, its buildings being taken over for police headquarters, the central prison, the law courts, and the government hospital.

Water supply to Jerusalem was a constant problem during this period. It was dependent mainly on the storage of rainwater runoff from the rooftops in cisterns dug out in the foundation rock. This system led to serious shortages in years of drought, and there were years when water had to be brought up from the coast by train (as in 1928). Matters were improved somewhat in 1918, when the army repaired the pipeline from Solomon's Pools, a short distance outside the city, to a reservoir in what is now the Romemah quarter. In 1920 this line was extended, and pumping machinery was installed at Solomon's Pools to increase the supply. Water was added from the ʿAyn Fāra springs in 1928, from the ʿAyn Fawwār springs in 1931, and

Water ration card for the Battei Varsha quarter, c. 1920.
Jerusalem, E. P. Gorodesky Collection.

from the more distant Wadi Qilt (on the way to Jericho) in 1935. It was only in that year, however, that Jerusalem's perennial dependence on the vagaries of rainfall was finally solved by the construction of a pipeline from Ra's al-ʿAyn on the Coastal Plain, replacing the old supply from five different sources and halving the cost of water.

Some of the early houses in Talpiyyot, a suburb south of Jerusalem, in the 1930s. Jerusalem Municipality Historical Archives. Photo Ben Dov, Jerusalem.

The Beit ha-Kerem suburb in 1928, five years after its establishment, Courtesy Keren Hayesod, United Israel Appeal, Jerusalem

THE DEVELOPMENT OF THE CITY. As the Jewish population increased—with a fillip due to the move from the Old City, as a result of the 1929 and 1936–39 attacks on them—new suburbs were built, some adjoining existing built-up areas and others less continuous (depending on where land could be bought). In the course of the years they formed one conurbation, including Romemah (1921); Talpiyyot (1922); Beit ha-Kerem (1923); Mekor Ḥayyim, Mekor Barukh, Reḥavyah, Kiryat Moshe, Naḥalat Aḥim (1924); Bayit va-Gan, Maḥanayim, Sanhedriyyah (1925); Kiryat Shemu'el (1928); Ge'ullah and Kerem Avraham (1929); Arnonah and Tel Arzah (1931). The character of these quarters was determined by the groups by or for whom they were established. Some were inhabited by Orthodox Jews, who could thus maintain undisturbed their religious practices and the quiet of the Sabbath. Others were established by professional groups or teachers, such as Beit ha-Kerem. Small workshops were concentrated in the commercial center (the center of the town) facing the Old City walls. Reḥavyah was designed for white-collar workers and people in the professions. By and large the character of each section was maintained, though as they grew into one another the social divisions were blurred. At the same time, the outward appearance of Jerusalem gradually changed in response to economic pressures, the increasing population, and the rising land value. Sir Ronald Storrs insisted on all buildings, private as well as public, being built of or faced with Jerusalem stone, which gives the city so much of its character. In the 1930s and 1940s, some relaxation was permitted, owing to the high cost of stone, so that in Reḥavyah, for example, some houses were built in concrete. Further afield, several kilometers from the center of Jerusalem, were Atarot (1920), Neveh Ya'akov (1924), and Ramat Raḥel (1925/26). At Atarot (Qalandiya) a small airport was built. The kibbutz of Ramat Raḥel, between Jerusalem and Bethlehem, was of special interest in its being the first attempt at combining agriculture with urban services (fruit growing with a laundry and bakery for the Jerusalem population). It also provided workmen for the city and ultimately became an extension of Talpiyyot and Arnonah.

Jerusalem was transformed from the neglected, poverty-stricken provincial town of Turkish times to a capital city. Among the public buildings erected in the years of British administration are the Pontifical (Jesuit) Biblical Institute (1927); the nearby French Consulate, the Catholic Church of All the Nations at the Garden of Gethsemane (1924); St. Andrew's Church (Scottish; 1927); the Nathan Straus Health Center (1928); the Jewish National and University Library on Mt. Scopus (1930); the Government House, later the headquarters of the UN Truce Supervision Organization, municipal offices, St. Peter in Gallicantu Church (1931), the Jewish Agency Compound (1932), the Y.M.C.A., with Jerusalem's first swimming pool (1933), the King David Hotel, the first of international standard in the city (1930); the Central Post Office; the Hadassah Hospital on Mt. Scopus; and the Rockefeller Archaeological Museum facing the northeast corner of the Old City wall (1938). Between 1938 and 1942 the al-Aqṣā Mosque on the Temple Mount was embellished with pillars of carrara marble, a gift from Mussolini. The earthquake in 1927 did considerable damage to the Augusta Victoria hospital on Mt. Scopus and to the Basilica of the Holy Sepulcher.

In 1936 the Palestine Broadcasting Service began operations, with offices and buildings in the city and the transmitting station in Ramallah. The Hebrew daily newspaper *Haaretz* appeared at first in Jerusalem but later moved to Tel Aviv. An older, established Jerusalem daily, *Do'ar ha-Yom,* had already closed down. On the other hand, the *Palestine Post* (later the *Jerusalem Post*), founded in 1931, remained in Jerusalem.

ARAB-JEWISH CLASHES. The development of the city was accompanied by disturbances that developed into violence against the Jews and the National Home provisions of the Mandate. The first outbreak occurred during 151

The Basilica of the Agony in the Garden of Gethsemane at the foot of the Mount of Olives, built 1919–24, on the ruins of a crusader church. The mosaic on the pediment of the façade represents Jesus offering his suffering to God. Photo David Eisenberg, Jerusalem.

Passover 1920. Despite the presence of a considerable number of British troops in the country, heavy attacks accompanied by looting were directed against Jews in Jerusalem. Before order was restored, five Jews were killed and 211 wounded, including several women and children; four Arabs were killed and 21 wounded. The Arab mobs had been incited by rumors that the Jews intended to take hold of the Muslim holy places. The 1921 riots in Jaffa and some of the Jewish settlements did not reach Jerusalem, but the creation of the Supreme Muslim Council by government order in that year and the election of Hajj Amin al-Husseini as its president promised trouble. He had earlier been appointed mufti of Jerusalem, over more moderate candidates, by the high commissioner in the vain hope that the responsibility and experience of office would moderate his violent anti-Zionist and anti-Jewish feeling. He con-

The Y.M.C.A., opposite the King David Hotel, built 1933.
Photo Zev Radovan, Jerusalem.

trolled the Muslim religious endowments, the waqf, and enjoyed the right to appoint and dismiss judges and other officers of the Shari'a courts and the patronage that went with these powers, though the salaries of the Shari'a judges were paid by the government. A more moderate Arab group, the National Defense Party, controlled by the influential Nashashibi family, was also formed in Jerusalem.

Signs of trouble, however, were not wanting. In 1925 a general strike of Arabs, which extended to Jerusalem, was organized in sympathy with the Arab revolt in Syria against French rule; again in 1926 there was a strike in protest against the official visit to Jerusalem of the French high commissioner in Syria, de Jouvenel. Quiet, nevertheless, was maintained until 1928. On Sept. 23, 1928, on the eve of the Day of Atonement, Jews introduced a screen to divide the men from the women during the service held at the Western Wall, but, to preserve the "status quo," the police forcibly removed it during the following day's services. In the name of the Supreme Muslim Council, the mufti

Members of the Revisionist youth movement, Betar, mustered for guard duty at the Western Wall, Ninth of Av, 1929. Courtesy Jabotinsky Institute, Tel Aviv.

declared that "the Jews' aim is to take possession of the Mosque of al-Aqṣā gradually." A General Muslim Conference met, presided over by the mufti. In the next few months building operations were carried out near the city wall, which the Jews saw as intentional interference with their praying. The heightened tension, with demonstration and counter-demonstration at the wall, burst into flame on August 23, 1929. Attacks by Arabs on Jews throughout the country, including Jerusalem (though more seriously in Hebron and Safed), lasted until August 29, when they were put down with the aid of troops rushed in from Egypt after 133 Jews and 116 Arabs had been killed and 339 Jews and 323 Arabs wounded in Palestine (most of the Arabs by troops or police). Jewish merchants abandoned the Old City and established the new commercial center outside the walls. After a British Commission of Inquiry, chaired by Sir Walter Shaw, reported on the political background of the outburst, an international commission followed (in 1930), but no agreement regarding the Western Wall could be reached. At the end of 1931 a Muslim Conference, attended by 145 delegates from all over the Muslim world, met in Jerusalem. Its public proceedings were not political and did not lead, as had been feared, to disturbances, but they further strengthened the mufti's position.

Tension remained high. On Oct. 13, 1933 the Arabs declared a general strike. A demonstration was staged at the government offices in Jerusalem, though prohibited by the government, and was dispersed by troops. Trouble spread to other parts of the country, and on October 28 and 29 there was renewed rioting in Jerusalem, but with one profound change: whereas the 1920–1921, and 1929 riots had been directed only against the Jews, they were now aimed against the government as well.

In 1936 troubles broke out again in Jerusalem, as well as in other parts of the country. A Supreme Arab Committee (later known as the Arab Higher Committee) was established, with the mufti as president. It resolved on a general strike and the nonpayment of taxes until Jewish immigration was stopped. Arab shops were closed in Jerusalem, as elsewhere, with those Arabs who refused to join being intimidated. The strike and more active disturbances continued until the arrival in Jerusalem of the Royal Commission, with Lord Peel as chairman, on Nov. 11, 1936. An atmosphere of tension nonetheless remained. At this time the population of Jerusalem was 125,000, of whom 76,000 were Jews.

In its report the Royal Commission recommended the partition of Palestine into two separate states—Arab and Jewish—with a new Mandate covering Jerusalem and Bethlehem (over an enclave "extending from a point north of Jerusalem to a point south of Bethlehem") with access to the sea "provided by a corridor extending to the north of the main road and to the south of the railway, including the towns of Lydda and Ramleh, and terminating at Jaffa." The policy of the Balfour Declaration was not to apply to this enclave, and "the only 'official language' should be that of the Mandatory Administration." Its revenues were to be provided by customs, duties, and direct taxation, and any deficit was to be made good by the British Parliament. Arabs and Jews in Jerusalem could opt for citizenship in the Arab or the Jewish state.

The Arab campaign of sabotage, intimidation, and murder, increasingly directed against moderately inclined Arabs, continued throughout 1937, with occasional Jewish reprisals. Jewish buses were bombed, and the potash convoy from the Dead Sea to Jerusalem was attacked. For several days in October, a curfew was imposed in the municipal area of Jerusalem. There were also attacks on Jewish transport on the main road connecting Jerusalem with the coast. Jewish reprisals culminated in November in large-scale attacks on Arabs and an Arab bus in Jerusalem by the Irgun Ẓeva'i Le'ummi (I.Ẓ.L.). To ensure the safety of worshipers at the Western Wall, a new road was opened through the Old City, avoiding the mainly non-Jewish quarters. Following an assassination attempt on the British inspector-general of the Palestine police force and the murder by Arab extremists of Jews and moderate Arabs, the Arab Higher Committee was declared unlawful and Ḥajj Amin al-Husseini was deprived of his office as president of the Supreme Muslim Council and his membership on the waqf committee. He fled to Lebanon; the Arab mayor of Jerusalem was deported to the Seychelles Islands together with other members of the Arab Higher Committee: and Daniel Auster, the Jewish deputy mayor, was appointed by the government to act as mayor—the first Jew to head the Jerusalem municipality. (In the following year a new Muslim mayor was appointed.)

Conditions worsened in 1938 with an intensified campaign of murder, intimidation, and sabotage, the Arab gang warfare now gradually developing on organized and, to some extent, coordinated lines, with still only isolated Jewish reprisals. Constant attacks were made on Jewish traffic to Jerusalem from the coast and armed robberies multiplied in the surrounding Arab villages by marauding parties seeking food, money, and lodging. Uncooperative Arabs and members of the Nashashibi family and party were murdered, the party having withdrawn from the Arab Higher Committee. In October, as the Government Report for 1938 states, "the Old City, which had become the rallying point of bandits and from which acts of violence, murder and intimidation were being organized and perpetuated with impunity, was fully reoccupied by troops" in an "operation of considerable magnitude." In the same year the British government sent out the Palestine Partition Commission (known, after its chairman, as the Woodhead Commission). It produced three plans, all providing for the Jerusalem area to remain under Mandate and outside the proposed Arab and Jewish states. Jewish proposals for the inclusion of "parts of Jerusalem" (reference being to the parts of the new town outside the Old City) were rejected, and in the end none of the proposals was adopted.

WORLD WAR II AND AFTER. After the outbreak of World War II, Jerusalem became a military headquarters. The German inhabitants of the quarter known as the German

157

Colony were interned or expelled, and their houses were
taken over by civilian and military personnel, while other
public buildings in the city belonging to German institutions were taken over by the government or army. Before
Britain's entry into World War II, its new anti-Zionist
policy, announced in the White Paper of May 1939, which
severely restricted Jewish immigration and land purchase
(one of a series of White Papers), led to mass protests and to
violent actions by the dissident Jewish I.Z.L. which, in May
1939, set fire to the Department of Migration. These actions
of violence continued until the outbreak of the war. In 1944
difficulties developed over the Jerusalem mayoralty,
when the mayor (a Muslim) died, and the Jewish deputy
mayor, who was appointed in his place, claimed full

Protest rally against the 1939 White Paper outside the Yeshurun
Synagogue. Courtesy Keren Hayesod, United Israel Appeal,
Jerusalem.

mayoralty, the population in the municipal area being estimated at 32,039 Muslims (21%), 27,849 Christians, and 92,143 Jews (61%). In the absence of agreement, the government finally appointed a Municipal Commission, all of whose members were British officials.

After 1944, when I.Z.L. and Loḥamei Ḥerut Israel (Leḥi) renewed their anti-government violence, Jerusalem was particularly involved. Many government buildings were blown up, culminating in July 1946 in an explosion that destroyed a wing of the King David Hotel housing government and military departments, with heavy loss of life.

In November 1947, when the United Nations decided on the partition of Palestine into a Jewish and Arab state, it also called for the internationalization of Jerusalem as a "corpus separatum." The Jewish authorities reluctantly accepted this, as well as other parts of the UN decision, but the Arabs rejected it. The Trusteeship Council of the UN appointed representatives of Australia, China,

Jerusalem railway station after the first Irgun Ẓeva'ı Le'ummi explosion, October 1946. Courtesy Jerusalem Municipality Historical Archives.

France, Mexico, the U.S., and Britain to work out plans for the administration of the area, but the UN General Assembly failed to reach a decision. In the meantime, the city, nominally still under British rule, was lapsing into anarchy. The Old City, including its Jewish population, was cut off from the new, while the areas outside the walls were divided between the Jews and the Arabs in warring camps. The British forces enclosed themselves against attacks by I.Ẓ.L. and Leḥi in barbed-wire areas in the New City cleared of Jewish inhabitants (these areas were known by the Jews as "Bevingrad," after the unpopular British foreign secretary). Jewish Jerusalem was put under virtual siege by Arab attacks on supply convoys on the one road from the coast, while the British troops did little or nothing to prevent the assaults. To cope with the emergency, the Jewish Agency and the Va'ad Le'ummi established the Committee of the National Institutions for Matters Pertain-

Princess Mary Avenue (now Shelomẓiyyon ha-Malkah St.), one of the "Bevingrad" areas fortified by the British in 1947. Courtesy Central Zionist Archives, Jerusalem.

Distributing bread during the period of martial law, 1946–47.
Courtesy Keren Hayesod, United Israel Appeal, Jerusalem.

ing to Jerusalem (shortened to the Jerusalem Emergency
Committee), headed by Dov Joseph. In April the six
Jewish members of the municipal council issued a procla-
mation to the Jewish citizens announcing that they had
assumed the functions of a municipality for the area under
Jewish control.

Arab Jerusalem did not suffer similarly as it was open to
the Arab-populated parts of the country to the north,
south, and east. Part of the Jewish Agency building in the
center of the city was blown up by Arabs, with loss of lives,
and the offices of the *Palestine Post* and a large residential
and shopping block in Ben Yehudah St. were blown up, the
last two almost certainly by anti-Jewish terrorists in the
British Police. The nearby Jewish settlements of Atarot and
Neveh Ya'akov to the north of Jerusalem, surrounded by
an Arab population, were abandoned. Deir Yāsīn, an Arab
village near the western outskirts of Jerusalem from which
attacks were launched on the adjoining Jewish areas, was
attacked by I.Z.L. and Leḥi, with 254 of its inhabitants
reported killed. A few days later a Jewish convoy taking
staff to the Hadassah Hospital on Mt. Scopus was attacked 161

The *Palestine Post* building (right) after the bomb explosion on February 1, 1948. Courtesy Jerusalem Municipality Historical Archives.

and destroyed, with 78 doctors, nurses, and others killed. This occurred only some 200 yards from the British military post that was responsible for safety on the road. The water pipeline from the coastal plain at Ra's al-'Ayn was cut. This presented the most serious threat to the Jews of Jerusalem, while it did not affect the Arabs, since a very large proportion of the Jews lived in houses built after construction of the pipeline and therefore lacked cisterns to catch the winter rains. Fortunately, a farsighted water engineer had earlier advised the Jewish authorities to make a survey of all Jewish-inhabited houses with cisterns and fill and seal them. When the pipeline was cut this supply, rationed and distributed by water trucks throughout the siege—even under continuous Arab shelling—saved Jewish Jerusalem.

Mt. Scopus with the Hebrew University and Hadassah Hospital and the adjoining Arab village, 'Isawiyya, became a Jewish-held enclave cut off from the New City, as did the Jewish Quarter of the Old City and areas to the south. Contact with these areas was occasionally possible only by troop-protected convoys. The streets dividing the Jewish

The Ben-Yehuda Street bomb explosion, February 23, 1948.
Courtesy Keren Hayesod, United Israel Appeal, Jerusalem. 163

Water rationing after the cutting of the pipeline at the end of May, 1948. Courtesy Central Zionist Archives, Jerusalem.

and Arab areas became front lines, barbed-wired positions, with posts on the Jewish side manned by members of the Haganah, I.Ẓ.L., and Leḥi. Control of the Arab side passed to armed Arab groups and then to the Transjordan army, the British-officered Arab Legion, which had not been withdrawn in spite of British promises. At midnight May 14/15, 1948, when the last of the British forces and

Arab Legion soldiers on the Old City wall, 1948. Courtesy Jerusalem Municipality Historical Archives.

government withdrew from Jerusalem, thus ending the Mandatory rule that had lasted since 1917, the Jews took control of the government buildings in the center of the town, including the general post office, the police headquarters and the broadcasting studios.

The Arab siege, however, continued for another two months, until it was broken by the construction of an alternate route through the hills from the coast (popularly called the "Burma Road") and the laying of a new water pipeline. The whole of western Jerusalem and the Mt. Scopus enclave were in Jewish hands, but Arab guns shelled the Jewish areas, killing 170 civilians and injuring a thousand. Food and water were still strictly rationed and the population was without electricity and fuel. To keep the bakeries going, oil was removed from all houses possessing central heating systems. As the Jews were cut off from the ancient cemetery on the Mt. of Olives, a temporary Jewish burial place was prepared near the Valley of the Cross, where a tiny landing strip was also set up for the occasional Piper Cub planes that flew Jewish leaders in and out.

Food convoy arriving in Jerusalem, February 1948. Courtesy
Central Zionist Archives, Jerusalem.

When the Arab countries invaded Palestine, Egyptian
and Iraqi troops approached the outskirts of Jerusalem,
joining the Arab Legion units. Ramat Raḥel changed hands
several times in fierce fighting before the Arab forces were
finally repelled. Meanwhile the Arab Legion closed in on
the Jewish Quarter of the Old City. On May 19, 1948, the
Palmaḥ breached the wall at the Zion Gate, but had to
withdraw. After intense fighting, with Jews and Arabs

The Jewish Quarter of the Old City in the 1940s. The large building in the center is the Tiferet Israel Yeshivah and behind it at right can be seen the dome of the Nisan Bak Synagogue. Courtesy Keren Hayesod, United Israel Appeal, Jerusalem.

confronting one another at a distance of only a few yards and Jewish supplies of food and ammunition almost exhausted, the Jewish Quarter of the Old City surrendered on May 27. Some 1,300 elderly men, women, and children, and wounded men were evacuated to the New City and others were taken prisoner. A general cease-fire was proclaimed on June 11, 1948, leaving East Jerusalem, including the Old City, to the Arabs in Transjordanian hands and West Jerusalem in Israel hands. Jerusalem being still under siege, the Provisional Government remained for the time being in Tel Aviv.

13 THE DIVIDED CITY (1948–1967)

For some time the position of Jerusalem remained uncertain. The city was divided in two by a cease-fire line running roughly north-south tangentially to the western wall of the Old City, the relations between the two sides being regulated by agreement between the local commanders of the Arab Legion and the Israel Defense Forces (I.D.F.). A resolution dealing with the temporary administration of the city had been adopted by a special subcommittee of the UN General Assembly, but was not carried by the Assembly itself. Egyptian troops still threatened the city from their positions in the Bethlehem area. Despite the establishment of the I.D.F. as the new state's only armed force, I.Z.L. and Leḥi units continued to exist in Jerusalem. On July 7 a special agreement for the demilitarization of the Scopus area was concluded between Israel and Transjordan.

During the ten days' fighting that followed the expiry of the first truce on July 7, 1948, the Israel forces broke the Egyptian lines and took Ein Karem (Ein Kerem) on the western outskirts of the city. On the night of July 16/17 the I.D.F. broke into the Old City from Mount Zion, while I.Z.L. and Leḥi forces breached the New Gate, but they were forced to withdraw a few hours before the second truce went into effect.

Count Bernadotte, the UN mediator, had proposed on June 27 from his headquarters in Rhodes that Jerusalem be handed over to Transjordan. The proposal had been categorically rejected by the Provisional Government of Israel. On July 26, two days after his arrival in the country, he proposed the demilitarization of the city, but this was also unacceptable to Israel, as it would have left the Jewish population defenseless. On August 1, to regularize the position, the Provisional Government declared Jerusalem to be occupied territory and appointed Dov Joseph as military governor. Bernadotte set up the UN Truce Supervision Organization, with its seat in the former Government House. The assassination of Bernadotte on Sept. 17 impelled the government to order the disbandment of the I.Ẓ.L. and Leḥi units, putting all armed forces in Jerusalem under I.D.F. command. In operation Yo'av (Oct. 15–22) the Egyptian forces in the south were isolated and withdrew, being replaced by the Arab Legion. On Dec. 13, 1948 the Transjordanian parliament confirmed the annexation of the Arab-controlled areas of Palestine and a week later the Transjordanian government appointed a new mufti of Jerusalem.

The population of the Israel-held area of Jerusalem took part in the elections to the Constituent Assembly (later called the First Knesset) in January 1949, and at the beginning of February the Provisional Government announced that Jerusalem was no longer to be considered occupied territory. The Knesset held its first sessions (Feb. 14–17) in the hall at Jewish Agency headquarters, where the members took the oath, Chaim Weizmann was elected president of the state, and the Transition Law (the "Minor Constitution") was adopted. According to article 8 of the armistice agreement with Jordan (April 3, 1949), a joint committee was to be set up to make arrangements for, inter alia, the renewal of the operations of the Hebrew University and the Hadassah Hospital on Mount Scopus and free access to the Jewish holy places in the Old City, the ancient Jewish cemetery on the Mount of Olives, and the institutions on Mount Scopus. However, although these matters were stated to have been agreed upon in principle by both sides, the article remained a dead letter, as Jordan refused to cooperate.

When the Jerusalem issue was again discussed by the UN General Assembly in November 1949, the Israel government opposed the idea of internationalization, but offered to sign an agreement with the United Nations guaranteeing the security of all holy places under its jurisdiction. On Dec. 10, however, the Assembly approved a resolution calling for international control over the whole city of Jerusalem and its environs and charged the Trusteeship Council to draft a statute for an international regime for the city. The Israel government reacted vigorously. On Dec. 13 it announced in the Knesset its decision to speed up the transfer of its offices to Jerusalem, proposed that the Knesset go back there, and proclaimed that Jerusalem was and would remain Israel's eternal capital. On Dec. 26 the Knesset resumed its sittings in the capital, meeting in a modest building (the Froumine building) in the center of town that had been erected for use by a bank. Both Jordan and Israel continued to oppose internationalization and the proposal was ultimately, in effect, dropped.

For a period of 19 years, Jerusalem was a divided city. In 1948 the population was estimated at 165,000: 100,000 Jews, 40,000 Muslims, and 25,000 Christians. The city's area was about 10 sq. mi. (28 sq. km.). The battles waged in and around Jerusalem for three-quarters of a year; the UN decision to internationalize the city, the transfer of the Arab center of gravity to Amman, and the establishment of the de facto seat of the government and the legislature in Tel Aviv were the causes of a precipitous decline in population on both sides of the front. The population of the Israel side (West Jerusalem) was estimated at only about 69,000 (including 931 Christians and 28 Muslims) in 1949, and that of the Jordanian side at about 46,000 as late as 1956.

EAST JERUSALEM. In May 1948, East Jerusalem was occupied by the Arab Legion. Its first act was the destruction of the Jewish Quarter, including almost all the synagogues (Ḥurvah, Nisan Bak, etc.) and Jewish institutions (*Battei Maḥaseh*, Yeshivat Porat Yosef, etc.). The ancient cemetery on the slope of the Mount of Olives was desecrated. Jerusalem was proclaimed the "second capital" of the Hashemite Kingdom of Jordan; it also became a

Ruins of the "Middle" Synagogue, one of the 16th-century Sephardi complex, destroyed during the sacking of the Jewish Quarter in May 1948. Courtesy Government Press Office.

district capital. East Jerusalem was entirely cut off from an approach to the Mediterranean coast, and the conversion of the former British military airfield of Qalandiya into a civil airport for the town alleviated its isolation only slightly.

Ruins of the "Ḥurvah" Synagogue, destroyed at the end of May 1948. Courtesy Government Press Office, Tel Aviv.

East Jerusalem now turned to the east bank of the Jordan, through which all its relations with the world at large were conducted. In the 1960s a direct road to Amman, via Abdullah Bridge, was added to the old Jericho-Salt road. Traffic to the north via the Sheikh Jarrāḥ quarter was dominated by Israel forces. This situation was slightly improved by the construction of a new road that connected the Mt. Scopus area to the vicinity of the Rockefeller Museum through the upper Kidron Valley, thus diverting the daily traffic from the border region. In 1948 East Jerusalem had been completely cut off from the Bethlehem-Hebron region and a very steep and tortuous road was built through Abu-Dīs, the lower Kidron Valley, and Beit-Sāḥūr. It was only after a few years that an improved, though also steep and tortuous road was constructed from

Jerusalem to Bethlehem, via Ra's-Maqābir and Ṣūr-Bāhir;

The Sephardi Porat Joseph Synagogue in the Old City, begun in 1914 and completed in 1923. The plaque below the *bimah* contains a tribute to the donor, Joseph Shalom of Calcutta, and his last message to the builders of the synagogue. Courtesy Central Zionist Archives, Jerusalem.

Desecrated graves in the Jewish cemetery on the Mount of Olives, 1967. Courtesy J.N.F., Jerusalem. Photo Albert.

Tombstones from the Mount of Olives used to build the walls of the Arab Legion barracks at al-ʿAzariyyah, on the Jericho road. Courtesy Government Press Office, Tel Aviv.

it was 10 mi. (17 km.) long, in comparison with the old road 3 mi. (5 km.) long through Talpiyyot, which was dominated by Israel.

The Jordanian-held part of Jerusalem had no electricity for several years until a new power station was built in Sha'fāṭ to replace the original one near the German Colony, which was in Israel hands. Water supply remained very poor after the line from Ra's al-'Ayn (Rosh ha-Ayin) was cut off, but a limited quantity was supplied by springs in the northeast of the city and a narrow water pipe was later laid from Solomon's Pools. The economy of East Jerusalem was based almost entirely on tourism, pilgrimages, and religious and research institutions. The only large factory was the cigarette works at al-'Azariyya. The Jordanian government was located in Amman, and Arab Jerusalem did not wield much political influence. Due to geographical conditions (the barrier of the Kidron Valley and its extensions), the city hardly developed to the south and only a little toward the east (Silwān, Ra's-al-'Amūd, al'Azariyya, Abu-Dīs) and on the slopes of the Mount of Olives. On the other hand, there was much construction on the northern side, and the the area between the Old City's northern wall and Wadi Joz (Jawz) became partly a shopping district (Saladin Street, Jericho Road, and their extensions) and largely a crowded residential district. The residential area of East Jerusalem, the greater part of which was not within the boundaries of the city itself, extended over a length of 7 mi. (15 km.) through Sha'fāṭ, Beit Ḥanīnā, and Qalandiya, almost reaching the outskirts of al-Bīra. The number of inhabitants, however, never surpassed 65,000, of whom about 25,000 lived within the walls of the Old City.

The relatively small number of luxury buildings erected in the eastern part of the city under the Jordanian administration included several large hotels, the largest of which—the Intercontinental—was built at the southern extremity of the Mount of Olives. In 1963, the "eastern" Y.M.C.A. was erected on the Nablus Road. Government House (after 1967, Israel Military Government headquarters) was situated on Saladin Street; the St. John Hospital for eye diseases and, next to it, the French Hospital and the British consulate-general were erected in Sheikh Jarrāḥ. The Dominus Flevit Church was built on the slope of the Mount of Olives (1953). Arab refugees were rarely seen in the city itself, except for the area of the improvised buildings in the destroyed Jewish Quarter and the remains of the German Compound. Their camps were situated in the south near Bethlehem (Dahīsha) and in the north (Kafr ʿAqab) and northeast (ʿAnatā). Because of the Israel enclave on Mt. Scopus, which dominated all principal roads to the town, and the proximity of the frontier to all the important parts of the city, a sense of uneasiness hovered over East Jerusalem throughout the period. The presence of the Jordanian army was felt everywhere and there were occasional clashes between sections of the local population and the Arab Legion soldiers. The outstanding events in the city during the period included the assassination of King Abdullah (1951), the fire in the Church of the Holy Sepulcher (1953), and the visit of Pope Paul VI (1964).

WEST JERUSALEM. The cessation of hostilities and the conclusion of the armistice agreement with Jordan left the Israel sector of Jerusalem situated at the eastern extremity of a "corridor" that was almost devoid of Jewish settlements. To the north, east, and south, the city was surrounded by hostile Arab territories. At first the city's population was diminishing and its political future was obscure. The Jewish city began to recover quickly, however, when it was proclaimed as the seat of the Knesset and the capital of the State of Israel at the end of 1949. Water supply was resumed, at first through an emergency pipe and later through pipelines of considerable capacity, whose sources were in the corridor and the coastal plain, and an immense water reservoir was built in the southwest of the city. The electricity network was connected to the national grid. On May 1, 1949 the first train since the war arrived in the city, after Israel had gained control of the entire railway track as a result of territorial arrangements with Jordan. A landing strip for light planes was constructed in the western part of the town.

The direct highway to Tel Aviv through Arab-held Latrun remained closed, but traffic to Jerusalem was renewed along the "Road of Valor," which was constructed from Ramleh through Naḥshon to the Hartuv junction, south of the War of Independence "Burma Road." Additional approach roads were constructed from Zorah through Ramat Razi'el to Ein Kerem and Castel (Me'oz Zion). Another road ascended through the Elah Valley to Zur-Hadassah and Ein Kerem, while an emergency track was laid out along the railway line from Hartuv to the Bar-Giora junction. Hadassah's hospital and other services were housed in rented premises in the center of the city, as its buildings remained isolated in the Israel enclave on Mt. Scopus and could only be reached every fortnight by a convoy under the protection of the UN. A new Hadassah Medical Center was built on a slope overlooking Ein Kerem. In addition to the hospital, the center grew to include a medical school, a training school for nurses, a school of dentistry, and a large range of clinics. The Hebrew University and its library, which had also been compelled to leave their buildings on Mt. Scopus, resumed their activities in the city, with provisional headquarters in the Italian Terra Sancta school, and in the early 1950s the construction of a new campus on Givat Ram, a hill between Reḥavyah and Beit ha-Kerem, was initiated. Campus buildings included a stadium, a synagogue, a planetarium, and the new National Library, inaugurated in 1961. On the western outskirts of the city, the Convention Center, Binyanei ha-Ummah ("National Buildings"), used for concerts, dramatic performances, exhibitions, and congresses, was built. In 1951, the 23rd Zionist Congress, the first to be held in Israel, took place there.

Immediately after the cessation of hostilities the only border-crossing point between Israel and Jordan was opened to the United Nations in Jerusalem off the historic road leading from Damascus Gate to Nabī Samwīl (and

The Franciscan Terra Sancta College, which served as one of the main buildings of the Hebrew University after Mt. Scopus became inaccessible. Courtesy Ministry of Tourism, Jerusalem.

Binyanei ha-Ummah, Jerusalem's exhibition building and concert hall. Photo David Eisenberg, Jerusalem.

the Coastal Plain). In time the "Mandelbaum Gate" (named after the owner of the destroyed building that had stood on the spot) became the official crossing point for tourists, with passport-control and customs offices. A second but unofficial crossing point existed for several years in the demilitarized zone around the former Government House, which had become the UN headquarters, in Ra's Maqābir.

In the late 1950s a start was made on the construction of the new government center, Ha-Kiryah, opposite the new university campus, housing the Prime Minister's Office and Ministries of Finance, the Interior, and later, Labor. A compound of one-story buildings was put up for the Foreign Ministry south of Romemah. On a hill to the southeast of and above Ha-Kiryah, the large Knesset building, which was built with the contributions of the Rothschild family, was completed in 1966. To the south of the Knesset are situated the Shrine of the Book and the Israel Museum (completed 1966–67). This ensemble of impressive buildings, which links the center of the city to the western districts (Kiryat Moshe, Bet ha-Kerem, and their extensions), added to the beauty of Jerusalem and visibly symbolized its position as the capital of Israel.

Although the UN General Assembly resolution of 1949 calling for the internationalization of Jerusalem was a dead letter, it was still on the record, and most countries, including the major powers, refused to recognize Jerusalem as Israel's capital, setting up their embassies and legations in Tel Aviv or its environs. President Weizmann continued to reside in Reḥovot, but after his death in 1952, diplomats went up to Jerusalem to present their credentials to his successor, President Ben-Zvi, and visit the Foreign Ministry and the Prime Minister's Office. Gradually, too, the boycott weakened and a number of missions moved to, or were established in the capital. In 1972, out of 46 foreign missions in Israel, 22 were in Jerusalem; those of two European countries: the Netherlands and Greece; 10 African: Central African Republic, Congo Brazzaville, Congo Kinshasa, Dahomey, Gabon, Ivory Coast, Liberia, 179

The Knesset building. Left foreground, the Shrine of the Book at the Israel Museum.

180   The Israel Museum, Jerusalem.

Malagasy, Niger, and Upper Volta; and 10 Latin-American: Bolivia, Chile, Colombia, Costa Rica, Dominican Republic, Ecuador, Guatemala, Panama, Venezuela, and Uruguay. In addition, 11 other countries maintained consulates or consulates-general in the city.

Besides numerous office buildings, the large Histadrut headquarters, and Heikhal Shlomo, the center of the Chief Rabbinate, were erected in the center of town. A branch of the U.S. Reform Rabbinical Seminary, the Hebrew Union College, was built near the King David Hotel, overlooking the Old City walls, and the buildings of the Academy of Sciences and Humanities overlooking the south of the city from Talbieh hill. Next to it are the presidential residence and the municipal theater. To the southwest, the town is dominated by Mt. Herzl, renamed when Herzl's remains were reinterred there in 1949. Since then, the summit of this hill has become a national cemetery where Vladimir Jabotinsky, J. Sprinzak, L. Eshkol,

Heikhal Shlomo, seat of the Israel Chief Rabbinate. Courtesy Government Press Office, Tel Aviv.

The president's residence.

182   The Jerusalem Theater.

Aerial view of a complex of public buildings in the Talbieh district, March 1971. Left foreground, the Jerusalem Theater, under construction; left background, the president's residence; center, the Van Leer Jerusalem Foundation, with the National Israel Academy for Sciences and Humanities to its right. Photo Werner Braun, Jerusalem.

and others are buried. On the northern slope of Mt. Herzl is a military cemetery, and toward the west is Yad Vashem, a memorial to the victims of the Holocaust, including a research center. On the western side, the town is enclosed by the bow-shaped Jerusalem Forest.

Many religious institutions have been established in Jerusalem in the years since 1948. These include the yeshivot of Belz, Netiv Meir, and Merom Zion; Yad ha-Rav Maimon and its religious college; etc. In the religious quarters an abundance of synagogues were built. New religious concentrations, resembling a second-generation Me'ah She'arim and its surroundings, were formed in the north of the city (Kiryat Mattersdorf) and in the west, at the entrance to Givat Sha'ul.

Extensive housing projects for new immigrants were erected along the armistice line in northern Jerusalem

Mount Herzl, with Herzl's tomb in the oval court. Photo Werner Braun, Jerusalem.

and in the northwest (Shemu'el ha-Navi St., Rome-mah Illit), as well as in Musrarah (Morashah). The main development of the city, however, took place in the south and southwest. The southern districts, Abu-Ṭūr (Givat Ḥananyah), Bak'a (Ge'ulim), the German Colony (Refa'im), and Katamon (Gonen), which were inhabited by Christians and Arabs until 1948, became completely Jewish, while among them and next to them large new housing projects were erected (Talpiyyot, Bak'a, Katamonim, the Rassco Quarter, Givat Mordekhai, etc.). On a height overlooking the city from the southwest, Bayit va-Gan expanded, and to the south of it Kiryat ha-Yovel, Kiryat Menaḥem, and Ir Gannim were established and filled with a population of tens of thousands. The former Arab villages

The building containing the eternal flame at the Yad Vashem Holocaust monument and memorial. Courtesy Ministry of Tourism, Jerusalem. Photo David Harris, Jerusalem.

Warning notice in the Musrarah quarter, on the Jordanian border, 1966. Courtesy Government Press Office, Tel Aviv.

185

The Katamon suburb, 1971. Photo David Eisenberg, Jerusalem.

of Māliḥa (Manaḥat), Deir Yāsīn (Kefar Sha'ul), and Liftā (Mei Nefto'aḥ) were expanded and repopulated; Ein Kerem was incorporated into Jerusalem, as was part of Beit Ṣāfāfā. On Mt. Zion, the Ministry of Religious Affairs established a new religious center around the reputed tomb of David, containing the Holocaust Vault and the Temple Observation Point, as a substitute for the lost Old City. To make up for the loss of the Mount of Olives, new cemeteries were consecrated in Sanhedriyyah and on Har ha-Menuḥot.

In order to diversify the sources of livelihood in the capital, considerable efforts were made by the Israel government to develop industry. Several small and medium-sized factories for electrical and metal products, pencils, pharmaceutics, etc. were opened and a large flour mill and silo was built. Publishing houses and printing became important branches of the economy. Industrial estates were built in Romemah, Mekor Barukh, Givat Sha'ul, and Talpiyyot by the Jerusalem Economic Corporation, in which about 90% of the shares were held by the government and the rest by various public bodies. Considerable impetus was also given to the tourist industry, and several large hotels were built (Kings, President, Holyland, Diplomat, etc.). After the solution of the water problem, several swimming pools were built. The University Stadium, a large sports field in the German Colony, and indoor facilities in the Histadrut building, provided opportunities for sports. Bet ha-Am (where the Eichmann Trial was held in 1961) contains a hall for lectures and theatrical performances and a large municipal library. More public parks and gardens were laid out and a Biblical Zoo was opened.

A number of factors contributed to give Jerusalem a distinctive character among Israel's cities: the larger proportion of families going back several generations, newcomers from Asia and North Africa, students and university personnel, and government and other public officials among its population; the dignified public buildings and picturesque, old-established neighborhoods; the almost universal use of stone or stone facing (except in some outlying districts) in both residential and public construction; and its position as the home of the foremost university and the seat of the president, the Knesset, and the government. It was an important center for exhibitions and conventions—national, world Jewish (notable the Zionist Congresses), and international, which, even if they transacted most of their business in Tel Aviv, usually held at least their ceremonial opening sessions in the capital.

The general tone of public and cultural activity was quiet and restrained: there were no sidewalk cafes and little night life. The city was visited from time to time by the Philharmonic Orchestra and the Tel Aviv-based theater companies, which performed at Binyanei ha-Ummah, Bet ha-Am, the Histadrut's Mitchell Hall or the distinctive Khan Theater, which had once been an Arab inn. Indigenous musical activities were provided mainly by the Broadcasting Services Orchestra and the Rubin Academy of Music. Art exhibitions were held at the Israel Museum, the Jerusalem Artists' House (which took over the premises of the Bezalel Museum), and private galleries.

Camp near the Monastery of the Cross for the Three- Day March, 1968. In the background are the buildings of Reḥavyah.

Courtesy Keren Hayesod, United Israel Appeal, Jerusalem.

Jerusalem also became an economic and administrative center for the villages in the "Corridor" (Bet Zayit, Mevasseret Yerushalayim, Me'oz Zion, Orah, Amminadav, Even Sappir, Bar Giora, Nes Harim, Mevo Betar, Ramat Razi'el, etc.), and the city was no longer threatened by isolation in a period of emergency. According to the census of 1961, the population was 166,300, including, it is estimated, several hundred Muslims and over 1,000 Christians. In 1967, the number of inhabitants was estimated at about 185,000.

SECURITY. As the border between Israel and Jordan ran through the middle of Jerusalem, there was constant vigilance on both sides. The Old City walls were hidden from view by high barriers across Jaffa Road and other streets, but from time to time Arab Legion sentries on the ramparts sniped at people in the streets of West Jerusalem and exchanges of fire developed. In April 1953, for example, the shooting went on for over 24 hours and in July 1954 it lasted for three days before a cease-fire was arranged through the UN observers. Occasionally, too, civilians in outlying districts were killed by Arab infiltrators. In September 1956 members of an archaeological convention examining antiquities near Ramat Raḥel were fired at from a Jordanian army post and four people were killed. There was a spate of incidents in June and July 1962, four Israelis being killed and five wounded. On the whole, however, the Jordanian authorities were not interested in making trouble and efforts were sometimes made, by informal contacts between local commanders on both sides, to reduce tension.

A constant focus of friction was the demilitarized zone on Mount Scopus. Every now and then the Jordanians would hold up the fortnightly convoy carrying replacements for the Israel police garrison that looked after the University and Hadassah buildings on the Mount and there was tension between the garrison and the inhabitants of the Arab village of 'Issawiya, in the Israel part of the demilitarized zone. In January 1958 Francis Urrutia, **189**

Convoy to the Israel guard on Mt. Scopus passing through the Mandelbaum Gate. Photo Zev Radovan, Jerusalem.

representing the UN secretary-general, made an unsuccessful attempt to get agreement on the implementation of Article 8 of the Israel-Jordan Armistice Agreement (see above). In May 1958, after Jordanian soldiers had opened fire on Israel patrols on the Mount, a UN officer, Col. George Flint, and four Israel policemen were killed by

Jordanian fire. This time Ralph Bunche, assistant to UN Secretary-General Dag Hammarskjöld, and then Hammarskjöld himself, visited Jerusalem and Amman in efforts to solve the problem, but without success.

MUNICIPAL AFFAIRS. After the departure of the British, an enlarged municipal committee was formed, consisting of the six Jewish councillors and representatives of the Va'ad ha-Kehillah and the Jewish quarters. In January 1949 a municipal council of similar composition was nominated by the Ministry of the Interior, with Daniel Auster as mayor and Reuven Shreibman (Shari) as deputy. In November 1950 the first municipal elections took place by the party list proportional representation system. The results reflected the fragmentation of the population on social, religious, and communal, as well as political and ideological, lines. The largest party in the new council, Mapai (Israel Labor Party), won only 25% of the votes and was closely followed by the United Religious Front (16%), General Zionists (16%), and Ḥerut (11%). The Progressives won 8% and a number of district and communal lists had 18% between them. Shlomo Zalman Shragai (Mizrachi Party) was elected mayor, with the support of a coalition consisting mainly of his own party, the General Zionists, and Ḥerut.

The city had difficult administrative, financial, and social problems to contend with. The staff had been accustomed to the oriental atmosphere of the Muslim mayoralty and the organization of finance and services was primitive. The citizens had not been in the habit of regularly paying rates, especially in the extensive slum areas. Orthodox districts, like Me'ah She'arim, were to a large extent a law unto themselves. The new mayor was hampered in dealing with these problems by dissension inside the coalition and obstruction by the opposition. In August 1953 an inquiry commission appointed by the Ministry of the Interior produced an unfavorable report and Shragai resigned, being succeeded by Yiẓḥak Kariv, of his own party. The difficulties persisted, however; in April 1955 the Ministry dissolved the municipal council and appointed a committee 191 of officials to run the municipality until the elections.

In 1955 the head of the Mapai list, Gershon Agron, was elected mayor with the support of Agudat Israel, the Progressives, and Aḥdut ha-Avodah. When Agudat Israel withdrew from the coalition, he retained his position with the aid of a defecting member of the National Religious Party. Agron died a few days before the 1959 elections and was succeeded by Mordekhai Ish-Shalom, who held the post until 1965. In that year Teddy Kollek, running a personal campaign on the Rafi ticket, won 20% of the votes and formed a coalition with Gaḥal (Ḥerut-Liberal bloc) and the religious parties. During the emergency preceding the Six-Day War in 1967, the opposition was invited to share in responsibility and an all-party administration was formed. After the 1969 elections, in which Kollek headed the united Labor-Mapam Alignment list, he was reelected at the head of an all-party coalition.

14 THE SIX-DAY WAR
AND AFTER REUNIFICATION

For Jerusalem the Six-Day War, despite its name, was in fact only a three-day war, from Monday morning (June 5, 1967) to Wednesday afternoon. The battles began with the Jordanian seizure of UN headquarters and their attempt to break through from there to the south of the city, to the accompaniment of indiscriminate shelling of the Jewish areas. The breakthrough was halted in time, and in a counterattack the Israel forces retook the UN headquarters, barred the Jerusalem-Bethlehem road, and occupied the village of Ṣur-Bāhir. At a later stage there were hard-fought battles to overcome opposition in the Arab Abu-Ṭūr quarter. The most difficult struggle, however, took place in northern Jerusalem, where Israel forces broke through to the Police School and Ammunition Hill slightly to the north of it. There was another breakthrough into Sheikh Jarrāḥ and the American Colony, and on the Tuesday all of East Jerusalem north of the walls of the Old City (Bāb al-Sāhira (Zahra), Wadi Joz) was seized. Contact was also made with the Israel enclave on Mount Scopus. On Wednesday, June 7, 1967, Israel forces broke through the Lions' Gate and took the Old City. United Jerusalem again became the capital of the nation. In the battles for the city and its surroundings about 180 Israel soldiers lost their lives, in addition to the civilians who were hit by shells, etc. As on many occasions in the city's history, the military thrust came from the west and the north, although the final breakthrough came from the east.

The damage caused by the three days of fighting, which was not severe, was repaired, mines were cleared away, military positions and protective walls were destroyed, barbed-wire fences were removed, the roads between the

Agron (formerly Mamilla) Road near the Jaffa Gate, with the wall protecting the Jewish section of the city between 1948 and 1967. Courtesy Keren Hayesod, United Israel Appeal, Jerusalem.

Agron Road after the removal of the wall at the end of the Six-Day War. Courtesy Keren Hayesod, United Israel Appeal, Jerusalem.

two parts of the town were joined, and all the gates of the Old City were once more opened. On June 22, the Knesset enacted a law bringing East Jerusalem within the framework of the administrative establishment and public services of West Jerusalem. The two parts of the city were officially reunited on June 28, when inhabitants from either side could visit the other for the first time in almost 20 years. East Jerusalem was connected to the Israel water supply network and the water shortage was overcome. The electricity network, however, was not united to that of Israel and continued to be operated by a Jordanian company.

The holy places of Christendom came under Israel rule. On 27 June, 1967, Prime Minister Eshkol met the religious heads of the Jewish, Moslem and Christian communities of Jerusalem and made the following statement:

"All the Holy Places in Jerusalem are now open to anyone wishing to pray in them, to the members of all religions, without discrimination. The Government of Israel has laid it down as a basic principle of its policy to guard the Holy Places, to ensure their religious and universal character, and to maintain freedom of access to them ... It is our intention to entrust the internal administration and the arrangements in the Holy Places to the religious leaders of the communities to which they belong."

On the same day, the Knesset enacted the Protection of Holy Places Law. It reads as follows:

"1. The Holy Places shall be protected from desecration and any other violation and from anything likely to violate the freedom of access of the members of the various religions to the places sacred to them or their feelings with regard to those places.

2. (a) Whoever desecrates or otherwise violates a Holy Place shall be liable to imprisonment for a term of seven years. (b) Whoever does anything that is likely to violate the freedom of access of the members of the various religions to the places sacred to them or their feelings with regard to those places shall be liable to imprisonment for a term of five years."

The Western Wall immediately after the end of the Six-Day War, 1967. Photo Werner Braun, Jerusalem.

On 29 November 1968, Prime Minister Levi Eshkol made it known that Israel would allow free access to the Holy Places even to the citizens of enemy Arab States.

One of the most important consequences of the unification of Jerusalem was the resumption of archaeological research within the Old City (in the Citadel, the Upper City, and near the western and southern walls of the Temple Mount), which, in addition to the scientific results, brought about a change in the landscape of the city. The ancient Jewish cemetery, which covers the slopes of the Mount of Olives, was restored. Efforts were made by the government of Israel and Israel public institutions to transfer their offices to Jerusalem, particularly the eastern section. Police headquarters were moved from Tel Aviv to a previously uncompleted Jordanian government building in Sheikh Jarrāḥ. Jerusalem is now distinguished by the duplication of many of its institutions, one of the last signs of the division of the town for 19 years. There are two Hadassah hospitals, two large museums, two Y.M.C.A. buildings, two university campuses, two electricity networks, two

Ben-Yehuda Street in Jerusalem's central business and shopping area, 1970. Courtesy Government Press Office, Tel Aviv.   197

airports (a small airport and the modern one near Qalandiya), many double consulates, and even two central bus stations.

Following the Six-Day War, united Jerusalem became the central attraction for tourists and many new immigrants. Thousands of Jewish students from the Diaspora, particularly from the United States, Canada, and Western Europe, study at the Hebrew University, and many of them remain to stay. By 1971, tourism to Jerusalem reached about 600,000 visitors a year. New immigrant centers, i.e., hostels for individuals and families, were established in Katamon Tet (1968) and Mevasseret Zion on a hill west of Jerusalem (1970).

Vast housing estates, some of them bigger than any development town in the country, were built across what had

Dancing at the Western Wall to celebrate the first anniversary of the reunification of Jerusalem, 1968. Photo Werner Braun.

been no-man's land, and on open tracts in East Jerusalem. The government's objective was to create a physical link between the two halves of the city as quickly as possible and thus forestall any international effort to redivide it. For this purpose some 4,000 acres were expropriated, almost all of it non-arable wasteland. Residents began moving into the first 2,000-unit development, Ramot Eshkol in Northern Jerusalem, a little more than two years after the war. Settlement soon followed in other new quarters nearby—which ranged from 230 to 2,100 units each—Givat ha-Mivtar, Ramat Dafna, the Sanhedriyyah Extension and French Hill.

Meanwhile, other massive projects were progressing in Jerusalem. On Mount Scopus, most of the ridge was leveled as the Hebrew University began expanding its small original campus into one capable of accommodating 14,000 students by 1976. Studies were resumed in the restored buildings from the fall of 1969. In the Old City, reconstruction of the Jewish Quarter was undertaken by a government-owned company, a task expected to take well over a decade, with as many old buildings as possible to be reconstructed and new buildings filling the gaps. The revitalized Quarter is to be the same size as it had been at the turn of the century but twice the size to which it had shrunk by 1948. In the valleys around the Old City work began on a National Park. In downtown Jerusalem, the first commercial and residential towers began to rise and plans were drawn up for a new central business district.

All this rapid development provoked heated public controversy in Israel and abroad over its visual impact on the city. Recognizing the significance of Jerusalem to much of the world's population, Mayor Teddy Kollek set up an international advisory body—the Jerusalem Committee—which included planners, educators and clergymen from 16 countries. The Committee met in Jerusalem in 1969 and 1970. One of its suggestions accepted by Mr. Kollek was the formation of a strong municipal planning arm to take responsibility for Jerusalem's planning out of the hands of government agencies. A Municipal Urban Planning Unit was set up in 1971 and Mr. Kollek invited a prominent British planner, Prof. Nathaniel Lichfield, to serve as chief town planner.

The reunification of the city brought about a revitalization of its economy. Jerusalem became the country's prime focus for tourism and the number of hotel rooms at the end of the Six-Day War, 2,750, was increased by 1,000 within five years. Six thousand more rooms were in the planning or construction stage. Industrial parks were established at Talpiyyot, Atarot and near Sanhedriyyah, the latter for science-based industries. The runway at Atarot Airport was lengthened in 1972 to permit the landing of medium-sized international airliners.

Whereas the population of Tel Aviv fell in the five years following the war and Haifa's remained roughly stable, Jerusalem's population increased by 15%. The national census on May 20, 1972 showed 304,500 persons living in the capital, an increase of 40,000 since the war, of whom the majority—some 25,000—were new immigrants. Unlike the poor immigrants from Asia and Africa who made up two-thirds of West Jerusalem's population before 1967, 70% of the new immigrants were from the Americas or Europe. Among the newcomers, 40% of the breadwinners were professionals as compared to 15% in the general Israel population.

Several major churches undertook large building programs in the city following reunification. At the initiative of Pope Paul VI, the Ecumenical Institute for Advanced Theological Studies was dedicated in 1972 on a hilltop in the south of the city. The Armenian Patriarchate constructed a seminary just inside the walls of the Old City to serve as the principal source of priests and teachers for the world's 5½ million Armenians. The Lutheran World Federation drew up plans for an international study center on the Mount of Olives below Augusta Victoria. Extensive repairs and construction work were also carried out by several churches on Mount Zion.

REUNIFICATION: PROGRESS AND PROBLEMS. With its reunification on June 28, 1967, Jerusalem restored its traditional character as a multi-national and multi-ethnic city. The population totaled about 265,000: 199,000 Jews and 66,000 Arabs. The non-Jewish population was composed of two religious sectors: the larger Muslim community of 54,000 (83%) and the various Christian factions numbering 11,000 (including 4,000 members of the Greek Orthodox Church, 3,600 of the Latin Church, and 1,200 Greek Catholics). The Jewish community thus comprised three-quarters of the population. The fact that it was the decisive majority was not novel, as a Jewish majority had existed in the city since the last third of the 19th century.

The municipal unification of Jerusalem brought into the city's boundaries areas that had been under Jordanian municipal jurisdiction before the Six-Day War (mainly within the boundaries defined during the Mandate period), as well as a broad area that had been organized under village councils or had not enjoyed municipal status. Consequently, population groups that had never been urban were included in the city's area and in the jurisdiction of the municipality and Israel government authority. The resulting population was most heterogeneous, from slum dwellers and semi-nomadic Bedouin to members of the upper middle class, who had moved beyond the limits of the Jordanian city and set up magnificent suburbs to the north. The Arab population was concentrated in these areas. About 33% of it (23,000) lived inside the Old City walls; about 38% (25,000) in the northern suburbs, most of them modern; and about 26% (17,000) in the southern parts, including the villages of Silwān, Abu Ṭūr, and Ṣur Bāhir.

The rate of natural increase among the Arab population, which is slightly less than double that of the Jewish, could increase the proportion of Arabs in the city from a quarter to a third within 20 years. The Israel government, realizing the potential difficulties of this situation, expended great efforts to provide more accommodation for Jews in the city

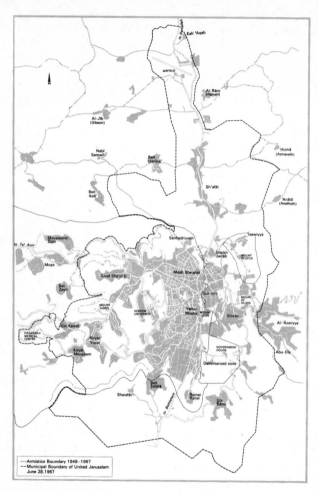

Map 6. Municipal boundaries of Jerusalem before and after the 1967 reunification. Based on D. Bahat, *Jerusalem—Its Epochs,* Jerusalem 1970.

Street corner near the Western Wall, 1969. Courtesy Government Press Office, Tel Aviv.

and to eradicate distinctions between the western and eastern parts. In 1967–69 there were only a handful of Jews living east of the former dividing line, but from the end of 1969, when the construction of new quarters began to be completed (e.g., Ramat Eshkol), the settlement of Jews in the eastern part of the city accelerated. In 1970 the government decided to add impetus to the establishment of Jewish quarters in the southern, northern, and northwestern parts of the Old City. As a result of these efforts, the number of Jews moving to Jerusalem reached 5,000 per year, twice as much as in the years immediately before the Six-Day War. In this 203 way the numerical balance between Jews and non-Jews was maintained in the unified city.

During the period of the city's division, the existence of two municipalities governed by states with such differing policies, rates of development, and character resulted in the development of two different cities. So different were their economic systems and social structures that it was sometimes difficult to believe that they were both parts of the same city. West Jerusalem quickly recovered from the damage it had suffered during the War of Independence, but from 1948 to 1967 its population decreased in proportion to that of the rest of the country; whereas in 1948 it had 9.6% of the total population of the State of Israel, at the end of 1960 this ratio had decreased to 7.7%. The economy of West Jerusalem was based mainly on a constellation of public services (government, university, Jewish Agency, and Hadassah) that employed about 30% of its labor force; about 17% was employed in industry, and 14% in business and banking. Tourism, in which Jerusalem has a relative advantage, did not play a central role. Only 13% of the hotels in Israel were located there, while 32% were in Tel Aviv. One of the major obstacles to the development of the city's economy was the fact that West Jerusalem had almost no economic hinterland, while in Haifa and Tel Aviv a great part of the economic activity extends to nearby townships and settlements and their scope of influence extends far beyond their municipal boundaries. The scope of Jerusalem's influence on the narrow underpopulated corridor that connects it with the coast was necessarily very limited.

In contrast to West Jerusalem, East Jerusalem under Jordanian rule retained its position as the largest city of the West Bank and it continued to serve as the center of a very broad economic and demographic hinterland. The city was the center of most of the financial institutions of the West Bank, as well as 85% of the tourist companies, and it also had the greatest concentration of the wholesale trade, the independent professions, and the trade in durable goods.

Production per employee in East Jerusalem was 50% higher than the average in the West Bank as whole, and the average income per person was also proportionally higher. Nevertheless, the economy of East Jerusalem was based mainly on one activity: tourism. The influence of every decrease in the number of tourists would extend to the various branches of the economy and result in crisis. The Jordanian authorities did not accord Jerusalem preferential treatment in relation to other cities. On the contrary, their policies of economic incentives and government aid were aimed basically at the capital, Amman, and the East Bank, as opposed to the West Bank, including Jerusalem. East Jerusalemites who wished to establish economic enterprises in their city had either to abandon their projects or implement them in Amman. Amman also received a distinct preference with regard to financial and cultural institutions. This policy led to a slowdown in the economic development of East Jerusalem and in acceleration in the development of the capital of the kingdom across the Jordan which was implemented mainly by entrepreneurs from the West Bank, primarily from Jerusalem.

Although the economic status of East Jerusalem was more stable than that of the western half of the city, a comparison of the two reveals a formidable gap in favor of the Jewish sector of the city. On the eve of the Six-Day War, the average yearly income per person in West Jerusalem was fourfold that of the eastern part. In West Jerusalem the income per person was estimated in 1965 as IL3,400 while in the eastern part it was only IL900. East Jerusalem contributed only 6–7% of the buying power of the unified city, in contrast to its 25% of the population. Under such circumstances it was extremely difficult to effect the economic integration of the two parts of the city and annul the effects of the war in a relatively short time. The Six-Day War resulted in a number of economic difficulties in East Jerusalem: the temporary cessation of tourism, on which the city's economy had been based; the loss of the Jordanian authorities and army as a source of economic demand; disruptions in trade between the various parts of the West Bank; the closing of the banks; the lack of liquidity; and the absence of economic stability. These brought about a serious economic crisis, which found immediate expression in mass unemployment. Four months after the war, unemployment in the eastern part covered one-third of the labor force, in contrast to 7–8% on the eve of the war. Especially affected were the building trades, transportation, and hotels. Services, such as restaurants, cafés, bakeries, and garages, which were also affected, recovered quickly due to rising demands from Israel tourists.

Within a few months, the process of economic disintegration ceased, and speedy action on the part of the authorities brought about a distinct improvement in the economic situation. The process of rehabilitation was accelerated by the huge public investments made in the city following the war, especially in construction. At the end of 1969 employment returned to its prewar level. About half of the businesses in East Jerusalem were better off than they had been on the eve of the war. The most outstanding improvement was in the situation of salaried workers. More than 5,000 workers and employees out of a labor force of about 18,000 were employed in West Jerusalem, earning salaries that were 150% higher than those they had received on the eve of the war. The recovery process had some negative manifestations, however. Price levels increased by 40–50%. About half of the businesses in East Jerusalem, especially those which could not compete with similar business in the western part of the city, were affected with varying degrees of severity.

The integration of the economic systems, and especially the implementation of the principles of a modern welfare state, brought about far-reaching changes in Arab society in East Jerusalem. The distribution of income and property became more equalized. Israel wages were paid to thousands of Arab workers, and a slow increase in the wages of Arabs employed in the Arab sector brought a general improvement in the standard of living. National Insurance,

Jews and Arabs working on a new housing project in the Ramot Eshkol area, January 1969. Courtesy Government Press Office, Tel Aviv.

especially birth benefits and benefits to families with many children, aided in the improvement of the status of women. Nevertheless, the damage to the relative economic position of the upper middle class brought complaints of "discrimination" and "Jewish control" of certain branches, especially the import of durable goods and tourism. Because of the atmosphere of long-range political insecurity that continued to exist among the Arabs of East Jerusalem, no plan for capital investments was implemented. The closing of Arab banks continued to influence the lack of liquidity and the scarcity of sources of credit. In view of developments from

1968, a warning has been voiced that the integration of East Jerusalem's Arabs into the city's united economy might lead to their concentration in low-income employment requiring manual labor. This trend can have undesirable social and inter-ethnic results.

Another unsolved problem is that of the employment of white-collar workers. With the unification of the city, many Jordanian government officials, travel agents, lawyers, etc. became unemployed. Only the Arab employees of the Jerusalem municipality and a small number of government employees (formerly Jordanian) were integrated into the institutions of the unified municipality and Israel government offices. Out of 500 people who worked in all levels of the Jordanian government on the eve of the war, only about 150 were absorbed, some of them in the military government. This problem was more of a political nature than an economic one. Some of the white-collar workers could not find employment in their professions for economic reasons; lawyers were not employed because they boycotted Israel courts. Most of them, however, especially civil servants on intermediate or senior levels, were unemployed because the functions they had fulfilled were transferred, with the change in authorities, to Israel government offices. The degree of integration of white-collar workers in the economic and administrative system became an important indicator for the reconciliation of Jerusalem's population to the new situation created by the unification of the city.

The unification of Jerusalem opened a new chapter in the complex relations between the Jewish majority and the Arab minority in the State of Israel. For the first time in its history, Israel had to absorb a developed Arab urban unit with advanced social stratification, considerable economic power, a high level of education, and a tradition of participation in the highest levels of government. Jerusalem, after its unification, became the greatest concentration of urban Arab population in the country. The percentage of high school graduates in East Jerusalem rose steadily under Jordanian rule, and in 1967, 38% of the males had completed high school and 9% had had higher education. The educational level of the Arab residents of the city was higher than that of the inhabitants of Judea and Samaria and even higher than the average of all the non-Jews in Israel, among whom the urban population was a small minority.

In contrast to the Arabs in Israel, who initially lacked an educated, stable urban class, the inhabitants of East Jerusalem lived for 20 years under independent Arab rule, during which it was the center of authority for the entire West Bank. The leadership of East Jerusalem was the major exponent of Arab-Palestinian nationalism and was integrated into the Jordanian establishment. Periodic disagreements with Amman aside, it was one of the outstanding elite groups in the Hashemite kingdom. When the city was unified, there were a considerable number of former ministers, ambassadors, members of parliament and senate, and senior officials in East Jerusalem, in addition to an efficient and capable municipal administration. In its attitude to Israel the East Jerusalem population was one of the most extreme elements in Jordan. The Palestine Liberation Organization was strong there, and many members of extremist parties, both right and left wing, resided in the city. As was customary in the Jordanian educational system, pupils were educated toward extreme pan-Arabism and revanche; even excerpts from the *Protocols of the Elders of Zion* were found among the teaching materials. The chauvinistic extremism stemmed, inter alia, from the fact that about 11,000 inhabitants of the city were formally refugees, i.e., the head of the family was born in an area that had been included in the State of Israel in 1948.

The Jewish population was agreeable in some respects and not agreeable in others to the improvement of relations with the Arab minority. The large number of oriental Jews and their Israel-born children—more than 50% of the Jewish population of the city—was significant in this matter, as this group was familiar with the Arabic language and the Arab way of life and culture and could theoretically serve as a bridge between the two segments of the population. However, the immigrants from Muslim countries who had come to Israel after the War of Independence (about a quarter of the total Jewish population) were, paradoxically, a potential cause of tension. Partly because they had suffered oppression and persecution in their countries of origin, they were sometimes influenced by latent urges to revenge in their attitude to the Arab population of East Jerusalem. Other sections of the Jewish population, mainly native Israelis and immigrants from Europe and English-speaking countries, lacked familiarity with Arabs and their way of life and often misunderstood them—either regarding them in an unrealistic romantic way or suspecting them as a hostile, alien element.

The two populations, which suddenly found themselves living in one city, bore the acute psychological influences of the Six-Day War, apart from the past legacy of the Jewish-Arab conflict. The Jewish population felt a sharp sense of release from the burden of fear that existed during the prewar period and euphoria over the unification of the city and the liberation of the Western Wall and the other holy places. The Arab population was astonished by the swift conquest of their city and suffered from a deep sense of shame after their decisive defeat. On the other hand, the factor that caused the greatest surprise among the Arab population was the humane and fair treatment accorded to them by the soldiers of the Israel Defense Forces. Influenced by Arab propaganda describing Jews as murderers of women and children, the Arabs awaited the worst. Fear gave way to astonishment and feelings of gratitude.

There was an initial atmosphere of goodwill and good-neighborliness that found dramatic expression on the "day of reunification" (June 28, 1967). When the barriers were removed and free movement between the two parts of the city was allowed, the Jewish and Arab masses mingled without incident. The atmosphere of peace and harmony in the city appeared unreal to those who witnessed it. Indeed, it lasted only a few short weeks, during which these feelings slowly abated. The two sides began to adjust themselves to the new reality. Repeated incidents and the loss of lives recreated the tension within the Jewish population. The Arab population found itself subject to a rule that, although tolerant and understanding, was nonetheless foreign, with which they could not and did not wish to identify, and to whose continued existence they could not reconcile themselves. The Israel authorities quickly learned the complex problems of the Arab sector and also found ways to solve them effectively. Nevertheless, several points of friction were created by a lack of understanding and knowledge of the mentality of the Arab population. This lack of understanding stemmed mainly from an approach to the population of East Jerusalem similar to that employed to the Arab population of the State of Israel before the war, disregarding the differences between the two communities. Likewise, attempts were made immediately to put into effect the procedures of Israel administration, without allowing the inhabitants of East Jerusalem sufficient time to adapt to the ways and means unfamiliar to them.

In the course of time, the inhabitants of East Jerusalem became accustomed to these procedures, and at the same time the Israel authorities became familiar with the feelings of the inhabitants on certain matters. This mutual adaptation erased most of the points of friction, the major one being the problem of taxes. The East Jerusalemites, accustomed to the Jordanian fiscal system, which levied low taxes, and in return rendered a low level of services, did not, at first, understand the principles of the Israel welfare state, demanding high taxation and providing a high level of services. Taxes connected with war and security caused additional complaints, since the inhabitants of East Jerusalem regarded their payment as "treason against the Jordanian kingdom," which was in a state of war with Israel.

In terms of their civil status, the inhabitants of East Jerusalem were Israel residents with Jordanian citizenship. (They could apply for Israel citizenship, but practically none of them did so.) This status allowed them to vote for and be elected to the Jerusalem municipality, but not to the Knesset. As Jordanian citizens, they could cross the cease-fire line and visit in Jordan, while they also had the right to move freely throughout Israel, like other residents. Despite the distinct improvement in many areas of relations with the authorities and the adjustment of the inhabitants of East Jerusalem to the way of life that developed in the unified city, relations were clouded by the fact that the population of East Jerusalem avoided all political coopera-tion that could be interpreted as voluntary acknowledge-ment of the unification of Jerusalem. Members of the Arab municipal council, who were invited to join the unified city council, refused to do so; lawyers refused to appear in Israel courts; companies refused to be registered as Israel companies; and the Shari'a courts refused to become part of the Muslim judicial system of Israel, despite a far-reaching compromise suggested by Israel. Nevertheless, the bound-aries between political cooperation, which was regarded as "treason," and the minimal reconciliation necessary for coexistence were very elastic. Thus, for example, the mass voting by inhabitants of East Jerusalem in the municipal elections of October 1969 was not viewed as collaboration.

Political tension remained latent most of the time, but it broke out a number of times and was expressed mainly in business strikes and demonstrations. Feelings of political frustration and tension were also nourished by a number of actions taken by the Israel authorities to insure the Jewish character of the city and enforce Israel control of the eastern part. In broad areas of the eastern part Jewish dwellings began to be erected. The acts of Arab terrorists aggravated the inter-ethnic tension. After one act of terror, which claimed a number of civilian casualties in West Jerusalem (the "Night of the Grenades," Aug. 18, 1968) young Jews attacked Arab civilians and damage was inflicted on Arab shops. Strong and unequivocal measures on the part of the Israel government and its major leaders put an end to the hooliganism, and later acts of Arab terror (such as the explosions which in 1968–69 killed and wounded many people in a marketplace, a supermarket, the students' cafeteria in the Hebrew University, etc.) did not elicit revenge on innocent Arabs. Nevertheless, the security forces increased their supervision over the Arab residents. Membership in terrorist cells and possession of arms caches were punished, inter alia, by the destruction of several houses and the confiscation of others. All these measures resulted in alternately rising and falling tension. A major event influencing the atmosphere between the communities was the short-lived shock of the fire in the al-Aqṣā Mosque on Aug. 21, 1969, which quickly abated when the culprit proved to be an insane Christian tourist from Australia, although the incident was blown up to major international proportions by all the Arab States.

In Jewish public opinion there were two different approaches to dealing with the Arab population. All Jews were ready to grant the Arabs full citizenship rights as individuals, but some would deny them the right of national political expression or separate representation, whereas others held that the Arabs should not only be granted individual rights but should be recognized as a national minority with legitimate aspirations of their own, entitling them to separate representation. This argument never came to a head, as the Arabs themselves refused to cooperate in any attempt at an interim arrangement and were not ready to accept any suggestion of separate representation or any kind of political organization.

By 1972 distinct progress had been made in the process of integrating the Arabs of East Jerusalem into the life of the city and inter-ethnic relations developed and improved, despite negative forces that operated throughout the period. Life had become almost completely normalized, apart from the political non-cooperation. Economic cooperation deepened and Arab merchants in Jerusalem were increasingly using Israel ports for their exports to other countries and for their imports, also becoming importers on behalf of Arabs in Judea and Samaria. At the same time, Israel goods predominated in the local market. Professional links between the two parts of the city increased. Other links were established between East Jerusalem and the rest of Israel, based on both economic ties and the spending of leisure time. Jerusalem's Arabs were turning increasingly to the municipality with their problems (including those related to governmental offices). Extensive building developed among the Arabs of East Jerusalem, several hundred units being constructed annually. Efforts were made to equalize the services provided in East Jerusalem with those in the West (including the connection of its electricity to the national grid). Problems were encountered especially in the more affluent areas (which had grown up without proper planning) in the preparation of roads, sanitation, and water as a result of the reluctance of the inhabitants to have their land utilized for such objects.

There were still fundamental political differences of approach between the Jewish majority and the Arab minority with regard to the future of the city. The integration of the communities and nationalities in Jerusalem was progressively implemented, mainly in the economic sphere and in areas necessary for municipal survival. There was little social contact between the two groups but the fact that thousands of Arab workers were employed in West Jerusalem led to significant contacts and new understanding. The deepening of reciprocal harmonious relations, however, ultimately depended upon the general solution to the Israel-Arab conflict.

Part Two

GEOGRAPHY
AND ARCHAEOLOGY

1 GEOGRAPHY

THE CLIMATE. Jerusalem's climate is Mediterranean, with a rainy, temperate winter and a hot, completely dry summer; there is a high percentage of solar radiation throughout the year, especially in the summer.

The annual rainfall in Jerusalem is about 20 in. (500 mm.). The rainy season continues from September to May, and approximately 30% of the annual rain falls by December, with 40% in February and March. There are about 47 rainy days annually on the average. On most of these days there is about 0.2 in. (5 mm.) of rainfall; 1.2 in. (30 mm.) of daily rainfall occurs about five or six times during a season; and once or twice there is as much as 2 in. (50 mm.). Particularly heavy rainfalls were recorded between Nov. 5 and Nov. 9, 1938, amounting to 8 in. (200 mm.) or 30% of the precipitation of that year. In the period from Dec. 13 to Dec. 23, 1951, over 14 in. (358 mm.) fell (57% of the annual rainfall). In the 100 years during which records of rainfall were kept (1840–1950), there were two years with less than 12 in. (300 mm.) of rainfall in the entire wet season, six years with less than 16 in. (400 mm.), and three years with more than 40 in. (1,000 mm.). Snow in Jerusalem is infrequent. When it does fall, it occurs mainly in January and February and can last about four or five days.

The average annual temperature in Jerusalem is 66°F (19°C). The average temperature in August, the hottest month, is 75°F (24°C) and in the coldest month, January, is 50°F (10°C). The average daily temperature from December to February is usually under 52°F (11°C). From the middle of February until the beginning of April, the temperature rises to an average of about 59°F (15°C). At the end of April it rises to about 68°F (20°C) and remains at that level till the end of July. In August it reaches 77°F (25°C), and from then till the end of October the daily average is about 68°F (20°C). The minimum temperature in the month of January goes down to 41°F (5°C). The maximum temperature during the *sharav* (heat wave) reaches 95°F (35°C). The regular wind in Jerusalem is a western one, but occasionally it is northwesterly or southwesterly. Winds do not originate in Jerusalem and its vicinity. Jerusalem is subject to heat waves during the months of May and June, as well as September and October. These periods are characterized by intensive heat and low humidity and usually last a few days. The humidity drops 30–40% below the average and the heat increases by about 27°F (15°C). The average daily humidity in Jerusalem is about 62%. The humidity drops until noon and rises toward evening. The amount of dew in Jerusalem reaches 0.8–1 in. (20–25 mm.) as an average during the 100 to 150 annual nights of dew.

FLORA. In Jerusalem, remnants of ancient trees are to be found, including the Jerusalem pine (*Pinus halepensis*, the tallest forest tree in Israel), the gall oak (*Quercus infectoria*), the common oak (*Quercus calliprinos*), the Tabor oak (*Quercus ithaburensis*), the Palestine terebinth (*Pistacia palaestina*), the mastic terebinth (*Pistacia lentiscus*), the arbutus, and the wild olive. Traces of ancient vegetation are found in Tel Arzah, on Mount Scopus, on the French Hill, in the Valley of the Cross, the German Colony, Ein Kerem, Bet ha-Kerem, Talpiyyot, and Agron Street.

BOUNDARIES. The only boundary of Jerusalem that remained unchanged after the Six-Day War (1967) was its western boundary. It descends southwest from Mount Ḥozevim to the village of Mei-Nefto'aḥ (Liftā) and west to Har ha-Menuḥot and from there to Kefar Sha'ul, Bet Zayit, Ein Kerem, the Hadassah medical center, Kefar Shalma, and Ir Gannim. The new boundaries of the city

Ancient olive tree in the Garden of Gethsemane. Courtesy Government Press Office, Tel Aviv.

were extended north, east, and south. North of Mount Hoẓevim, the boundary includes the villages of Sha'fāṭ, New Beit Ḥanīnā and Qalandiya to the airport at Atarot, and then returns eastward to the Jerusalem-Ramallah highway, encompassing within the boundaries of the city the hilly area between Jerusalem and Atarot. The eastern boundary includes the natural mountainous framework of Jerusalem: Mount Scopus, the Mount of Olives, the village of Al-Ṭūr, the Old City, and the village of Silwān. The new boundary on the south includes the villages of Ṣūr Bāhir and Beit Ṣafāfā and continues the length of the Valley of Rephaim to the juncture with the western border. Greater Jerusalem within these borders has an area of 26,250 acres (105,000 dunams) and forms one organic unit.

TOPOGRAPHY. The watershed of the region passes through the city in a north-south direction via Mount Scopus, the Sanhedriyyah quarter, Romemah, Maḥaneh Yehudah, Terra Sancta, the Y.M.C.A., Givat Ḥananyah, the Mandatory Government House (later the headquarters of the UN observers), Talpiyyot, and Ramat Raḥel. There are some mountain ridges branching off the watershed to the east and west. On the low eastern ridge, which descends to the river bed of Kidron, the ancient city was built. A western ridge divides the Christian and Armenian quarters of the Old City and ends on Mount Zion. It was here that the upper city was built. A number of ridges penetrate to the west and south of Jerusalem: the ridge of Beit Yisrael, the ridge on which the Mandatory Government House stands, the ridge of Ha-Kiryah (Israel government center), the Kiryat ha-Yovel ridge, the Gonen ridge, and the ridge of Ir Gannim. The ridges and the branches of the mountains form valleys that greatly influence the structure of the city. These are divided into two groups: those facing Naḥal Kidron in the east, and those facing Naḥal Sorek in the west. Naḥal Ben Hinnom, which demarcates the south-western boundary of historical Jerusalem, flows into Naḥal Kidron. Another tributary of the Kidron is Naḥal Egozim, which divides the Bet Yisrael quarter from Mount Scopus. Naḥal Sorek borders Jerusalem on the north and the west. In the south the Valley of Rephaim is a tributary of Naḥal Sorek.

The topography of Jerusalem forms five main natural basins. The eastern basin includes the Old City and the drainage basin of Kidron and Ben Hinnom. The northern basin includes the Romemah, Tel Arzah, and Sanhedriyyah quarters. The southern basin includes the German and Greek colonies, Ge'ulim, Talbiyah, Mekor Ḥayyim, Bet ha-Kerem, Bayit va-Gan, Kiryat ha-Yovel, Ein Kerem, 219 and Ir Gannim. The central basin includes the government center (Ha-Kiryah), the Hebrew University, and the Israel Museum. As most of the ridges and the valleys extend in a north to south direction, only a few extending from east to west, the city has developed lengthwise. Mount Scopus is 2,700 ft. (827 m.) and the Mount of Olives is 2,640 ft. (805 m.) high, whereas the Old City is some 200–260 ft. (60–80 m.) lower. Mount Herzl and Bayit va-Gan are 2,340 ft. (835 m.) high, whereas nearby Ein Kerem is only 2,230–2,300 ft. (650–700 m.) high.

2 THE OLD CITY

The present-day massive stone walls of the Old City built c. 1537 under the Turkish sultan Suleiman the Magnificent, enclose a smaller area than that of the Second Temple period. The location of its seven gates (Herod's, Damascus, and New gates in the north, Jaffa Gate in the west, Zion and Dung gates in the south, and St. Stephen's (Lions') Gate in the east) is thought to be identical to that of the gates of antiquity.

Inside the walls of the Old City, where all the inhabitants lived until the middle of the 19th century, four quarters are distinguished: in the northwest corner, the Christian Quarter, grouped around the Church of the Holy Sepulcher; in the southwest, the Armenian Quarter; in the center and northeast, the Muslim Quarter; and, in the southeast, the Jewish Quarter. From St. Stephen's Gate westward to the Holy Sepulcher runs the Via Dolorosa, which passes through the Muslim Quarter and is flanked by several churches, monasteries, and Christian charitable institutions. The artificially flattened ground on Mt. Moriah, where both the First and the Second Temple stood (since King Herod's time supported by the pillars and vaults of the vast subterranean "Solomon's Stables") today bears two of the holiest shrines of Islam: the Dome of the Rock (Omar Mosque) and the al-Aqṣā Mosque. The Temple Area is surrounded by the colossal Herodian enclosure wall, preserved in the east, south, and west; a larger section of the Western ("Wailing") Wall, the most venerated site in Jewish tradition, was bared to view after 1967, and archaeological excavations further south, north, and west have added to the knowledge of the city's structure

The western part of the Old City wall built by Sultan Suleiman in c. 1537, with the Jaffa Gate Citadel on the right. Courtesy Ministry of Foreign Affairs, Jerusalem.

in the Second Temple period and historical events of those and later times. Between the Western Wall and the Armenian Quarter lies the Jewish Quarter, which had to surrender in the 1948 fighting. Under Jordanian rule, this quarter deteriorated, and all its synagogues were systematically destroyed. Following the Six-Day War (1967) reconstruction was started there, and in 1972 the re-built complex of four Sephardi synagogues (Yohanan ben Zakkai, Eliyahu ha-Navi, Istambuli and "Middle" synagogues) was consecrated.

3 THE NEW CITY

As a result of the gradual population rise, space within the confines of the walls of the Old City became ever more crowded, particularly in the narrow Jewish Quarter. Jews were therefore the first to found new quarters outside the walls; in 1858 Mishkenot Sha'ananim was built west of the Old City, soon followed by Yemin Moshe and by Naḥalat Shivah in the northwest. At about the same time, churches began to establish hostels and other institutions outside the walls for the benefit of the growing flow of Christian pilgrims: the buildings of the Russian Compound are notable among these.

The New City spread mainly toward the northwest along the road leading to the port of Jaffa. From this direction most goods were brought and pilgrims, both Jewish and Christian, arrived from overseas and enlivened trade in the city. In the first Jewish quarters the houses were crowded together, primarily for security reasons; the Yemin Moshe quarter was even surrounded by a wall and its gates closed every evening. Those first quarters which the inhabitants built exclusively with their own means (e.g., Naḥalat Shivah) were shabby in appearance and lacked uniformity in style and layout. Others, where construction was partly or wholly financed by philanthropists (like Yemin Moshe, which was aided by Sir Moses Montefiore and bears his name), were better planned, generally with rows of houses of one or two stories. The Me'ah She'arim quarter took on particular importance. Founded in 1874 by pious Jews from the Old City, it has remained a stronghold of Jewish Orthodoxy.

At the end of the 19th century, the first garden suburbs

made their appearance; those of non-Jews (e.g., German Colony and Greek Colony, Katamon, etc.) preceded modern Jewish quarters (Reḥavyah, Bet ha-Kerem, Talpiyyot, etc.). In all these it was attempted to lend beauty to the individual house and surrounding garden, and to plan streets, water, sewage and electricity networks along rational lines while details were kept within the framework of the urban outline scheme.

The British Mandatory authorities aimed to preserve Jerusalem's beauty and historical treasures. All outer house walls had to be built of the fine local stone, which is both durable and in harmony with the landscape. Rules were issued limiting the height of structures and floor space percentage relative to plot area, and care was taken to retain open spaces and preserve the skyline, particularly of sites of natural beauty and historical interest. An effort was made to fit the main roads to traffic densities, and a ring road was planned to connect the outer suburbs with each other. On the other hand, the authorities rejected industrialization as not befitting Jerusalem's character, and they did not encourage a rapid population growth.

4 CITY PLANNING (1948–1972)

In the first years of the State of Israel, the most pressing tasks facing the city of Jerusalem were repair of the damage caused in the War of Independence, absorption of new immigrants, and preparation of a new outline scheme fitting in with the border which then divided the city between Israel and Jordan; at a later stage came zoning into residential, commercial, administrative, cultural, and industrial units.

With the Hebrew University campus, the Knesset, and the Israel Museum as pivotal points, a large center of legislative, administrative, cultural, and commercial institutions was laid out. The whole area was well integrated in the general plan of the capital. Care was taken to conserve and restore sites of archaeological and historical interest, to maintain open spaces and develop green belts.

Jerusalem's hilly topography was taken into account: the ridges and upper slopes, which are well drained in winter and cool and agreeable in summer, were reserved for building, while valleys were earmarked for parks, gardens, and fruit orchards.

The de facto borders that surrounded Israel Jerusalem left the west as the only direction for the city's expansion. It was therefore decided to let the outline scheme hinge on the huge Binyanei ha-Ummah (Convention Center) at Romemah, the dominant height of the Jerusalem urban area which lies astride the main western entrance of the city. Accordingly, the existing commercial center was planned to expand northwestward to Romemah. The buildings of the government ministries (Ha-Kiryah) and the new Knesset edifice, surrounded by lawns and gardens, adjoin this area to the south. Still further south lie the impressive campus of the University and the National Library, the Israel Museum, and related institutions. This whole complex is thus situated between older quarters in the east and the expansion belt of residential suburbs (Kiryat Moshe, Bet ha-Kerem, Bayit va-Gan, Kiryat ha-Yovel, etc.) in the west and southwest. The Hadassah Medical Center is the extreme point of westward expansion.

Contrary to the British view, industry is now regarded as an element indispensable to Jerusalem's economy. Owing to the city's geographical position, light industries are easiest to develop here. In addition to the enlarged existing industrial area at Tel Arza in the northwest, a second, at Givat Sha'ul in the west, was developed.

Owing to economic and security considerations, the planning authorities regarded the road system linking the capital to the rest of the State as particularly important. After the War of Independence, a single highway to Tel Aviv in the northwest was open; the railway line became usable again after border corrections in the Israel-Jordan armistice of 1949. Since then, additional roads, which converge on the city from the west and southwest, were constructed.

As elsewhere in the country, the large new suburbs in the west and southwest (Katamon, Kiryat ha-Yovel, etc.) were laid out as self-contained neighborhood units. Prior to 1967, they had to absorb many newcomers settling in Jerusalem and aid in thinning out the overpopulated older quarters further east, some of which had been earmarked for replanning and reconstruction. In an outer circle around these suburbs spread a green belt of parks, forests, and playgrounds. Landscaping and planting of parks and lawns accentuated sites of historical interest all over the city. Although the law prescribing the facing of buildings with natural stone was relaxed in part of the city to prevent unnecessary rises in the cost of popular housing, it was retained for all representative sections of the city.   227

Growth and Planning Since Reunification (1967). Immediately after the Six-Day War, all military installations, fences, and shell-proof concrete walls which had separated the two parts of the city were removed, and the connecting streets and roads paved and opened. Next, unseemly structures obstructing the view of the Old City wall were torn down, the wall itself and its gates painstakingly repaired, and the first gardens of a planned green peripheral belt planted in front of it. Inside the Old City, hovels were demolished close to the Western Wall. Two additional rows of its ashlars, hidden in the rubble, were uncovered and a wide square in front cleared, paved, and rendered suitable for prayer. The reconstruction of the Jewish Quarter and its historic synagogues was started and institutions of religious study moved in, their pupils forming the nucleus of the Old City's renewed Jewish community. South of the Temple Mount, archaeological excavations were started early in 1968. The slight damage caused to Christian churches and institutions during the fighting was speedily repaired and church building and renovation work (e.g., on the Holy Sepulcher), which had been in progress prior to June 1967, were resumed. Jerusalem's boundaries were redrawn, giving the capital a municipal area of 107 sq. km., the largest in the country.

One of the main problems of the Jerusalem master plan lay in reconciling the desire for a continuous built-up area with the necessity to preserve and enhance numerous historical sites, sacred to three world religions, such as the entire Old City, the Kidron and Ben Hinnom gorges, the "City of David" to the south, Mount Scopus and the Mount of Olives, and many more. Both inside and outside the Old City walls, gardens were laid out or were planned, while other areas to the east and south were earmarked as public open spaces or sites for preservation and reconstruction.

Another difficult task, which after June 1967 assumed great urgency, lay in securing efficient traffic arteries leading
228 through and around Jerusalem. The existent main thor-

oughfares had become totally inadequate, particularly Jaffa Road, which carried the bulk of both urban and interurban traffic. A network of new broad roads was blueprinted in order to provide alternative approach routes from all directions, to enable vehicular traffic to cross the municipal area to destinations beyond it (e.g., from Bethlehem directly to Ramallah) without clogging Jerusalem's main arteries. Adequate parking facilities had also to be provided throughout the city. The numerous protected historical sites and edifices and, primarily, Jerusalem's hilly terrain rendered this program highly expensive, as entire complexes of nonessential buildings would have to be demolished. In addition, earth-moving work, on a very large scale, would have to be carried out and long road tunnels excavated in the ridges.

In order to arrive at an acceptable joint solution to the traffic, social, and economic problems, planners preferred not to concentrate industry, commerce, administration, tourism, etc., each in a separate area, but rather to distribute them evenly throughout the city, thus shortening the distances between residential quarters and sites of employment and more evenly spreading traffic flow during rush hours. As more and more government ministries and other central offices moved to the capital, an increasing need was felt to depart from the original plan of concentrating all government buildings in Ha-Kiryah and to distribute them over other sections, including East Jerusalem.

The Hebrew University saw the return of its original campus atop Mount Scopus, where, beginning with the Harry S. Truman Research Center, an intensive restoration and building program was launched in 1968, comprising lecture halls and dormitories for thousands of students. Other institutes of learning, e.g., yeshivot, Christian theological seminaries, etc., were constructed in various parts of the city.

In view of the growing need for tourist accommodation and services in Jerusalem, large sums of public and private capital were invested in hotel building, and suitable sites were earmarked for these purposes throughout the city. The capital attracted increasing numbers of industrial enterprises, particularly in the electronics and other science-centered industries, for which new areas were set aside in the south, north, and northeast.

New housing developments called for the largest share of both space and investments. While the southwest (Kiryat ha Yovel, etc.) continued to serve as the sector of intensive apartment building, and vacant lots elsewhere were increasingly being used for new constructions, a concentrated effort was being directed toward the favorable terrain in the north, beyond the former armistice line. New residential quarters, including Ramot Eshkol and the French Hill quarter, both under construction since 1968, promised to provide accommodation for tens of thousands of citizens, both Jews and non-Jews, and to link western Jerusalem with Mount Scopus in the east and Sha'fāṭ in the north.

In 1971, construction was started of four large suburbs in the city's outer periphery: Neveh Ya'akov in the north, beyond Sha'afat; Ramot in the northwest, in the direction of Nabi Samwil (the highest spot in the Jerusalem Hills); Giloh, on the ridge dominating the city's southern approaches, and a fourth quarter in the southeast, on the slope of Government House Hill facing the Judean Desert. Certain details in the city's quick building process engendered discussions, both between experts and in the wider public. While interested parties, especially of the hotel trade, sought to minimize restrictions on the height of new structures, particularly on the high ground circling the Old City, public opinion in general favored stricter architectural control and painstaking conservation of ancient, or otherwise outstanding, edifices.

The advisability of a large conurbation centered on Jerusalem is a debatable point. Most experts hold that such a development should not be encouraged, so as not to spoil the landscape on the approaches to the city, of singular beauty and great spiritual significance to mankind. In the long run, however, it may prove difficult to prevent an at least partial amalgamation of satellite towns like Bethlehem or Ramallah with the capital on which their economy is largely dependent. The solution appears to lie in detailed planning and landscaping, protecting skylines and open spaces wherever necessary, locating new suburbs where they least interfere with the scenic vistas, and reducing buildings to a height tolerable from the aesthetic point of view.

5 ARCHAEOLOGICAL RESEARCH

Since the mid-19th century, when the earliest research was carried out in Ereẓ Israel, Jerusalem has been the main attraction for archaeologists because of its historical and religious significance. The fact that Jerusalem was populated by layer upon layer of ancient civilizations and included many sites sacred to the various religions made methodical archaeological research a difficult and challenging task. Investigation of the ancient remains on the surface began at the beginning of the 19th century. An appreciable part of the scientific surveys by E. Robinson (1824, 1852), T. Tobler (1845), C. J. M. de-Vogüé (1853, 1861) are devoted to ancient Jerusalem and contain descriptions and sketches of some of the remnants found on the surface. These works are particularly important because subsequent building activities in the city covered a good part of the remains. Charles Wilson (1864–66) conducted the first detailed survey and published an exact map of the city.

BIBLICAL PERIOD. *The City and Its Fortifications.* Charles Warren (1867–70) was the first to try to follow the line of the ancient wall by excavations, pits, and tunnels. In the S.E. corner of the Temple Mount he discovered what he identified as the wall of the Ophel, which continues for 750 ft. (230 m.) to the south on the top of the eastern slope of the two hills on which ancient Jerusalem was built. Although Warren perceived correctly that this wall was of later date than the First Temple, those who followed him assumed that at least the lower part of the wall belonged to the Jebusite city and to the City of David. Warren's work turned the attention of archaeologists to the eastern hill

Warren's dig at the southeastern corner of the Temple Mount, showing Herodian layers of the wall of the Mount (1) and adjoining it (2) what Warren identified as the wall of the Ophel. This was subsequently proved to be of a much later period, probably Hasmonean. In the background are the Mt. of Olives (3) and the Kidron Valley (4). Photo David Eisenberg, Jerusalem.

south of Jerusalem, whose form was like an elongated triangle based on the Temple Mount—the eastern side being the Kidron Valley, and the western side the Tyropoeon Valley, which divides the eastern from the western hill. This area, with the exception of the Temple Mount, is called the City of David in archaeological terminology.

Clermont-Ganneau and H. Guthe (1881) found additional sectors that extended the line of the "Jebusite wall" along the eastern slope of the City of David. In the southern end of the City of David, at the opening of the Tyropoeon Valley near the Siloam Pool, F. J. Bliss and A. C. Dickie (1894–97) discovered massive sectors of walls that served to dam the opening of the Tyropoeon Valley and fortify this weak point, which was the lowest in the whole city. They also discovered the continuation of the wall on the slopes of the western hill above the Ben Hinnom Valley. The lower of the wall's two levels was mistakenly attributed by them to the period of the First Temple. (This opinion served as the basis for including the western, as well as the eastern, hill in the Jerusalem of the early monarchy.) M. Parker's expedition (1909–11) dug in the area of the Gihon Spring and the slope above it, where an additional sector of the wall was discovered (the results of Parker's expedition were published by L. H. Vincent). The southern end of the City of David was investigated by the Weill expedition (1913–14, 1923–24), which revealed additional built-up sectors of the line of fortifications.

R.A.S. Macalister and J. G. Duncan (1923–25) excavated a considerable area in the north of the City of David over the Gihon Spring. They discovered sectors of the wall, towers, and revetment whose early use they attributed to the Jebusite city and subsequent use to Jerusalem during the period of David and Solomon. Inside the line of fortifications they uncovered a number of population strata, the lowest of which they attributed to the Canaanite and the Israelite cities. The J. W. Crowfoot and G.M. Fitzgerald expedition (1927–28) dug close to the area mentioned above. The results of the systematic excavation show that most of the remnants discovered there cannot be dated earlier than the Roman and Byzantine periods. They were additions to the system of fortifications then accepted as belonging to the Jebusite city—the splendid gate (the "Gate of the Valley"), which is above the Tyropoeon Valley in the west of the city (the width of the wall in the area of the gate is approximately 28 ft. (8.5 meters)). K. Galling, G. Dalman, J. Simons, L.H. Vincent, M. Avi-Yonah, N. Avigad, B. Mazar, and other scholars published theoretical studies based on these findings, while the efforts of archaeologists were directed to other areas of ancient Jerusalem.

There is a difference of opinion concerning the basic problem of the topography of ancient Jerusalem: the area of the city in the biblical period, particularly since the time of David and Solomon. Those who accepted the narrow concept (Galling, A. Alt, Mazar, and Avi-Yonah) claimed that the area of Jerusalem in that period spread over the extension of the City of David—the eastern hill between the Kidron Valley and the Tyropoeon Valley—at the top of which stood the Temple and the king's palaces within the boundaries of the Temple Mount and its vicinity, as they are today. The exponents of the wider concept (Vincent, Simons, Dalman and others) claim that the western hill, Mount Zion, and the Armenian and Jewish quarters of the present day should be added to this area. For their conclusions in this matter, the scholars employed the descriptions in the Bible far more than they used the archaeological findings then available.

The excavations of Kathleen Kenyon (1961–67) opened a new period in the history of archaeological research of the city. She dug in many places, although in limited areas, in the eastern and western hills and a few inside the Old City. The fact that the areas of excavations were so limited was detrimental to the important conclusions she published. On the other hand, in the great cut A, which was carried out between the Gihon spring and the sectors of the upper wall discovered by

Kathleen Kenyon's excavations in the eastern hill, south of the Temple Mount. Photo Werner Braun, Jerusalem.

Macalister and Duncan in 1925, the key to understanding the topography and the boundaries of the city in biblical times was made clear. The system of fortifications discovered by Macalister and Duncan was found to have been built on the remnants of the biblical city, which were demolished with the destruction of Jerusalem at the end of the First Temple period. It thus becomes clear that the line of fortifications discovered by Macalister and Duncan did not precede the Return to Zion or the Hasmonean period. This conclusion also holds for the rest of the remnants of fortifications discovered on the top of the eastern slope described above.

A series of soundings on the eastern slope of the western hill confirmed the opinion that there was no continuation of Israelite population west of the Tyropoeon Valley. Kenyon's cut A was deepened in some places to the rock, where ceramics were found from the Early Bronze Age and the Middle Bronze Age. The most ancient architectural structure was a thick wall built from hunks of rock in the Middle Bronze Age, discovered at the bottom of the slope, some 82 ft. (25 m.) above the Gihon spring. This was the wall of Jerusalem until the eighth century B.C.E. During the reign of Hezekiah a new wall, whose width was approximately 18 ft. (5.5 m.), was built in the same place.

The discovery of the site of the city walls in the biblical period solved another difficult problem, i.e., the relation between the entrance to Warren's shaft (see Water Supply, below) and the line of the upper wall, which in the past had been attributed to the period of the Jebusite city and the City of David, placing the upper entrance to the ancient waterworks outside of the fortified area. Such an arrangement would have differed completely from those in every other ancient city and negated the very purpose for which the waterworks were constructed, i.e., to ensure a regular supply of water in the event of a siege. The inclusion of this water system within the limits of the fortified city, as a result of the discovery of the new range of walls, solved this problem.

Organizing the city's area was a problem because of the narrowness of its circumference, due to the steepness of its eastern slope. This problem was overcome by a series of graduated terraces filled in with stones and supported by stone walls that rose from the base of the city—the eastern wall—upward. According to Kenyon, this system was used in Jerusalem from the 14th century B.C.E. and throughout the Israelite period. It should be identified with the "Millo," mentioned in I Kings 9:15. Today it is clear that the Canaanite city extended only on the eastern hill, and its area was approximately 15 acres (60 dunams). There is ceramic evidence from the tenth century B.C.E. of the extension of the population northward to the Temple Mount, which had been built by Solomon as the upper city (the administrative and religious center). Its total area was then approximately 120 dunams. Remnants of buildings of hewn stone and proto-Aeolian capitals, found by Kenyon, hint at the splendid buildings of Jerusalem in the period of the kings (similar to those in Samaria and Megiddo). While Kenyon produced archaeological evidence of the development of the ancient city on the entire eastern hill and Temple Mount, excavations carried out after the Six-Day War (1967) produced new evidence about the history of the western hill and the area today known as the Old City. In his excavations at the Citadel, Johns (1934–40) found ceramics from the late Israelite period not prior to the seventh century B.C.E. This fact was proved in the excavations of R. Amiran and A. Eitan (1968–69), in which floors of dwellings from that period were discerned. Similar ceramics were discovered close to the rock by Tushingham, working with Kenyon, in the soundings made in the Armenian Quarter and the Muristan Bazaar.

In N. Avigad's excavations (1969ff.) in the center of the Jewish Quarter, parts of buildings dated to the end of the Israelite period were discovered for the first time, in addition to late Israelite ceramics. His main find (1970) was a segment of the city wall, some 130 ft. long by 25 ft. broad (40 m. by 8 m.), running in a northeast–southwest direction across the western hill. B. Mazar's excavations (from 1968 onward) south of the Temple Mount uncovered a whole series of tombs hewn in the rock whose style suggests Phoenician influence and which he dated to the ninth-eighth century B.C.E. Their site is beyond the Tyropoeon Valley on the beginning of the rocky slope of the western hill. It is clear that this sector had not been included in the limits of the city in the period when it evidently served as a cemetery for the aristocracy. It is therefore now possible to conjecture cautiously that in the late eighth century B.C.E. an Israelite settlement was initiated on the western hill. The buildings which were dug out in the 1960s by Kenyon provide clear signs of the Babylonian conquest of the year 586 B.C.E. and serve as physical evidence of the destruction of Jerusalem at the end of the First Temple period.

The "Daughter of Pharaoh Tomb" of the First Temple period, hewn out of the rock in Siloam village. Above the entrance to the square structure are the remnants of an inscription in ancient Hebrew characters. Photo David Eisenberg, Jerusalem.

239

Necropolises. The graves discovered by Parker (1909–11) on the slope above the Gihon are the most ancient finds in Jerusalem. They were dated to the beginning of the Early Bronze Age. Kenyon discovered a series of graves from the Middle Bronze Age on the Mount of Olives. Graves rich in remnants from the Middle Bronze and Late Bronze Ages were found near the Dominus Flevit Church and were excavated by S. Saller (1954). Graves with many important implements of the Late Bronze Age were also found in Naḥalat Aḥim (Amiran, 1961) and in the area of the UN headquarters. A series of graves of the First Temple period cut into rock were found east and west of the City of David. In some of them, the influence of the Phoenician style is noticeable in the planning of the hewn graves, as well as in the cemetery area. As early as 1865 F. de Saulcy investigated the monolithic "Tomb of the Daughter of Pharaoh." Clermont-Ganneau examined a series of graves hewn in the rock of the Siloam village (among them was the grave with the inscription "[   ]yahu who is over the house"). In the southern end of the City of David, Weill (1913–14) found monumental tombs that he identified as the graves of the House of David, but it seems that this identification requires further proof. A summary study of the graves and accompanying inscriptions in the Kidron Valley and village of Siloam was made by Avigad (1945–47). A new survey of all the graves hewn in rock in Siloam was made by D. Ussishkin (1968). (For tombs discovered by Mazar south of the Temple Mount, see above.)

SECOND TEMPLE PERIOD. *The City and Its Fortifications.* Remains from the period of the Second Temple, and particularly from the time of King Herod (37–4 B.C.E.) served as a starting point for archaeological research. Terms and names connected with the period are mainly obtained from the descriptions of the city by Josephus. In 1867–70, Wilson and Warren were engaged in an investigation of the Herodian walls of the Temple Mount. Warren's description and precise sketches of the topography of

Jerusalem, particularly of the structure of the Herodian walls, are still in use. "Robinson's Arch" and "Wilson's Arch" were studied in detail and the nature of their original function was examined. Warren uncovered a part of the foundation of the first arch of "Robinson's Arch" (revealed in its entirety by Mazar from 1969 and the concept of its having served as the base of an extensive bridge was abandoned). He investigated the Herodian subterranean structure in the south of the Temple Mount, which is called "Solomon's Stables." He also correctly identified the site of the Antonia fortress, adjoining the northwest corner of the Temple Mount, which was investigated by Clermont-Ganneau (1871) and Vincent and Marie-Aline de Sion (1955; the foundation and stone floor of the fortress can be seen today in the cellars of the monasteries at the start of Via Dolorosa, for example in the convent of the Soeurs de Sion). C. N. Johns (1934–40) revealed three fortification systems in the

"Robinson's Arch." Photo David Eisenberg, Jerusalem.

court of the Citadel near Jaffa Gate. The two earlier systems belonged to the Hasmonean period and the third to the period of Herod. The most impressive remnant is Phasael's Tower, commonly called David's Tower (its original remnants are preserved to a height of 66 ft. (20 m.). It became clear that on the eastern side the city's fortification system rested on the walls of the Temple Mount and on the western side on the Citadel.

The remnants of the First Wall were uncovered south of the Citadel around Mt. Zion, along the Valley of Hinnom to the Kidron Valley. Schick and H. Maudsley (1871–75) located remnants of half a house in the rock that served as a base for the wall and its towers in the western sector between the Citadel and Mt. Zion. In the section between Mt. Zion and the Kidron Valley, Bliss and Dickie uncovered two fortification systems; the earlier was mistakenly ascribed to the period of the First Temple, but later comparisons with the findings of Johns' excavation in

Photograph taken during C. N. Johns' excavations at the Jaffa Gate Citadel, showing two Hasmonean fortification systems (1 and 2) and the remnants of Herod's Phasael Tower (3).
242 Courtesy Israel Department of Antiquities, Jerusalem.

the Citadel show that it belonged to the Hasmonean period. The remnants of the walls found at the top of the eastern hill, which had been attributed to the First Temple period, were shown by Kenyon's excavations to belong to the continuation of the First Wall, which extended to the southeastern corner of the Temple Mount. Sections of the line of the First Wall, which descend eastward from Phasael's Tower directly to Wilson's Arch on the Temple Mount, were revealed by Warren in the area of the markets of the Old City.

The line of the Second Wall was reconstructed on the basis of the sources, rather than on archaeological findings (the scientific contentions of a number of scholars about this wall are influenced by the location of the Church of the Holy Sepulcher in this area). Fixing of the course of the Second Wall north or south of this church determines the degree of scientific authenticity in the identification of this building, which, according to Christian tradition, is outside the course of the Second Wall. Established facts, however, are few. The line of the wall began at the First Wall near the Citadel, passing the area of the Church of the Holy Sepulcher, and reaching the Damascus Gate. Below this gate R. W. Hamilton (1931–37; 1938) and J. B. Hennessy (1964–66) uncovered a gate from the late Roman period, and under its foundations was found an Herodian construction, thought by Hamilton and Avi-Yonah to be the original gate of the Second Wall. Hennessy's attribution of the remains below the Damascus Gate to the time of Agrippa I, regarding them as part of the Third Wall, is based on insufficient evidence. From there the wall turned to the southeast toward Antonia. Kenyon dug near the Muristan Bazaar in the Old City and reported locating the fosse that is cut in the rock of the Second Wall, thus placing the area of the Church of the Holy Sepulcher outside of the market quarter fortified by this wall. Most scholars date the building of the Second Wall to the Hasmonean period.

The course of the Third Wall, the construction of which was begun at the time of Agrippa I (37 C.E.) is in dispute.

Vincent, Simons, Kenyon, and Henessy fix the course parallel to the line of the Turkish Wall in the northern part of the Old City of today. The opinion of E. L. Sukenik and Mayer (1925–27), however, seems better founded. They identify the Third Wall with the line of the wall they uncovered along a distance of approximately 1,600 ft. (500 m.) from the Italian Hospital to the W.F.Albright Institute of Archaeological Research. (Sectors of wall, towers, and gate were revealed parallel to the northern wall of the Old City, approximately 1,600 ft. (500 m.) to the north.) Sections of this wall had been examined by Robinson (1838), V. Schultze (1845), and C. Schick (1878).

Additional portions of the wall are still being disclosed today in digs along its course, which begins at the Citadel, continues northward to the Russian Compound, turns northeast to the northern Kidron Valley, and there turns southward to the northeastern corner of the Temple Mount. The wall is built carelessly and is far simpler than the Herodian walls. This description is in keeping with the historical conditions at the time of its construction; it was begun in the day of Agrippa I and completed hastily before the outbreak of the revolt in 66 C.E. in order to protect the "New City."

The excavations of Macalister and J. G. Duncan, J. W. Crowfoot and G. M. Fitzgerald, and Kenyon on the eastern hill revealed the usual remnants of domiciles from the period of the Second Temple. Kenyon produced conclusive archaeological evidence as to the date of the destruction of those buildings, which coincides with the destruction of Jerusalem in 70 C.E. (Her other conclusior. that settlement on the eastern slope of the western hill did not begin before the time of Agrippa I, does not accord with the findings of other archaeologists.)

Remnants of the buildings of the Upper City were first revealed in the excavations of the Citadel. Amiran and Eitan (1968–69) revealed two levels of building; the earlier belongs to the Hasmonean city, while the later is from Herodian times and was demolished with the destruction of

Jerusalem. Avigad's excavations (1969ff.) in the Jewish Quarter disclosed remnants from the Hasmonean and Herodian periods. Beautiful architectural details and large quantities of plaster fragments, painted with a variety of geometric designs and plants, suggest the existence of a splendid building from the Herodian period. A seven-branched *menorah*—one of the most ancient known examples—engraved with great precision was found on one of the plaster fragments. Also uncovered was the large dwelling of the Bar Kathros family, rich in findings, which was completely covered with an accumulation of ash from the fire that razed it at the time of the destruction of the Upper City in 70 C.E.

The layout of the area around the southwestern corner of Temple Mount is becoming progressively clearer due to Mazar's excavations (beginning 1968). Alongside the southern wall of the Temple Mount a wide street, paved with stone slabs, leading to Hulda's Gates, was discovered.

B. Mazar's excavations along the west wall of the Temple Mount, showing "Robinson's Arch" (1), and the base of a pillar (2). Herodian stones (3) were reused by the Umayyads. Photo David Eisenberg, Jerusalem.

B. Mazar's excavations near the south wall of the Temple Mount, revealing remains of the Umayyad period (eighth century C.E.). Below the street skirting the wall on the left was discovered a Herodian pavement leading to Huldah's Gates. In the background is the dome of the al-Aqṣā Mosque. Photo David Eisenberg, Jerusalem.

It was supported by a high wall on its southern side, which separated it from the continuation of the slope of the eastern hill. The extent of the remains of "Robinson's Arch" was revealed. A monumental stairway was uncovered leading from the plaza in front of the Temple up to the street in front of one Huldah gate (the "Double Gate"). Remains of a parallel stairway led up to the other Huldah Gate (the "Triple Gate"). The details of the southern and western walls of the Temple Mount serve as an example of the Herodian building system. The extent of the work and the expanse of the area involved resulted in the discovery of thousands of small items (pottery, coins, etc.).

A summary of archaeological research today shows that the Second Temple city grew from the ancient kernel of the City of David and part of the western hill, in which the returnees to Zion settled. Dynamic expansion began when Jerusalem became the capital of the Hasmonean kingdom in the second century B.C.E. and the capital of the Herodian kingdom in the first century B.C.E. By then most of the area of the western hill was built up, and the population began to spread to the northern areas of the city—the "New City"—which reached its peak on the eve of the revolt in 66 C.E., when the area of the fortified city extended over 1,800 dunams (450 acres).

Necropolises. The burial areas of Jerusalem form a belt surrounding the city from Sanhedriyyah in the northwest, through Givat ha-Mivtar, Mt. Scopus, the Mt. of Olives, and the hill of the UN headquarters, to Talpiyyot and Ramat Raḥel in the south. A few graves were also found west of the city. Hundreds of rock-hewn tombs—some simple and some very elaborate—were uncovered. The inside plan of the tombs is simple, as was the custom then. On the sides of central rooms are burial rooms that contain separate sepulchral chambers. The bones of the poor were gathered in limestone ossuaries. Some of the larger tombs have decorated fronts influenced by the architectural style of the West and by the east Hellenistic style; the combination created a hybrid style, which may be defined as Jewish 247 art of the Second Temple period. As early as 1863 de Saulcy cleaned out the tombs of the kings and discovered there the decorated sarcophagi that probably belonged to the family of Queen Helena of Adiabene. Clermont-Ganneau completed the excavation of those tombs in 1867. He also partially cleaned the tomb known as Absalom's Tomb (1891). In 1891 Schick published the discovery of the tomb of the House of Herod, found near the site on which the King David Hotel was built later. In 1924 N. Slouschz cleared Absalom's Tomb. From 1926 to 1940 E. L. Sukenik studied approximately 40 Jewish funerary complexes in the city (such as the tomb of the Nicanor family discovered on Mt. Scopus). Avigad investigated the various burial sites of Jerusalem, especially in the Kidron Valley (1945–47). Jason's Tomb from the Hasmonean period was excavated in Reḥavyah by L. Raḥmani (1954), who also investigated the burial sites of Sanhedriyyah (1961). In 1968 V. Tsaferis excavated several tombs at Givat ha-Mivtar, northeast of the city. One of them contained 35 burials, including one of a young man called Yoḥanan, who had died by crucifixion. Hundreds of limestone ossuaries and simple graves were disclosed on the western slope of the Mt. of Olives, near the Church of Dominus Flevit, by P. B. Bagatti and J. T. Milik (1953–55). The major findings in this cemetery are from the Herodian period; however, it was used from the Hasmonean period to the Byzantine period.

THE LATE ROMAN PERIOD. After the destruction of the Second Temple and the suppression of the Bar Kokhba revolt (135 C.E.), the boundaries of the city became narrower. Remnants of the late Roman city, whose name was changed to Aelia Capitolina in the second century C.E., were uncovered in a number of places in the Old City. In the buildings of the Tenth Roman Legion, stationed at the time in Jerusalem, were found marks of its seal (LXF) on white tiles and clay pipes. In the excavations in the Citadel by Johns (1934–40) and Amiran and Eitan (1968–69), many remnants were revealed of the permanent camp of the Tenth Legion. Similar remnants were found in the excavations of Avi-Yonah on Givat Ram (1963, 1969). The new line of fortifications was uncovered extending from the area of the Citadel and continuing under the line of the Turkish Wall of the Old City. Hamilton (1937–38) and Hennessy (1964–66) revealed sectors of this wall and its towers on both sides of the Damascus Gate. The gate of Aelia Capitolina was found under the Damascus Gate, and an inscription mentioning the Roman name of the city was found fixed upon the gate. At the beginning of the Via Dolorosa, above the remnants of Antonia, a Roman triumphal arch, now called Ecce Homo, was discovered. Clermont-Ganneau investigated it in 1873–74. Kenyon (1961–67) found that the Muristan Area in the Old City, which in her opinion had not been included within the boundaries of the Second Temple city, had been filled in and leveled at that time for settlement purposes. The soundings of J. Pinkerfeld (1949) in the foundations of "David's Tomb" on Mt. Zion disclosed a previous level built from stone. In his opinion it probably contains remnants of a fourth-century synagogue. In Mazar's excavations (beginning 1968) dwellings from this same period were found. An inscription engraved on a stone tablet dates to the days of Septimius Severus (beginning of the third century C.E.) and is dedicated to the emperor and his family. The southern aqueduct was duplicated in Roman times by a high-level line from Ein Etam.

THE BYZANTINE PERIOD. During this period Jerusalem flourished anew. The city became the focal point for Christian pilgrimages. The main changes concentrated around sites associated with Christian tradition. Near these sites, churches, monasteries, and hospices were built. The city again spread out over the eastern and western hills to the south of the Temple Mount. The excavations of Macalister and Duncan, Crowfoot and Fitzgerald, Weill, Hamilton, Kenyon, and Mazar reveal remnants of streets, dwellings, and public buildings covering the south of the city, which was once again encircled by a wall. Remnants of that wall had been discovered by Warren near the Ophel, 249 and long sectors were uncovered above the Valley of Hinnom by Bliss and Dickie. The construction of this wall is dated to the middle of the fifth century C.E. and is connected with the building activities of Empress Eudocia in Jerusalem. Mazar concludes from his findings that the Byzantine buildings near the Western Wall were destroyed by the Jews in preparation for the rebuilding of the Temple in the time of Julian (362–63).

Avigad's excavations carried out in the Jewish Quarter (1970) revealed a bathhouse whose accessories were well preserved and a part of the Nea Church, built by Justinian in the sixth century C.E. Some of these have been incorporated into newer buildings. The Church of the Holy Sepulcher was examined in part by Wilson (1863), M. Harvey (1933–34), and V. Corbo (1961–63). The original church was founded in the fourth century C.E. The entrance, contrary to the accepted form, is in the east. This change resulted from the architectural incorporation into the church of the site of the Holy Sepulcher, which was surrounded by a special round structure; the "Rock of Golgotha" was included as well. The order of the White Fathers and Ch. Mauss (1863–1900) excavated the remnants of the church built above the Pool of Bethesda. Nearby they found remnants of a second Byzantine church that had been incorporated into the crusader Church of St. Anne. Bliss and Dickie (1894–97) dug above the Siloam Pool and uncovered the remains of the Church of Eudocia. J. Germer-Durand, who dug in the eastern slope of Mt. Zion at the end of the 19th century, revealed dwellings and a church. P. G. Orfali (1909, 1919–20) excavated the remains of the Gethsemane Church in the Kidron Valley. Vincent (1959) and Corbo (1959) discovered the remains of the Church of the Ascension on the top of the Mt. of Olives. Avi-Yonah (1949) discovered remains of a church and a monastery in the area of Givat Ram. Bagatti and Milik (1953–55) uncovered a cemetery of the Byzantine period in Dominus Flevit on the Mt. of Olives.

The Byzantine city was destroyed with the Persian

Remnants of a Byzantine double gate used as decoration on the 16th-century Ottoman wall. Photo David Eisenberg, Jerusalem.

conquest in 614 and the Muslim conquest in 638. Parts of numerous Byzantine structures served as building material for the Muslim structures that were constructed in the city 251

Herodian stone at the city's southern wall, with an inscription probably cut by a Jewish pilgrim c. fourth century C.E.: "And when you see this your heart shall rejoice and your bones shall flourish like young grass" (Isa. 66:14). Courtesy Israel Exploration Society, Jerusalem, Excavation of the Southern Wall.

by the end of the seventh century and in the eighth century. Much evidence of that was found in the excavations of Mazar (beginning 1968). It became clear that a large structure was built close to the southern wall of the Temple Mount in the period of the Umayyads at the beginning of the eighth century. On one of the stones in the Herodian Wall of the Temple Mount, Mazar discovered an inscription that he believes was engraved by a Jewish pilgrim in the fourth century C.E. The text of the inscription was taken from Isaiah 66:14; "And when you see this your heart shall rejoice and your bones shall flourish like young grass." This inscription undoubtedly indicates that among the masses of Christian pilgrims who arrived in Jerusalem during the Byzantine period, there were Jewish pilgrims visiting the ruins of the Temple Mount.

6 WATER SUPPLY

FIRST AND SECOND TEMPLE PERIODS. The location of Canaanite Jerusalem on the eastern ridge near the riverbed of the Kidron was closely related to the discovery of the only water source in the entire area on the eastern slope of the ridge. This was the Gihon Spring, which supplied 7,000–40,000 cu. ft. (200–1,100 cu. m.) daily during periods of 30–40 minutes, with interruptions of four to ten hours (according to the season). As early as the middle Canaanite period, the inhabitants of Jerusalem dug a tunnel to assure the water supply in the event of a siege. At first they attempted to sink a shaft straight down to the water level, but did not succeed because of the hardness of the rock. They then dug an angular tunnel with stairs; at its end was a shaft ("Warren's shaft") 43 ft. (13 m.) high, which descended to the level of the spring and through which water could be drawn without the enemy's knowledge. It is possible that this system was the "gutter" *(zinnor)* mentioned in the account of the conquest of Jerusalem by David and his warriors (II Sam. 5:8). In addition to the tunnel, near the spring were several open canals extending southward that carried the excess spring water to the fields and gardens along the Kidron riverbed. At the end of the eighth century B.C.E., Hezekiah, king of Judah, initiated the excavation of a new 1,765 ft. (535 m.) tunnel which extended from a level of 2,086 ft. (636 m.) to 2,080 ft. (634 m.), passing in the form of two arches under the hill of the City of David. This tunnel conducted the waters of the Gihon to the Siloam (Shiloaḥ) Pool in the valley between the two hills. The well-known Siloam inscription recounts the excavation of the tunnel and the "day of the tunnel" in which "the stone cutters made their

Hezekiah's tunnel, which brought water from the Gihon Spring to the Siloam Pool. Constructed before 701 B.C.E. Courtesy Israel Department of Antiquities, Jerusalem.

way toward one another ax-blow by ax-blow." The excavation of this tunnel was a considerable engineering feat, and since then the waters of the Gihon have flowed to the Siloam Pool. The pool was initially covered and hidden from enemies, as discovered in excavations.

In earliest times the inhabitants of Jerusalem had already increased the meager supply of the Gihon Spring by digging cisterns and pools. Of the two types of reservoirs, the cisterns are more difficult to make, but they are better for preserving water against evaporation. After the discovery of waterproof lime mortar, the number of cisterns in the ancient city grew equal to (if not greater than) the number of houses. The most famous is a double cistern known as Struthion (Gr. *strouthos*—"ostrich"), which is located under the court of the Antonia Fortress southwest of the Temple; its maximum dimensions were 160 ft. (49m.) in length, 23 ft. (7 m.) in width, and 56 ft. (17 m.) in depth. A great number of cisterns were dug in the area of the Temple Mount, the largest among them being the "Sea," whose capacity was 140,000 cu. ft. (12,000 cu. m.). There were two other cisterns of 94,000 cu. ft. (8,000 cu. m.) and 60,000 cu. ft. (5,000 cu. m.) capacity.

The major pools in the area of Jerusalem are the Siloam Pool at the southern end of the central valley; the Snake Pool (Birkat al-Sultan) in the Hinnom Valley; the Pool of Towers (Hezekiah's Pool) north of the Fortress; and Mamilla Pool (first mentioned in the Byzantine period), located between the Jaffa Gate and the watershed line. Three of the ancient pools are not open today: the Ḥammām al-Shifā' Pool in the upper central valley, which may be the biblical "Upper Pool"; the Pool of Israel, which served as a ditch for the northern boundary of the Temple Mount; and the Sheep Pool, also north of the Temple Mount at some distance from it. The latter is mentioned in the New Testament (John 5:2-4), where it is called Bethesda (Beit Ḥisda), and apparently also in the Copper Scroll from the Dead Sea caves. It is a double pool and has two levels. The New Testament states that healing powers were attributed to it, and excavations of the site have revealed that a health rite took place there during the Roman period. The lower of the two pools was probably used for washing sheep, which were then sold for sacrifices at the nearby Temple.

At the end of the Second Temple period, it was clear that the growing city could not be supplied from the waters collected in the cisterns and pools, especially during mass gatherings of the three pilgrimage festivals. Pontius Pilate therefore decided to build an aqueduct from the springs of the 'Arrūb River near Hebron. It was an open canal which passed through four tunnels near Bethlehem. In order to preserve the gradient of the water level, which assured a steady flow from the springs to the Temple Mount, the aqueduct wound along the 2,574 ft. (766 m.) contour line so that although the direct distance from the 'Arrūb River to Jerusalem is no more than 13 mi. (21 km.), the aqueduct was 42 mi. (68 km.) long. On its way southward, it also collected the waters of Ein Etam (Solomon's Pools), south of Bethlehem. During the rule of Septimius Severus, a second aqueduct on a higher level was added, extending from Solomon's Pools to Jerusalem. The latter crossed the valley near Rachel's Tomb via a line of pipes operated by syphon pressure, which in many cases split the stone links.

FROM THE ROMAN PERIOD. From the Roman period to the end of the Ottoman period, Jerusalem's water supply was based mainly on rainwater collected in the city's cisterns and pools. The original Spring of Gihon had long been blocked; its location was unknown, and its waters flowed through Hezekiah's tunnel to the Siloam Pool. According to Christian tradition, these waters were used by Jesus to heal the blind man (John 9:7), and the site thus became sacred to Christians. As early as the fourth century C.E. the pilgrim of Bordeaux mentions a pool surrounded by colonnades used for bathing for healing purposes. The empress Eudocia built a church and a hospital above the pool. In the early Muslim period as well, the waters of the Siloam were regarded as having special powers, but in the course of generations the pool was neglected, and the tunnel of Hezekiah became partially blocked. The waters of the Gihon, which had ceased to flow through the tunnel, broke out to the Kidron River. Thus the Gihon Spring was rediscovered in the 14th century, and its name reappears for

Underground tunnel believed to be part of the aqueduct, discovered during B. Mazar's excavations near the southwestern wall of the Temple Mount. The aqueduct brought water into Jerusalem from springs near Hebron. Courtesy Hebrew University, Jerusalem.

the first time in a Jewish source from the 16th century. With the rediscovery of the Gihon, the site of the spring was consecrated. Christians established it as the spot where Mary had washed Jesus' swaddling clothes and therefore called it the "Virgin's Fountain." The waters of the Gihon Spring today flow again through Hezekiah's tunnel to the new Siloam Pool built in the 19th century.

During the Ottoman period the waters of the Gihon were drawn and sold in the streets of Jerusalem, but in the 19th century they became polluted from sewage water reaching the spring, and today are used only for watering the flower beds of Kefar ha-Shilo'ah (Silwān). The Rogel Spring served Jerusalem throughout the generations as a secondary source of water. During the Ottoman period its waters, like those of the Gihon, were drawn and sold in Jerusalem, but its major importance lies in its being the main source of the water for Kefar ha-Shilo'ah.

A number of changes occurred in later times in the system of public pools known from the Roman period. With the concentration of Jerusalem on the western hill, the pools at the lower part of the central valley were neglected. The ancient Siloam Pool was apparently reconstructed during the Byzantine period, but was later neglected, filled with silt, and called by the Arabs the Birkat al-Ḥamrā' (Pool of the Red Earth). The pool of Ḥammām al-Shifā', near Bāb al-Silsila (the Chain Gate) of the Temple Mount, was known from medieval times, but was later blocked to enable the collection of subterranean waters, which were drawn from the pool via a shaft. The pool of Beit Ḥisda (Bethesda) continued to be in use in the Byzantine period and was called the Probatike pool, but was later blocked. Likewise, the Struthion pool fell into disuse.

Crusader sources mention three pools in Jerusalem: Lacus Legerii, northwest of the Damascus Gate, outside the city walls (today, Arḍ al-Birka); Lacus Germani, the ancient Snake Pool rebuilt by Germanus in 1176 (today known as Birkat al-Sultan in the Hinnom Valley); and Lacus Balneorum, the "Pool of Baths" (the ancient Pool of

Towers) called Birkat Ḥammām al-Biṭrīq and Hezekiah's Pool by Christian travelers. This pool is joined by an aqueduct to the Mamilla Pool, which is at the head of the Hinnom Valley. The Mamilla Pool itself continues to be mentioned in the Umayyad period. The three latter pools were reconstructed and renovated during the Mamluk and Ottoman periods. The Arabic name Birkat al-Sultan was given because of the expansion and renovation carried out on it by Sultan Suleiman the Magnificent in 1537. Other pools in Jerusalem, the dates of whose construction are not clear, are St. Mary's pool near the eastern wall of Jerusalem and the al-Hajj pool north of the city wall, opposite the present-day location of the Rockefeller Museum. Plastered cisterns in the courtyards of houses served as a major source of water throughout all the periods. In the mid-19th century, 950 cisterns were counted in the Old City, while at the end of the Ottoman period the cisterns of the entire city, including the suburbs outside the walls, numbered 6,600, with a total capacity of over 17,000,000 cu. ft. (500,000 cu. m.). In 1919 the British determined that the total capacity of the cisterns and pools of Jerusalem, including those on the Temple Mount, was approximately 53,000,000 cu. ft. (1,500,000 cu. m.).

The local sources, however, were not sufficient to meet the needs of the city, and throughout most of the periods water continued to be conducted to Jerusalem from the area of the ʿArrūb springs and Solomon's Pools. The use of the aqueduct during the Byzantine period is known from a Greek inscription that prohibits the cultivation of land at a distance of 15 cubits from the aqueduct. The reference is apparently to the aqueduct on the lower level, which was built at the time of the Second Temple and continued to be used during this period. It is reasonable to assume that this aqueduct was also in use during the Muslim and crusader periods, and it is known that it was rebuilt during the Mamluk period, when the third pool was also built at Solomon's Pools, south of Bethlehem. Waters collected there were conducted to Jerusalem via the aqueduct. At the beginning of the Ottoman period, the lower aqueduct continued to function, and Suleiman the Magnificent even built a number of *sabīls* (public fountains) that received their waters from the aqueduct. At the beginning of the 18th century, however, a clay pipe was built into the aqueduct, and its operation entailed difficult engineering problems. The pipe was blocked and often went out of use. Various attempts to improve the aqueduct in the 19th century were unsuccessful, but at the beginning of the 20th century the clay pipe was rebuilt as far as Bethlehem, and from it a narrow iron pipe conducted a limited amount of water—about 180 cu. m. daily—to Jerusalem.

The problem of water supply was very grave at the end of the Ottoman period, to the extent that Jerusalem's inhabitants were compelled to buy water brought by train or on the backs of animals from a considerable distance. With the British conquest (1917) the need for an immediate solution to the water problem arose. The cisterns in the city were purified, and the first water project built by the British army was based on the water sources in ʿAyn ʿArrūb. The old well there was renovated, a pump was built, and an iron pipeline 15 mi. (24 km.) long was laid down to the reservoir in the Romemah quarter. In 1921 Solomon's Pools were renovated, as was an ancient water project in Wadi al-Biyār which lies south of pools for collecting rainwater. Waters from this wadi and from the area of al-Khaḍr as well as spring water in the vicinity, were collected in Solomon's Pools and pumped from there to the iron pipelines from ʿAyn ʿArrūb. In 1924 the water was conveyed from ʿAyn Fāra in the bed of Wadi Qilt, north of Jerusalem. This project considerably increased the amount of water supplied to Jerusalem. At the same time, around 1,400 cubic meters were supplied daily from the outside, but there was still considerable use of private cisterns. With the fast growth of West Jerusalem, the water problem again became grave and the need arose for an additional abundant source of water. In 1934 the pipeline from the abundant springs at Rosh ha-Ayin (Raʾs al-ʿAyn) near the coast was built, finally solving the problem of the water supply for the city till 1948. During the Israel War of Independence (1948) West Jerusalem suffered from lack of water because several pumping stations of the Rosh ha-Ayin pipeline were captured and damaged by Arab forces. Later the government of Israel built a new pipeline from the same source which supplied West Jerusalem with water. The reunified city, after the Six-Day War (1967), was supplied from the Israel western as well as the southern and northern sources which served East Jerusalem during the Jordanian rule.

7 CARTOGRAPHY

Ever since map-making began, the geographical position of Jerusalem was shown on most of the manuscript maps of the world, such as the maps at the cathedral of Herford and of the Ebstorf monastery. It appeared, of course on the "Tabula Peutingeriana" and on all the maps of the Near East and the Holy Land. The cartographical symbols employed on these maps are of the conventional semi-pictorial design and therefore do not provide any information on particular features of the city.

PICTORIAL MAPS. The earliest topographical description of Jerusalem is the bird's-eye view of the "Holy City of Jerusalem," the central piece of a map of the Holy Land preserved on the mosaic floor of a ruined basilica at Madaba, in Transjordan. The mosaic, dated between 560 and 565 C.E., depicts an oval-shaped city surrounded by walls, with six gates and 21 towers. It shows the "Cardo maxima," the colonnaded main thoroughfare, together with four smaller streets and 36 other features of the city—such as public squares and buildings, churches, and monasteries—and contains the oldest presentation of the Western Wall. This "map" shows Jerusalem as viewed from the west, whereas during the following centuries the city was predominantly portrayed from the east, since the view from the Mount of Olives encompassed the most important sections of the medieval town (i.e., all the parts of the Temple Mount and most of the stations of the Via Dolorosa). Typical examples of this mode of presentation are: the large map engraved by Erhard Reuwich, a Mainz woodcutter and printer, after drawings made by him on the spot in 1483; the woodcut made by Jacob Clauser for Sebastian Muenster's cosmography (published 1544 in Basle); and the copper engraving reproducing a drawing made in 1682 by Cornelis de Bruin. These productions were often copied by the many artists who were unable to paint pictures based on personal observation.

HISTORICAL MAPS. Another approach is represented in the work of the biblical scholars who, for religious reasons, intended to clari-

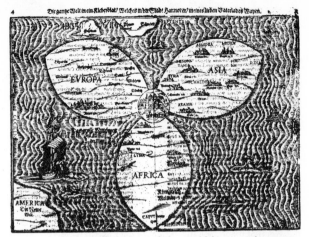

Jerusalem shown as the center of the world in a woodcut map
by Heinrich Buenting in his *Itinerarium Sacrae Scripturae,*
Helmstadt, 1581. Haifa, Maritime Museum. Photo Sadeh, Haifa.

fy the state of the city during different periods of biblical history,
concentrating mostly on New Testament times. These map-makers
were often unfamiliar with the topography of the city and derived
their knowledge from the literary sources at their disposal, i.e., the
Bible, the works of Josephus and classical Greek and Latin writers,
and certain passages of the Talmud. Best known among these maps
are the works of the Dutch astronomer Pieter Laiksteen (dated
1544 and republished in 1573 by Benito Arias-Montano), Christian
van Adrichem (Cologne, 1584), and the Rev. Thomas Fuller
(London, 1650). Other maps, mostly engraved by Dutch craftsmen,
appeared in many editions of the Bible and became very popular as
an aid to understanding the text.

COMPARATIVE MAPS. Laiksteen opened a new chapter of
cartographic development with his twin set of town maps, the first
attempt to present a comparative topography of New Testament
Jerusalem and the walls and buildings in the city of his own time by
graphic means. The prime motive for the creation of such maps was
the desire to defend the authenticity of the holy places. The
correctness of their location was piously accepted by countless
generations of pilgrims, but with the spread of the Reformation in   263

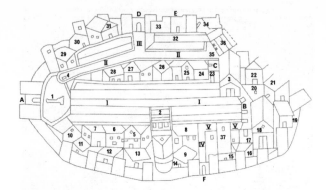

Gates: A—Damascus Gate (Gate of the Column), B—Zion Gate, C—Dung Gate, D—Eastern Gate, E—Golden Gate, F—Jaffa Gate. **Streets:** I—Main north-south road (Cardo), II—Road of the Valley, III—Street of the Eastern Gate, IV—Street from Jaffa Gate to the Temple Mount (Decumanus), V—Street leading to Mount Zion.

Buildings: 1—Column inside Damascus Gate, 2—Church of the Holy Sepulcher, 3—New Church (Nea), 4—Entrance Gate to Street II, 5—Palace of the Patriarch, 6—Clergy House of same, 7—Hospital, 8—Forum, 9—Bath which became the Baptistery of the Church of the Holy Sepulcher, 10—Monastery of St. Serapion, 11,12—Unidentified, 13—Monastery of the Spudaei, 14—Unidentified, 15-17—Monasteries near the Tower of David, 18—Church on Mount Zion, 19—Diaconicon of same, 20—Clergy House of same, 21—Baths above Siloam Pool, 22—Church near the Pool, 23—Tetrapylon at crossing of main streets, 24—Church of the 'Holy Wisdom' (Hagia Sophia), 25, 26—Unidentified, 27—Monastery of St. Cosmas and St. Damianus, 28—Public bath, 29—Palace of the Empress Eudocia, 30—Structure above the Sheep Pool, 31—Church near the Sheep Pool, 32—Temple area, 33—Remains of Antonia Fortress, 34—Corner Church of St. James, 35—Entrance to the street of the Western Wall, 36—Western or Wailing Wall, 37—Tower of David.

Schematic drawing of the Jerusalem section of the Madaba map, with identification by M. Avi-Yonah. From *Atlas of Israel*, 1970. Courtesy Survey of Israel, Jerusalem.

Jerusalem depicted as an oval, walled city on a detail from the Madaba map mosaic, 560–565 C.E. Courtesy Israel Department of Antiquities, Jerusalem.

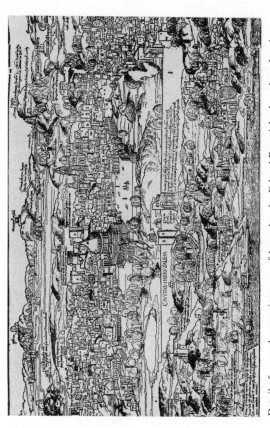

Detail of a wood engraving map of Jerusalem by Erhard Reuwich, based on drawings made during his visit in 1483 and printed in B. von Breydenbach, *Reise ins Heilige Land*, Mainz, 1486. New York Public Library, Spencer Collection.

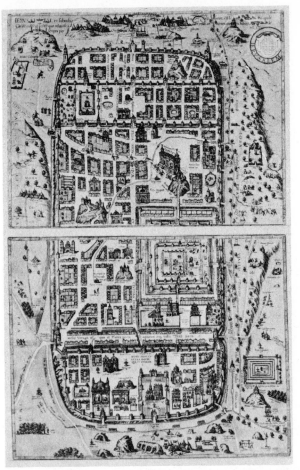

"Jerusalem et Suburbia Eius," a two-page color engraving of the Holy City and its environs by Franz von Hoghenberg after Christian von Adrichem (1572–1618). Jerusalem, Israel Museum.

16th-century Europe, an ever growing number of pilgrims—mostly from Britain and Germany—disputed the ecclesiastical tradition promulgated by the Franciscan friars in their capacity as the officially appointed "Custodians of the Holy Land." In view of the fact that Empress Helena's Church of the Holy Sepulcher was not outside the present walls of the city, as suggested by the Gospels and Jewish tradition, an endless discussion arose, culminating in 1883 with Charles C. Gordon's identification of Jeremiah's Grotto with Mount Calvary. In order to decide this dispute, the actual course of the city walls during Roman times had to be ascertained, as the position of the Third Wall would automatically establish the location of the "True Calvary." The first map designed to solve this problem was made by the Franciscan friar Antonio degli Angelis, who lived in Jerusalem and Bethlehem from 1569 to 1577. Friar Antonio constructed a town plan based on fairly exact observations and/or actual measurements and delineating the course of the Third Wall. This map, published in 1578 by a monastery in Rome, was lost and is known only from a 1584 bibliographical note by Christian van Adrichem. The map was later republished and appeared in 1609 as a plate in Bernardino Amico's *Plans of the Sacred Edifices of the Holy Land.* This engraving was the work of Antonio Tempesta, but the artwork for a further edition, published in 1620, was entrusted to Jacques Callot. These two important artists added many "improvements" and embellishments, but Natale Bonifaci made a modest engraving for Johann Zuallart's travelogue (Rome, 1587). Bonifaci's version has often been copied, mainly for pilgrims interested in pictures suitable as illustrations for their reports, and has been reproduced in many 17th-century travel books of the Holy Land.

SURVEY MAPS. In 1818 an Austrian physician, Franz Wilhelm Sieber, traveled through the Near East, spending 42 days in Jerusalem. He decided to produce an exact map based on reliable measurements because he was aware of the "mistakes and curious differences existing between all the plans published up to now" and was interested in furthering the "very important study of biblical history." He walked in and around the city and, in the disguise of a botanist or as a doctor dispensing medical advice to the population, acquainted himself with the terrain and determined the geographical position of the places he chose as points of observation. He took "approximately two hundred geometrically correct bearings, ascertained the course of the Kidron Valley, the circumference of the walls, and the position of the Temple and the

268

JÉRUSALEM, Ville capitale de la Palestine, sous David et Salomon et qui célèbre par son temple et les republiques voysines qui en sont Princes, étoit bâtie et par les Musulmans qui la concernent. Elle est superbe autrefois sous la domination des Turcs; il y a un couvent de Cordeliers qui paye un tribut au Grand Seigneur.

Vallée de Josaphat

Torent de Cédron

Hand colored etching of Jerusalem by an 18th-century French artist. Jerusalem, Israel Museum.

269

mosques." His many excursions helped him fill in many smaller details, corrections and additions. His nicely engraved map appeared as an appendix to the report on his travels (Prague and Leipzig, 1823; Prague, 1826).

Until that time the Muslims placed formidable difficulties in the way of an accurate survey. In 1818 Sieber had to camouflage his work of map making as Cornelis de Bruin, the Dutch landscape painter was obliged to do in 1682. During the 19th century, however, the change of political climate in the Near East provided foreign scholars with much more liberty to execute their research. The decisive point in the development of Jerusalem cartography was reached after the bombardment of Acre, when the presence of the British fleet afforded the Corps of Royal Engineers the opportunity to conduct surveys in the country. One party was dispatched to Jerusalem and, in 1841, worked openly for six weeks in and around the city without encountering any opposition. The official completion of the survey was marked by the officer in charge, Col. R. A. Alderson, personally taking the measurements of the Citadel. This was the first time that Jerusalem was mapped for nonreligious (i.e., military) considerations. Another survey, made by the Royal Engineers in 1864–65, was also conducted for purely secular reasons: it was sponsored by a benefactress eager to improve Jerusalem's water supply. This work, the Ordnance Survey, is still the basis for all reliable maps of the city. Besides these British efforts, other nations (France, Germany, Italy, Netherlands, and the United States) have contributed to the mapping of the city and the topographic recording of its surrounding. These maps, while rarely offering new intelligence about fundamental facts, often serve as documentary evidence on the progress of settlement, the construction of new buildings, etc. The same information can be derived from the maps accompanying various guide books. All these maps were made by foreigners acting without any assistance from the Turkish government. No official survey of the territory was made until the British Mandatory administration established its own survey department, which prepared and printed many useful maps. After 1948 its work was taken over by the Survey of Israel, which enlarged the scope of publications considerably.

Part Three

IN JUDAISM

1 IN THE BIBLE

Interestingly, Jerusalem is mentioned in the Pentateuch only once, and that incidentally, by the name of Salem (Gen. 14:18), in connection with Melchizedek. The injunctions to worship God "in the site that He will choose" (e.g., Deut. 12:4) do not specifically refer to Jerusalem. The obscure verse "On the mount of the Lord there is vision" (*yera'eh;* Gen. 22:14), referring to the mountain in the "land of Moriah" on which Isaac was nearly sacrificed (Gen. 22), may signify an identification of the mountain with the site of the Temple; however, definite evidence for the designation of the Temple Mount by the name "Mt. Moriah" is found only in a source from the Second Temple period (II Chron. 3:1).

The uniqueness of Jerusalem as the royal city and the center of the worship of the Lord dates from the period of David (II Sam. 6-7; 24:18-25; I Chron. 21:18-22:1). During the First Temple period, when the Temple Mount was referred to as "Mt. Zion," the name "Zion" also occasionally embraced the whole of Jerusalem (cf. e.g., I Kings 8:1; Isa. 1:27). The promise of an eternal dynasty (II Sam. 7) delivered by Nathan to David in conjunction with the question of the erection of a Temple in Jerusalem, also implied eternity for Jerusalem as the royal city and the city of the Temple, although its name is not explicitly mentioned. The conception of the eternity of Jerusalem in the Bible is related to the monarchy of the House of David, and must be understood as part and parcel of it.

During the reign of Solomon, the unique status of Jerusalem as the royal city was established by the erection of the Temple, which invested the monarchy, as well as the

עולם חלק מלך שלם הוציא לחם ויין והוא כהן לאל וגו'

Illustration in an Italian manuscript, 17th–18th century, of the verse, "And Melchizedek King of Salem brought forth bread and wine; and he was priest of God the Most High." (Gen. 14:18). Harrison Miscellany, p. 16. Ardmore, Pa., Sigmund Harrison Collection.

site, with an aura of holiness. In the prayer of Solomon (I Kings 8), in which the Temple is considered a house of worship, "the city" ("which Thou hast chosen") is linked with the "house." The Temple is perceived as the eternal seat of the Lord ("a place for Thee to dwell in forever"), and there is no doubt that this conception of a double eternity—that of the dynasty of David and that of the symbolic residence of the Lord—imparted sanctity to the whole city.

In Psalm 78:68 the choice of Mt. Zion symbolizes the choice of Judah after the abandonment of Ephraim and Shiloh, and the Temple on Mt. Zion is conceived as a continuation of the Tabernacle of Shiloh. In Psalm 132, which describes the bringing of the Ark to the City of David, Zion is conceived not only as a city chosen by the Lord for the monarchy but also as the place and seat of the Lord—His resting place and His abode; in other verses, it is explicitly stated that the Lord has attached, or will attach, His name to Jerusalem (e.g., II Kings 21:4). Psalm 122 is a hymn of admiration and love to Jerusalem (cf. Ps. 87). Royal justice ("there thrones for judgment were set, the thrones of the House of David"; Ps. 122:5) is particularly emphasized as the virtue of Jerusalem—possibly in the wake of the reforms of Jehoshaphat (II Chron. 17:4–11).

It is perhaps in contrast to this that Jeremiah foresees (3:17) that in the days to come "Jerusalem shall be called the throne of the Lord"—the symbol of divine righteousness and justice (cf. Ps. 89:15), a quality that is attributed to the throne of David. In the prophecy of Jeremiah (33:16), the ideal Jerusalem is also called "The Lord is our righteousness," with reference to the justice and mercy which will be dispensed in days to come by the king, upon whom this title is also conferred (23:5–6; 33:15). The expression "habitation of righteousness and holy hill" (Jer. 31:22 (23)) is also to be explained as referring to Jerusalem even though it is seemingly applied to "the land of Judah and its cities" in general. Isaiah's "city of righteousness" (Isa. 1:26; cf. 1:21, 27)—an epithet for Jerusalem—is to be understood not as a poetic expression but as a reference to its mission to dispense justice and righteousness and to be the seat of the judges. It is not impossible that in all these appellations, there is also an echo of the name Zedek which was borne by the pre-Israelite kings of Jerusalem—Melchizedek and Adoni-Zedek (Josh. 10:1)—and which was possibly derived from an ancient name of the town.

The greatness and the splendor of Jerusalem are described in the Bible in hyperbolic poetic imagery: in Psalms—"beautiful in elevation, the joy of all the earth" (48:3 (2)); "the perfection of beauty" (50:2), and so on; in Lamentations, expressing yearning for the past—"full of people . . . great among the nations, princess among the cities" (1:1), "the perfection of beauty, the joy of all the earth" (2:15). In the Song of Songs (6:4), the beloved is compared to Jerusalem (and to Tirzah), the symbol of beauty and loveliness. In the "Song of Ascents" (Ps. 122, 125, and 132), the pilgrims praise Jerusalem in hyperbole; in Psalm 137, "Zion" and "Jerusalem" are symbols of the whole country, and their destruction ("the day of Jerusalem") is a symbol of the Exile.

In the Prophets and in Lamentations, the name and the concept of Jerusalem are frequently employed to represent the whole of Judah; Jerusalem embodies the conduct and the deeds of Judah and is occasionally identified with Judah, as well as with the whole of Israel, for good or ill. Sometimes, however, the parallel between "Jerusalem" or "Zion" on the one hand, and "Judah," the "cities of Judah," or "Israel," on the other, emphasizes—in praise or in disparagement—not that which is common to them but the central, independent status and the special features of the elected city. The "daughter of Jerusalem" and the "daughter of Zion" also signify both the city and the kingdom, either as an expression of affection or as a designation of the sinful city and nation. Prophetic literature reflects different trends in the historical-religious conception of Jerusalem according to the conditions and circumstances in which the prophet waged his struggle against idolatry and in support of the belief in the Lord. In opposition to the heathen notion that the power of the Lord of Israel over Jerusalem is no different from that of the gods of Damascus, Arpad, Hamath, and others over their respective cities, Isaiah, during the reigns of Ahaz and Hezekiah, emphasized the idea of the uniqueness of Jerusalem: as the city of the Lord of Israel, the true God, its status and fate differ from that of all other cities whose gods are no more than idols (10; 29; 30; 31; 33; 37; 38); even the mighty Assyrian conqueror shall not vanquish Jerusalem, which is assured of divine protection for the sake of the honor of His name and the name of David, His servant. It appears that as a result of the miraculous salvation of Jerusalem from the hands of Sennacherib, in accordance with the prophecy of Isaiah, the sense of the uniqueness and the might of the city became implanted within the nation; those Psalms that stress Jerusalem's title "city of God" and God's intervention as its protector (e.g., 46; 48; 76; 87) apparently belong to this period.

Isaiah's conception was, however, given to distortion, and it turned into a belief in a quasi-magic immunity which the city, and the "Temple of the Lord" which was in it, bestowed upon its inhabitants. Jeremiah rose against this new idolatrous conception; he rejected—seemingly in contrast to Isaiah—any distinctiveness attributed to Jerusalem. He maintained that the divine protection of the city was contingent upon the people's following the ways of God; if they forsook God, Jerusalem would be abandoned to the historic fate of all the other cities which fell before the Babylonian conqueror and were destroyed (7; 17; 19; 21; 25; 27; 34, et al.). The gap between the mission of Jerusalem—to be "the faithful city . . . full of justice" (Isa. 1:21)—and its actual state as " . . . rebellious and defiled, the oppressing city" (Zeph. 3:1) preoccupies all the prophets, who react to this discrepancy in pain or in anger. For Ezekiel, this gap between the vision and the reality becomes the cornerstone of his prophecy concerning Jerusalem before its destruction. All the faults and the sins of Israel, from the time they left Egypt until the days of the prophets, are attributed to Jerusalem, which is described as having surpassed Samaria and Sodom in its corruption and wickedness. In a cruel itemization, Ezekiel enumerates the "abominations of Jerusalem" (16; 22; 23; et al.); he is the only one of the prophets from whose words it is inferred that the anticipated destruction is to be regarded as an irreversible decree.

All the prophets share the expectation of an exalted future for Jerusalem—a loftiness which includes both physical splendor and a sublime religious-spiritual significance; this anticipation refers at times to the near future and at times to the end of days. Jeremiah's vision of the rebuilt Jerusalem (30:18–19; 31:37–39) is a realistic one, and it includes a detailed demarcation of its enlarged area, the whole of which will be "sacred to the Lord." Zechariah (8:3–5) also anticipates that Jerusalem will be called "the faithful city, and the mountain of the Lord of Hosts, the holy mountain"; its streets will be filled with "old men and old women" and "boys and girls" will play there. Ezekiel raises the Holy City of the days to come above actual and historic reality; it is only indirectly implied that he is referring to Jerusalem—whose name is not mentioned at all and whose site is not indicated: "a city on the south . . . up on a very high mountain" (Ezek. 40:2). Its description (45:1–8; 48:8–22, 30–35) does not evoke the image of an ordinary city or even of a royal city or capital but that of a background for the Temple, a city entirely sanctified to God, the abode of the Divine Presence, whose name will be "the Lord is there." The image of Jerusalem at the close of the Book of Zechariah (14:16–21) is similar, but—unlike in Ezekiel—the sanctity of the city of the Temple is of a universal nature, which will be recognized by all the nations. The description of "the mountain of the House of the Lord" and "the House of the God of Jacob" as the place from which learning, justice, and peace will emanate to all the nations (Isa. 2:2–4; Micah 4:1–3) identifies the mountain and the house with Zion and

Jerusalem. The chapters of consolation in the Book of Isaiah (40–66) contain an abundance of expression of fervent love for Zion and Jerusalem, on the one hand, and descriptions of its future greatness and splendor in a hyperbolic poetic style, on the other. When the universal character of the center of divine worship is emphasized (56:7; 66:18–21, et al.), there is no clear distinction between the Temple and the city. In the prophetic descriptions of the visionary Jerusalem and its history, there are numerous miraculous eschatological elements (Isa. 24:23; 27:13; 54:11–12; Ezek. 47:1–12; Joel 4:2, 12–21; Zech. 12, 14).

2 IN HALAKHAH

Because of its special characteristic holiness, Jerusalem is treated in the *halakhah* differently from other cities. "Jerusalem was not divided among the tribes" (i.e., there could be no permanent ownership of it), and thus even outside the field of the sacrifices and Temple services, there are several laws which do not apply to the city. In other walled cities a house which was not redeemed by the seller within one year of the sale remained in the permanent possession of the purchaser and did not revert to the seller in the Jubilee year; this law did not apply to Jerusalem (BK 82b; and see Ar. 9:6 and 32b; Z. M. Pineles, *Darkah shel Torah* (1861), p. 165). In Jerusalem it was also forbidden to rent houses to pilgrims; they were to be given lodgings gratis, and according to Eleazar b. Simeon it was even forbidden to rent beds (Tosef. Ma'as. Sh. 1:12; see S. Lieberman *Tosefta ki-Feshutah*, 2 (1955), 722ff.). Indeed, it was customary for the residents to vacate their homes (ARN¹, 35, 104, cf. Tosef. Suk. 2:3) for which service they received the skins of the sacrificial animals (Tosef. Ma'as. Sh. 1:13). These special laws clarify the Mishnah: "No one ever said 'The place is too confined for me to lodge in Jerusalem'" (Avot. 5:5; Yoma 21a).

The laws of the *'eglah 'arufah* ("broken-necked heifer"), the *ir ha-niddahat* ("town to be destroyed for idolatry"), and "plagues in buildings" did not apply to Jerusalem (BK 82b; cf. Tosef. Neg. 6:1). The first law requires the elders of the city nearest to a murder victim to decapitate a heifer in a ceremony whose purpose is twofold: to disclaim responsibility for the crime and to expiate the defilement of their land incurred by the blood spilt (Zev. 70b). But this law

279

does not apply to Jerusalem because its citizens do not own the city's land and they do not belong to one tribe. A city which had gone over completely to idolatry had to be totally destroyed because the sins of the people were conceived of as being visited in their property as was also the understanding of the phenomenon of "leprosy in buildings." Thus these laws did not apply to Jerusalem which could not be punished for the sins of its inhabitants.

A whole series of *halakhot* were intended to remove from Jerusalem anything which would increase ritual impurity. Therefore no trash heaps were allowed which could produce insects, nor was it permissible to raise chickens which peck at trash heaps (BK 82b; but see Eduy. 6:1). Places of burial were allowed only outside the walls of Jerusalem; in addition no existing graves were maintained in Jerusalem "except for the graves of the House of David and the grave of Huldah the prophetess which have been there from the times of the early prophets" (Tosef. Neg. 6:2). When there was a funeral procession (Sem. 10), the remains of the deceased were not taken through the city (Tosef. Neg., *loc. cit.,* and see S. Lieberman, *Tosefet Rishonim,* 3 (1939) 190). In particular, the prohibition against leaving a corpse in Jerusalem overnight was strictly enforced, except for the honor of the deceased (BK 82b; Sifra, Be-Ḥukkotai, 6:1).

During the pilgrim festivals the laws of impurity were relaxed in Jerusalem; food and drink of the *am ha-areẓ* were then considered ritually clean, and an *am ha-areẓ* was believed if he said that he had not touched an earthen vessel, for during the festivals everyone was considered a *ḥaver* (Ḥag. 26a; Yad, Metamei Mishkav u-Moshav 11:9). It seems, however, that at the end of the Second Temple period the opposition to excessive restrictions also increased: "On one occasion they found (human) bones in the wood chamber, and they desired to declare Jerusalem unclean. Whereupon R. Joshua rose to his feet and exclaimed: Is it not a disgrace that we declare the city of our fathers unclean!" (Zev. 113a; Tosef. Eduy. 3:3).

A regulation intended to enlarge the building area within Jerusalem can be seen in the *halakhah* which says of Jerusalem that "It may neither be planted nor sown nor plowed . . . and trees are not put in it, except for the rose garden which existed from the time of the early prophets" (Tosef. Neg. 6:2; BK 82b). The rose garden—like the graves of the House of David and Huldah the prophetess—is a remnant of a period when these *halakhot* were not in force. Possibly the same reason explains both, namely, the desire to prevent the reduction of available land for expanded housing facilities necessary to accommodate a growing population in the city, and lodging places for pilgrims. According to the *halakhah* the area of the city itself may be enlarged only under special conditions: "Additions are not made to the city [of Jerusalem], or to the Temple compartments except by king, prophet, Urim and Thummim [Oracle], a Sanhedrin of 71, two [loaves of] thanksgiving, and song; and the *bet din* walking in procession, the two loaves of thanksgiving [being borne], after them, and all Israel following behind them." (Shevu. 14a; and see Sanh. 1:5). During the Second Temple period there was no Urim and Thummim. Abba Saul relates that the area of Jerusalem was enlarged only twice (Tosef. Sanh. 3:4; TJ, Sanh. 1:5, 19b, TB, Shevu. 16a). It is perhaps possible to explain the *halakhah* that a foreign resident is not allowed to live in Jerusalem in terms of demographic policy (Tosef. Neg., 6:2). Even if security is posited as the reason for this law, it is not, however, necessary to date it to the period of the war with Rome.

That Jerusalem, as a meeting place for pilgrims, was also a place of business, is likewise reflected in the *halakhah*. The rabbis decreed that in Jerusalem the hour must be recorded on legal documents insofar as many documents were written by one person on the same day for people who did not know each other. Thus it was important to know whose document was written first (Ket. 10:4). A location known as *"even ha-to'an"* ("depository stone," BM 28b; see Yad, Gezelah va-Avedah 13:1) was especially set aside in

Jerusalem for announcing and claiming lost articles.

Jerusalem was also noted for its customs, some of which were related to its special nature as a city of pilgrims. R. Simeon b. Gamaliel said: "There was a great custom in Jerusalem: A cloth was spread over the doorway. As long as the cloth was spread the guests may enter; when the cloth was removed from the doorway the guests were not permitted to enter." According to R. Samuel b. Meir (Rashbam), this refers apparently to uninvited guests who happened to be in the city for the festival and "who knew that they could eat there and they would go there to eat" (BB 93b; see Tosef. Ber. 4:9; S. Lieberman, *Tosefta ki-Feshutah,* 1 (1955) 62f.). It is related of the dignitaries of Jerusalem themselves that "not one of them would go to a meal until he was invited and not one of them goes to a meal until he knows who dines with him" (Lam. R. 4:4, Sanh. 23a). The different types of food were illustrated on the tablecloth "because of the fastidious people so that none of them should eat anything harmful" (Lam. R., *loc. cit.*).

People of integrity in Jerusalem would not sign documents unless they knew who the joint signatories were. They did not sit in judgment unless they knew who sat with them (Sanh. 23a; see *ibid.,* 30a). When the Torah Scroll was removed from the Ark or returned to it they would walk behind it in respect (Sof. 14:14). There was a custom in Jerusalem to educate the boys and girls to fast on fast days. When a boy was over 12 years old "they used to bring him before every priest and elder in order to bless him, to strengthen him, and to pray for him" (*ibid.,* 18:5).

R. Eleazar b. Zadok testified that in Jerusalem there were groups of people who volunteered to carry out specifically those commandments between man and his neighbor. Some attended engagement festivities, others marriage feasts, others festivities surrounding the birth of a child or circumcisions, while still others gathered bones (of the dead). "Some went to the house of celebration, others to the house of the mourner" (Tosef. Meg. 4:15). The laws concerning the festivals were prominently and elaborately observed in Jerusalem. Wherever they went on Sukkot the people of Jerusalem did not leave their *lulavim* behind (Tosef. Suk. 2:10, Suk. 41b). They used to bind the *lulav* with chains of gold (Suk. 3:8). There was no courtyard in Jerusalem which was not lit up by the light of the water-drawing festival (*ibid.* 5:3).

Even after its destruction, Jerusalem retained its holiness, and special *halakhot* continued to be observed. The second tithe is not separated in Jerusalem since it is now forbidden to redeem it (Yad., Ma'aser Sheni 2:1–4). When praying one is obligated to face Jerusalem and if he "stands in Jerusalem he should turn his heart toward the Temple" (Ber. 30a). Entrance to the Temple Mount itself is forbidden because of ritual impurity; one who comes to pray may approach only as far as the Temple Mount. The obligation of making pilgrimage to Jerusalem remained in force, but in addition one is obliged to mourn the destruction of the city. Besides the fasts and the established days of mourning, and especially the Ninth of Av, one is forbidden to eat meat or drink wine on any day in which he sees Jerusalem in its destruction (Tosef. Ned. 1:4). One who does see Jerusalem in its destruction says: "Zion has become a wilderness, Jerusalem a desolation" (Isa. 64:9) and rends his garment. One who rends his garment for Jerusalem should not rend it further for the other cities of Judah (MK 26a). One should really mourn the destruction of Jerusalem every day and in every place; it is, however, impossible to mourn too much. "The sages have therefore ordained thus. A man may whitewash his house, but he should leave a small area unfinished in remembrance of Jerusalem. A man may prepare a full-course meal, but he should leave out an item of the menu in remembrance of Jerusalem. A woman may put on all her ornaments except one or two, in remembrance of Jerusalem" (Tosef. Sot. 15:12–14; BB 60b).

3 IN THE AGGADAH

The abundance of aggadic statements dealing with Jerusalem may be divided into three classes: those dealing with the Jerusalem of historical reality from its capture by David until the destruction of the Second Temple; statements and homilies about the Jerusalem that preceded and followed this historical city; and those dealing with the "ideal" Jerusalem of the Messianic age.

THE HISTORIC CITY. Lavish are the praises of Jerusalem in the *aggadah*, which invest it with all desirable qualities and virtues. There is no beauty like that of Jerusalem (ARN[1] 28, 85). Of the ten measures of beauty that came down to the world, Jerusalem took nine (Kid. 49b). A man who has not seen Jerusalem in its splendor has never seen a beautiful city in his life (Suk. 51b). Even Jerusalem's lack of delicious fruit and hot springs was turned into grounds for praise: "R. Isaac said: Why are there no fruits of Ginnosar in Jerusalem? So that the festival pilgrims should not say: 'Had we merely made the pilgrimage to eat the fruits of Ginnosar in Jerusalem, it would have sufficed for us,' with the result that the pilgrimage would not have been made for its own sake. Similarly R. Dostai b. Yannai said: Why are the hot springs of Tiberias not in Jerusalem? So that the festival pilgrims should not say: 'Had we merely made the pilgrimage to bathe in the hot springs of Tiberias, it would have sufficed for us,' with the result that the pilgrimage would not have been made for its own sake" (Pes. 8b; and see Sif. Num. 89).

Extravagant accounts were given of the size of Jerusalem and the numbers of its inhabitants were magnified in order to glorify it (Lam. R. 1:1 no.2). According to R. Hoshaiah, there were 480 synagogues in Jerusalem, each including a school for the study of the Bible and another for the study of the Mishnah (TJ, Meg. 3:1, 73d), and in addition there were 394 *battei din* (Ket. 105a). Jerusalem was known by 70 names, all expressions of affection and esteem (Ag. Song 1:1, line 125ff.), as well as by the Name of the Holy One blessed be He (BB 75b). Among the ten miracles wrought in Jerusalem are: "No person was stricken in Jerusalem, no person ever stumbled in Jerusalem, no fire ever broke out in Jerusalem, no building ever collapsed in Jerusalem" (ARN¹ 35, 103).

The people of Jerusalem were renowned for their wisdom: "R. Yose said: Wherever a Jerusalemite went, they would spread out for him a soft seat and place him on it in order to hear his wisdom"; the Midrash tells a number of stories about Athenians who came to Jerusalem and were impressed by the wisdom of the people and about Jerusalemites who went to Athens and surprised its inhabitants by their wisdom (Lam. R. 1:1 nos. 4–14). The people of Jerusalem were of distinguished birth and those of other places sought to marry them. "A provincial who married a woman from Jerusalem gave her her weight in gold, and a Jerusalemite who married a woman from the province was given his weight in gold" (Lam. R. 1–2, no. 2). The Jerusalemites were distinguished for their beauty (BM 84a: "R. Johanan said, I am the only one remaining of Jerusalem's men of outstanding beauty"). There are many references to the pleasant customs of "the nobility of Jerusalem and of the gentle-minded in Jerusalem" (Lam. R., *loc. cit*). The inhabitants of Jerusalem were granted atonement for their sins daily (PdRK, ed. Buber, 55b).

These statements reflect the views of the sages about Jerusalem and its people during the period of the Second Temple, and in their light they considered the reason for its destruction. Some sages declared: "We find that the First Temple was destroyed because they were guilty of practicing idolatry and incest, and of shedding blood, which applied to the Second Temple too"—and this despite all the qualities for which the Jerusalemites were praised. On the other hand, Johanan b. Torta maintained "... but in the Second Temple period we know that they studied the Torah, were strictly observant of the *mitzvot* and of the tithes, and every kind of good manners was found among them, but they loved money and hated one another without cause" (TJ, Yoma 1:1, 38c; TB, Yoma 9b). As an illustration of causeless hatred there is the story of *Kamẓa and Bar Kamẓa given by R. Johanan as the cause of the destruction of Jerusalem (Git. 55b), which was also blamed explicitly on a deterioration in relations between men (BM 30b: "Jerusalem was only destroyed ... because they based their judgments [strictly] on the letter of the law and did not go beyond its requirements."). This line was followed by other *amoraim* (Shab. 119b: "Jerusalem was destroyed only because the small and the great were made equal ..., because they did not rebuke one another ..., because scholars were despised in it ..."), while others laid the blame at the door of man's transgressions toward God ("because the Sabbath was desecrated in it ... because the reading of the *Shema* morning and evening was neglected"; *ibid.*). Although here proofs are deduced from biblical verses, the reference is to the destruction of Jerusalem in general and not specifically to that of the First Temple.

THE EXTRA-HISTORICAL CITY. The history of Jerusalem begins with an *aggadah* on the creation. "At the beginning of the creation of the world the Holy One blessed be He made as it were a tabernacle in Jerusalem in which He prayed: May My children do My will that I shall not destroy My house and My sanctuary" (Mid. Ps. to 76:3). Eliezer b. Jacob held that Adam offered a sacrifice "on the great altar in Jerusalem" (Gen. R. 34:9). According to one view Adam was created from a pure and holy place, the site of the Temple (PdRE 12; Gen. R. 14:8; TJ, Naz. 7:2, 56b: "he was created from the site of his atonement"), while another maintained that all the world was created from Zion (Yoma 54b).

In an extension of the vision of Isaiah (2:2) "that the

mountain of the Lord's house shall be established as the top of the mountains, and shall be exalted above the hills," Jerusalem is pictured by a Diaspora Jew of the second century B.C.E. as "situated in the center of the land of Judah on a high and exalted mountain" (*Letter of Aristeas*, 83). In a *baraita*, the view of the Temple as the highest place is connected with the verse (Deut. 17:8): "Then shalt thou arise, and get thee up unto the place which the Lord thy God shall choose," which shows that the Temple is higher than the rest of Erez Israel, and Erez Israel than all other countries (Kid. 69a). Associated with this description of the Temple and Jerusalem is the idea that the place is also the center of the world and the *tabbur ha-arez* ("the navel of the earth"), a well-known Greek concept. Philo also described Jerusalem "as situated in the center of the world" (*Legatio ad Gaium*, 294) and Josephus states that Judea "stretches from the River Jordan to Jaffa. The city of Jerusalem lies at its very center, and for this reason it has sometimes, not inaptly, been called the 'navel' of the country" (*Wars*, 3:51–52). This idea is also found in the Midrash: "As the navel is set in the middle of a person so is Erez Israel the navel of the world, as it is said: 'That dwell in the navel of the earth' [Ezek. 38:12]. Erez Israel is located in the center of the world, Jerusalem in the center of Erez Israel, the Temple in the center of Jerusalem, the *heikhal* in the center of the Temple, the ark in the center of the *heikhal*, and in front of the *heikhal* is the *even shetiyyah* ["foundation stone"] from which the world was started" (Tanḥ. B., Lev. 78; and see Sanh. 37a; Song R. 7:5 no. 3). The antiquity of this *aggadah* is attested by a parallel in the Second Book of Enoch (23:45; Cahana's edition) in which the metaphor "the navel of the earth" is connected with the site of Adam's creation ("And that Melchizedek will be priest and king in the place of Araunah saying, In the navel of the earth where Adam was created ..."). These *aggadot* and others like them make Jerusalem the place where the decisive events in man's history, as recounted in the book of Genesis, occurred (see Gen. R. 22:7; PdRE 23, 31). The

The *even shetiyyah* ("foundation stone") over which the Dome of the Rock is built, regarded by Jewish and Islamic tradition as the center of the world. Photo Richard Cleave, Jerusalem.

identification of Mount Moriah, on which Solomon built "the house of the Lord" (II Chron. 3:1), with "one of the mountains" in the land of Moriah, on which Abraham bound Isaac on the altar, predates the special holiness of Jerusalem and its choice as the site of the Temple to before David's capture of the city and connects this with the promise given to the patriarch Abraham. To the name by which it is first mentioned, Salem ("peace" or "perfection," Gen. 14:18) was added *yirah* ("reverence," in Gen. 22:14) after the *Akedah*, both combining to form the name Jerusalem (Gen. R. 56:10).

The designation, "daughter of Zion," which is often used in the Bible to refer to the people of Israel, presumes the metaphor of Jerusalem as the mother, and this is also found in the apocryphal and apocalyptic literature (IV Ezra 10:7; I Bar. 4:9; II Bar. 3:1) as well as in Midrashim (PR 26:131b; Yal. Mak. on Ps. 147:2, no. 4 in the name of the Tanh.). The term "mother" had a special significance for Hellenistic Jewry: in referring to Jerusalem as the "metropolis," they expressed the idea that the Diaspora communities were settlements founded on the initiative of the mother city, Jerusalem (Philo, *In Flaccum*. 45–46; *Legatio ad Gaium*, 281). But in the *aggadah* the term metropolis had a different connotation. Of Jerusalem, the "navel" of the earth and the light of the world (Gen. R. 59:5), R. Johanan said that "it is destined to become the metropolis of all countries" (Ex. R. 23:10), and in the future all nations would be "daughters of Jerusalem" (Tanh. B. Deut. 4).

THE IDEAL JERUSALEM. The statements of the sages on the Jerusalem of the future are for the most part connected with and based on prophetic visions on this subject. Through close scrutiny of every detail of these visions and by accepting every metaphor and parable as factual, they wove fanciful and extravagant legends. Some, however, not content with inferences from biblical passages, added their own ideas. It is an aggadic tradition, said Samuel b. Nahmani, that "Jerusalem will not be rebuilt until the exiles are gathered in, and if anyone tells you that the exiles have gathered together but Jerusalem is not rebuilt, do not believe it" (Tanḥ. No'aḥ 11). In time to come God will rebuild Jerusalem and never destroy it *(ibid.)*, and it will be rebuilt with fire (TJ, Ber. 4:3, 8a). In the future, said R. Johanan, the Holy One blessed be He will raise Jerusalem by three *parasangs* (BB 75b); "Jerusalem will be extended on all sides and the exiles will come and rest under it," and it will reach the gates of Damascus (Song R. 7:5 no. 3). Simeon b. Lakish said, "The Holy One blessed be He will in days to come add to Jerusalem more than a thousand gardens and a thousand towers" (BB 75b; Mid. Ps. to 48:13; and see Kohut, Arukh, 4 (1926), 24). In the future the Holy One blessed be He will bring forth living waters from Jerusalem and with them heal everyone who is sick (Ex. R. 15:21). The borders of Jerusalem in time to come will be full of precious stones and pearls, and Israel will come and take their jewels from them (PdRK 137a). The Holy One blessed be He will build Jerusalem of sapphire stone "and these stones will shine like the sun, and the nations will come and look upon the glory of Israel" (Ex. R. 15:21). Simeon b. Gamaliel declared that "all nations and all kingdoms will in time to come gather together in the midst of Jerusalem" (ARN¹ 35, 106).

Jerusalem of the future is connected with the heavenly Jerusalem. The widespread concept of the heavenly Temple, which owes its origin to Isaiah's vision (Isa. 6), is the source of the aggadic idea of a heavenly Jerusalem *(Yerushalayim shel Ma'lah)*. In an homiletical interpretation of the verse: "The Holy One is in the midst of thee, and I will not enter into the city" (Hos. 11:9), R. Johanan said "The Holy One blessed be He declared, 'I shall not enter the heavenly Jerusalem until I can enter the earthly Jerusalem.' Is there, then, a heavenly Jerusalem? Yes, for it is written [Ps. 122:3]: 'Jerusalem, that art builded as a city that is compact together'" (Ta'an. 5a). Another homiletical interpretation stating that the heavenly Jerusalem is located directly opposite the earthly Jerusalem is derived from the verse (Isa. 49:16): "Behold, I have graven thee upon the palms of

My hands; thy walls are continually before Me" (Tanḥ., Pekudei, 1), and this Jerusalem is in the heaven known as *zevul* (Ḥag. 12b). While the heavenly Temple was fully prepared before the world was created (Tanḥ. B., Num. p. 34), the heavenly Jerusalem "was fashioned out of great love for the earthly Jerusalem" (Tanḥ., Pekudei, 1). This distinction is unknown in apocalyptic literature. In the Syriac Apocalypse of Baruch (4:3) God says that the heavenly Jerusalem is "prepared beforehand here from the time when I took counsel to make paradise."

While apocalyptic literature (IV Ezra 10) and Paul (Gal. 4:26) stress the contrast between the heavenly and the earthly Jerusalem, the *aggadah* emphasizes their affinity. Thus in time to come, it is stated in apocalyptic literature (I Enoch 90:28–29; IV Ezra 7:26, 10:54), the heavenly Temple and the heavenly Jerusalem will descend and be established in the place of the earthly Temple and earthly Jerusalem. "For in a place where the city of the Most High was about to be revealed no building work of man could endure." This view—adopted by the Christians, who repudiated the belief in a restoration of the earthly Jerusalem—was rejected by the *aggadah*, which states that the earthly Jerusalem will extend and rise upward until it reaches the throne of Divine Majesty (PdRK 143b; and see Tanḥ., Zav, 12; PR 41:173a). It is only in later apocalyptic literature written in Muslim countries in the Geonic period that the idea reappears of the heavenly Jerusalem coming down to earth wholly built and entire.

4 IN THE LITURGY

STATUTORY PRAYER. In the liturgy the Jew of every land gave full expression to the vow taken "by the rivers of Babylon"—"If I forget thee, O Jerusalem, let my right hand forget her cunning" (Ps. 137:5). The mention of Jerusalem was obligatory in all the statutory prayers, and it is largely used (together with Zion) as a synonym for Erez Israel as a whole (in point of fact, references to Erez Israel are rare). The most important of the many references is the 14th blessing of the daily *Amidah,* which is entirely devoted to Jerusalem. It begins "And to Jerusalem Thy city return in mercy . . . rebuild it soon in our days" and concludes, "Blessed art Thou, O Lord, who buildest Jerusalem." On the Ninth of Av a moving prayer of comfort to "the mourners of Zion and the mourners of Jerusalem" and for the rebuilding of the city (called *Naḥem* after its opening word) is added to this blessing in the *Amidah* of *Minḥah,* and the concluding blessing is changed to "who comfortest Zion and rebuildest Jerusalem." The first of the last three blessings (common to all the *Amidot*), an invocation for the restoration of the sacrificial system, concludes with the words "and may our eyes behold Thy return in mercy to Zion. Blessed art Thou, O Lord, who restorest Thy Divine Presence unto Zion." The same combination of prayer for Jerusalem with the hope for the restoration of the Divine Service in the Temple is the theme of the fourth blessing of the *Musaf* on the New Moon and festivals (the Sabbath *Musaf* refers to the return to "our land"), while the *Ya'aleh ve-Yavo* prayer includes one for "the remembrance of Jerusalem Thy holy city." The third benediction of the Grace after Meals, largely devoted to Jerusalem, includes a prayer for Jerusalem, Zion, the

292

restoration of the Davidic dynasty, and the rebuilding of the Temple. It concludes with the same benediction as the 14th blessing of the *Amidah*, with, however, the addition of the word meaning "in His mercy."

וְיַעֲלֶה וְיָבֹא וְיַגִּיעַ וְזִכְרוֹן מָשִׁיחַ בֶּן דָּוִד עַבְדֶּךָ
וְזִכְרוֹן יְרוּשָׁלַיִם עִיר קָדְשֶׁךָ וְזִכְרוֹן כָּל עַמְּךָ בֵּית יִשְׂרָאֵל
לְפָנֶיךָ לִפְלֵיטָה לְטוֹבָה לְחֵן וּלְחֶסֶד וּלְרַחֲמִים וּלְחַיִּים
(לר"ח) וּלְשָׁלוֹם ❖

(לשבת) בְּיוֹם הַשַּׁבָּת הַזֶּה ❖ בְּיוֹם רֹאשׁ חֹדֶשׁ הַזֶּה
(לפסח) בְּיוֹם חַג הַמַּצּוֹת הַזֶּה ❖

(לשבועות) בְּיוֹם חַג הַשָּׁבוּעוֹת הַזֶּה ❖ (לסוכות) בְּיוֹם חַג הַסֻּכּוֹת הַזֶּה
(לשמיני העצרת) בְּיוֹם שְׁמִינִי חַג הָעֲצֶרֶת הַזֶּה
(לראש השנה) בְּיוֹם הַזִּכָּרוֹן הַזֶּה ❖

זָכְרֵנוּ יי אֱלֹהֵינוּ בּוֹ לְטוֹבָה ❖ וּפָקְדֵנוּ בוֹ לִבְרָכָה ❖ וְהוֹשִׁיעֵנוּ בוֹ
לְחַיִּים ❖ וּבִדְבַר יְשׁוּעָה וְרַחֲמִים חוּס וְחָנֵּנוּ וְרַחֵם עָלֵינוּ
וְהוֹשִׁיעֵנוּ כִּי אֵלֶיךָ עֵינֵינוּ כִּי אֵל (אלך) חַנּוּן וְרַחוּם אָתָּה ❖

וּבְנֵה יְרוּשָׁלַיִם עִיר הַקֹּדֶשׁ
בִּמְהֵרָה בְיָמֵינוּ ❖ בָּרוּךְ אַתָּה

The city of Jerusalem depicted at the head of the prayer for the rebuilding of the Holy City in *Seder Birkat ha-Mazon,* a manuscript of the Grace after Meals, Mikulov, Moravia, 1728. Copenhagen Royal Library, Cod. Heb. 32, fol. 5v.

The *Lekhah Dodi* hymn is an impressive example of the longing for Jerusalem as it found its expression in the liturgy. Designed as a hymn of welcome to "Princess Sabbath," no less than 6 of its 9 stanzas are devoted, explicitly or implicitly, to the yearning for Jerusalem.

IN PIYYUT. The theme of Jerusalem figures prominently in *piyyut*, but its implications and frame of reference are greatly extended. Whereas in the statutory prayers the theme is confined to the actual Jerusalem, in the *piyyut* Jerusalem is also the embodiment of an idea: it is a symbol of Israel's glorious past and her hopes for the future, an image of the heavenly Jerusalem whose gates directly correspond to those of the temporal Jerusalem. The various biblical names for Jerusalem are found in the *piyyut*, as well as new names suggested by the context in which Jerusalem appears in the Bible. There are hundreds of relevant *piyyutim* and many were adopted in the *mahzorim, kinot*, and *selihot* of the various rites. If Jerusalem was the "chiefest joy" of Israel when it dwelt in its own land, after the Exile, the deprivation from it became the "chiefest mourning." It is thus the theme of *piyyutim* on occasions of joy, such as weddings; of sadness, as in the *kinot* of the Ninth of Av; and of solemnity, such as the *selihot*. One of the earliest of such *piyyutim* for marriages is *Ahavat Ne'urim me-Olam* by Eleazar Kallir, which contains the following stanza:

שַׂמְּחוּ אֶת יְרוּשָׁלַם בְּשִׂמְחָה
וְגִילוּ בָהּ בְּהַצָּלָה וּרְוָחָה
כִּי לָעַד לֹא יַנִּיחֶנָּה
וְלֹא לְעוֹלָם לָנֶצַח יַאֲנִיחֶנָּה

Gladden Jerusalem with gladness
And rejoice in her with deliverance and well-being,
For He shall not neglect her forever,
Nor shall He eternally abandon her to sighing.

The theme (of joy) is common to all such *piyyutim* in honor of the bridegroom. One of the best constructed *piyyutim* on Jerusalem is included in the *selihot* for the third day of the Ten Days of Penitence according to the

Lithuanian custom. It is a 22-stanza abecedarius, beginning with the verse:

יְרוּשָׁלַיִם אֶת ה׳ הַלְלִי דָּגוּל מֵרְבָבוֹת

Jerusalem, praise the Lord, distinguished among myriads

Each strophe starts with the word Jerusalem, followed by the alphabetical acrostic word and concludes with a biblical quotation in which the last word is Jerusalem. The *piyyutim* of *Ne'ilah* for the Day of Atonement include both the stanza from the *Avadnu me-Erez Hemdah* of R. Gershom b. Judah of Mainz:

הָעִיר הַקּוֹדֶשׁ וְהַמַּחֲזוֹת
הָיוּ לְחֶרְפָּה וּלְבִזּוֹת
וְכָל מַחֲמַדֶּיהָ טְבוּעוֹת וּגְנוּזוֹת

The Holy City and its environs
Have been shamed and disgraced
And all her glories engulfed and plunged into oblivion.

and the acrostic poem of Amittai b. Shephatiah of the tenth century in Italy beginning,

אֶזְכְּרָה אֱלֹהִים וְאֶהֱמָיָה
בִּרְאוֹתִי כָּל עִיר עַל תִּלָּהּ בְּנוּיָה
וְעִיר הָאֱלֹהִים מֻשְׁפֶּלֶת עַד שְׁאוֹל תַּחְתִּיָּה

I remember, O God, and lament
When I see every city built on its foundation
And the City of God degraded to the nethermost pit.

Almost every *paytan*, whether of Erez Israel (e.g., Yannai, Kallir, Yose b. Yose) or of the Diaspora (e.g., Saadiah b. Joseph Gaon, Abraham ibn Ezra, Joseph b. Abraham Gikatilla) composed a *piyyut* on this theme. Each expressed his praise and longing for Jerusalem. Kallir calls it "the city of strength"; Saadiah sees "the streets of the city full of rejoicing"; Ibn Ezra sings of the "beloved Zion"; a *paytan* called Isaac refers to it as "Jerusalem the Crown of Glory"; Abraham b. Menahem as "the joyous city"; while for Israel b. Moses Najara, in his well-known Aramaic table hymn, *Yah Ribbon*, it is "the best of all cities."

In his love songs which express passionate yearning for Jerusalem, Judah Halevi excels all others and earned the title "the Singer of Zion." His famous *Ziyyon Ha-Lo Tishali*, included in the *kinot* for the Ninth of Av, gave the lead to the *kinot* which are called "Zionides" because they commence with the word Zion. Jerusalem to Judah Halevi is "beautiful of elevation, the joy of the world, the capital of the great king" (cf. Ps. 48:3). It is "the site of the throne of the Messiah" and "the footstool of God"; it is at times also spoken of as the "city of the universal God". Ezekiel's mention of the two sisters "Oholah the elder, and Oholibah her sister"—personifications of Samaria and Jerusalem (23:4)—became a fruitful theme for the *paytanim*, often in the form of a dialogue between them. The *piyyut* on this theme by Solomon ibn Gabirol, *Shomeron Kol Titten*, is well known, being included in the *kinot* of the eve of the Ninth of Av in the Ashkenazi rite. Jerusalem and Samaria engage in a dialogue; the former maintains that the destruction of the Temple is the cruelest possible blow; Samaria retorts that at least the descendants of Judea still exist, while hers are lost. Oholibah answers that the repeated persecutions and exiles have been worse than death. The *piyyut* ends with the prayer, "Renew our days of old, as Thou didst say, 'The Lord will rebuild Jerusalem.'"

Another recurring motif is the contrast between "my departure from Egypt" (from bondage to freedom) and "my departure from Jerusalem" (from freedom to bondage). There are *piyyutim* with this refrain by, among others, David b. Samuel ha-Levi, Ephraim b. Jacob, and David b. Aleksandri, and an example can be seen in the *Esh Tukad be-Kirbi* included in the *kinot* of the Ninth of Av in the Ashkenazi rite.

The poems and *piyyutim* on Jerusalem, although individual compositions, express the longings and love of the whole Jewish people. Their inclusion in the various rites clearly testifies that throughout the ages Jerusalem continued to be at the very center of the Jews' emotions and cultural heritage.

Since the establishment of the State of Israel, and especially since the 1967 Six-Day War, there has been a growing feeling that the *piyyutim* on Jerusalem which emphasize its utter destruction and desolation should no longer be recited. Similarly a revised version of the *Naḥem* prayer, based on variants, particularly the Palestinian version which begins *Raḥem*, composed by E. E. Urbach, is recited in some synagogues.

5 IN KABBALAH

According to the homilist Baḥya b. Asher, the dual ending of the Hebrew word for Jerusalem (*Yerushalayim*) indicates that there is a heavenly Jerusalem corresponding to the earthly Jerusalem (see Aggadah: above). It contains a "holy palace and the prince of the Presence is the high priest" (commentary on *Sefer ha-Komah*). Following the *aggadah*, the Holy Land is the center of the world and in its center is Jerusalem, whose focal point is the Holy of Holies. All the good in the world flows from heaven to Jerusalem, and all are nourished from there. In Kabbalah Jerusalem therefore symbolizes the lowest *Sefirah, Malkhut* ("kingdom"), which mainly rules over the world. The mystical drama behind the history of Jerusalem is expressed in various essays: Ḥayyim Vital, for example, interpreted the war between Tyre and Jerusalem as a battle between impurity and holiness. Jerusalem is surrounded by mountains so that the forces of the *sitra aḥra* ("the left side," the demonic powers) cannot penetrated its sanctity, and in the teaching of the Zohar, the angels of the *Shekhinah* are the guardians of the walls. According to Naḥmanides and Baḥya, Jerusalem is therefore especially suitable for prophecy and its inhabitants have a "superior advantage," for "no curtain separates it [Jerusalem] from God" and He wishes to be worshiped there. The prayers of all Israel rise to heaven via Jerusalem, which is the gateway to the heavens. The walls of Jerusalem will eventually approach the Throne of Glory and then there will be complete harmony in the realm of the *Sefirot*.

As the messianic belief did not occupy a special position in Spanish Kabbalah, Jerusalem did not attain a particular status beyond the customary mystical-symbolic homiletic interpretations. After the expulsion from Spain (1492), there is evidence of a preference for Safed over Jerusalem. The Messiah will first reveal himself in Galilee and then will go up to Jerusalem.

Until the 16th century, only a small number of kabbalists lived in Jerusalem. However, from the 17th century on, many kabbalists were attracted to Jerusalem, including entire groups, like those around Jacob Ẓemaḥ, Meir Poppers, and Gedaliah Ḥayon. Shabbateans especially tended to look toward Jerusalem. One author even wrote as if he lived in Jerusalem. Of special note (and still standing) is the *bet midrash*, Bet El, founded by Shalom Sharabi, which served as a center of Kabbalah in the East for 150 years. Its students excelled in asceticism and in prayer according to Lurianic meditations *(kavvanot)*.

The Bet El Synagogue which served as the center of kabbalist life in Jerusalem from the middle of the 18th century. It was established by the Yemenite rabbi Shalom Sharabi, who compiled the kabbalistic prayer rite, *Nahar Shalom*. Courtesy Shiver, Netanyah.

299

6 IN MODERN HEBREW LITERATURE

HASKALAH. The historical perspective with which the Haskalah literature invested Jerusalem gave the city a sense of reality if not immediacy. The *maskil*, though he wanted to assimilate into European culture, also tried to preserve his historical identity; he thus not only recalled his ancient past but vivified it. The yearning for the past glory of Israel was, however, a nostalgia for the almost irretrievable. Thus one of the major trends in the Haskalah, not unlike European literature in this respect, was a harking back to a "Golden Age." This, however, was not born out of a desire to return to the Land of Israel, which was only to grow strong much later in the wake of disappointment with the Enlightenment.

Haskalah literature not only celebrated the glory of ancient Jerusalem but also lamented the Jerusalem laid waste, the bondage, and the exile. Two of the earliest Hebrew Haskalah writers, Ephraim and Isaac Luzzatto, celebrated the glories of Israel's past; their panegyrics were interwoven with a strain of infinite longing to be echoed later by Micah Joseph Lebensohn (Mikhal). Jerusalem also figured prominently in the rational allegorical strain in Haskalah writings, e.g., *Emet ve-Emunah* ("Truth and Faith"; in *Kol Kitvei Adam u-Mikhal*, 3 (1895)), by A. B. Lebensohn, where the city is the seat of wisdom. Against the symbolic landscape of Jerusalem, Micah Joseph Lebensohn wrote a number of semi-epical poems: *Shelomo ve-Kohelet, Moshe al-Har Avarim,* and *Yehudah Halevi*. In *Moshe al-Har Avarim* Moses stands on Mount Avarim and "his eye is turned toward Jerusalem." Judah Halevi is

depicted as journeying to the Land of Israel where he meets

with desolation and ruin. Standing before the gates of Jerusalem the medieval poet falls into a trance and sees the host of the dead of Zion pass before his eyes. The modern poet thereby gives a kaleidoscopic view of the woeful legions of the Jews who died for Jerusalem and Zion.

Ahavat Ziyyon ("Love of Zion," 1853), a historical novel set in Jerusalem in the time of Ahaz, by Abraham Mapu, is a colorful pageant of the ancient past. Sensitively imitating the speech of biblical Hebrew, the author captured the rhythm of life of the ancient Hebrews. Divested of any mythical analogies, symbols, or nostalgia his graphic rendering of life in Judah where Jews were free in their own homeland stirred the hearts of a ghetto generation. While Jerusalem in the novel is the backdrop of the action, it is also the symbol of the Haskalah, a harmonious reconciliation between beauty and morality. Mapu also mourned the ruin of Jerusalem which is the leitmotif of *Ayit Zavu'a* ("The Painted Vulture," 1857), a savage attack on Jewish obscurantism, whose butt is Lithuanian Jewry. Jerusalem, seen through the eyes of one of the characters who sits on Mount Zion contemplating its desolation, is described with an immediacy seldom found among Haskalah writers.

Judah Leib Gordon, a later Haskalah writer, expressed his love of Zion more directly than other *maskilim* and in this sense is as much a writer of the renascence period as of the Haskalah. Though he never joined Ḥibbat Zion and had misgivings about the return of the Jews to their ancient homeland, 20 years before the movement's inception Gordon wrote *Al Har Ziyyon she-Shamam* (1862; in *Kitvei Yehudah Leib Gordon* (1953)) urging the people to rebuild Zion. Among his poems on Jerusalem are *Ahavat David u-Mikhal* ("The Love of David and Michal") and *Bein Shinnei Arayot* ("Between the Teeth of the Lions"), an epic poem on the war between Judea and Rome. The theme of the latter, a people fighting for its liberty against overwhelming odds, is exemplified through the tragic story of a Jewish warrior who fought at the gates of Jerusalem, only to be taken captive to Rome and pitted against a lion in the 301 arena. The poet's anguish over a nation whose ancient glory is no more suffuses the poem.

RENASCENCE PERIOD (1880–1947). In late Haskalah literature there is no clear distinction between belles lettres and writings of a social and publicistic nature. This division was effected in the renascence period when issues vital to the Jewish community were in literary writing either subsumed to the aesthetic element or were so well integrated that their militancy was muted. The great poets of the time, such as Ḥ. N. Bialik and S. Tchernichowsky, excluded the Zionist issue from most of their works. Thus the Zionist poets of the renascence movement are not the literary giants of modern Hebrew literature but minor bards such as M. M. Dolitzki, who wrote reams of poetry on Jerusalem, most of which is sentimental and trite. A minor poet, N. H. Imber, is remembered by virtue of his poem *Ha-Tikvah* (about 1876).

Jerusalem features prominently in the historical dramas of the period, some of which were a continuation of the allegorical-biblical literature of the Haskalah. In J. L. Landau's *Aharit Yerushalayim* ("The Last Days of Jerusalem," 1886) the protagonists expound ideas about freedom and the glory of Israel.

Major writers of the later renascence period (1920–47) returned to the theme of Jerusalem. Although some used it merely as an image, symbol, or backdrop for the development of their plot, they invested the city with a flesh and blood reality. J. Ḥ. Brenner wrote a number of works against the background of Jerusalem, such as, *Shekhol ve-Khishalon* ("Bereavement and Failure," 1920) in which he decries the Jerusalem of the *kolel* and *halukkah;* and *Mi-Kan u-mi-Kan* ("From Here and There," 1911). Some of Yaakov Cahan's historical plays, *David Melekh Yisrael* (1921), the King Solomon trilogy, and others, are set in biblical Jerusalem. In *Aggadot Elohim* ("Legends of God," 1945), a saga of the Jewish people from the time of creation to the resurrection, Cahan strikingly describes the desolation of Jerusalem which at the same time he sees as a symbol of redemption. He also edited the anthology *Yerushalayim be-Shir ve-Ḥazon.*

Dramatists of the caliber of Mattityahu Shoham also made Jerusalem the pervading motif of some of their works. The theme of *Ẓor vi-Yrushalayim* (1933) is a culture conflict expressed through the characters: Jezebel, Elijah, and Elisha. Jezebel is associated with Zor (Tyre), the center of Phoenician culture, the seat of idolatry identified with the flesh. Elisha, at first attracted to Jezebel, dissociates himself from her. Jerusalem symbolizes the ideal society, the rule of the spirit. Elisha's self-denial and resistance to the temptations of Jezebel is in contrast to an earlier tragic emphasis in Shoham where the Jewish protagonist is overpowered. While it is a play of high dramatic quality, it is not theatrical. The characters never become flesh and blood but remain symbolic or allegorical figures. *Ha-Ḥomah* ("The Wall," 1938), a drama by Aharon Ashman, is set in the time of Ezra and Nehemiah. Jerusalem merely serves as a background for the dramatic action. Nathan (Bistritski) Agmon's *Be-Leil Zeh* (1934), renamed *Leil Yerushalayim* ("Jerusalem Night," 1953), an impressionistic play in which the dialogue is fragmentary and the characters symbolic, dramatizes the crisis in modern Jewish history as manifested in the conflict between the conservative Jew who acquiesces in exile and the demand for redemption. While Jerusalem is the physical setting in many of these works the city also functions as a symbolic landscape for the play.

During this period of national revival much drama, prose, and poetry was written in which the theme of the return to Zion did not focus on Jerusalem, but rather on pioneering and the pioneer. Although the naturalistic and realistic schools did not take up Jerusalem as a motif, there were exceptions, among them Yehoshua Bar-Yosef's *Be-Simta'ot Yerushalayim* ("In Jerusalem Alleys," 1941), a dramatization of the tragic disintegration of a family. A conflict of generations and values, whose tragic "dissolution" is in madness, unfolds against the background of the timelessness of Jerusalem.

Yehuda Karni in his Palestine period infused the individualistic motifs of his earlier poetry with a nationalistic theme in which Jerusalem is the eternal symbol of the Jewish people and the embodiment of its destiny. He thus deviated from the realistic trend prevalent in Palestine wherein Jerusalem was a backdrop to contemporary social problems. In his book of poems, *Shirei Yerushalayim* ("Songs of Jerusalem, 1944), the hopeless stagnation and decay of 20th-century Jerusalem against the canvas of its historical continuity is portrayed as ephemeral and transient.

A lyrical and personal note runs through Ya'akov Fichmann's poems on Jerusalem whose wistful mood expresses an undefined longing. The poet, like a prowler, stealthily surprises the city in its most intimate moments. Onto these he projects his own moods. In the sonnet *Jerusalem,* Fichmann captures Jerusalem in a moment in which all of time is gathered, and in which "Dead splendor rests on furrows of new life."

Jerusalem is central to a number of Shmuel Yosef Agnon's works, especially to his major novels: *Ore'ah Natah Lalun* (1940; *A Guest for the Night,* 1968), *Temol Shilshom* ("The Days Before," 1946), and *Shirah* (1971), each of which treats the Jerusalem motif differently. The action in *Ore'ah Natah Lalun* is set in a small Galician town to which a traveler from Jerusalem, drawn by childhood nostalgia, has come to spend the night. The two main symbols in the work, the town's *bet ha-midrash* and Jerusalem, interact on a level beyond the immediate realistic scene. They are also interwoven into the surrealistic images often producing a sense of eeriness and unreality. On every level of the story Jerusalem functions both as a real place in time and space and as a symbol. The surrealistic atmosphere of the town and the town itself have reality by virtue of the fact that Jerusalem in *Ore'ah Natah Lalun* has real existence. In *Temol Shilshom* Jerusalem also functions on several different levels; most of the action takes place in the city during the period of the Second

Aliyah. *Shirah* is set in the Jerusalem of the 1930s and describes, often satirically, the life of German-Jewish and other intellectuals at the Hebrew University. Other works of Agnon in which Jerusalem is either the setting, theme, or functions as a symbol are: *"Tehillah," Sefer ha-Ma'asim* ("The Book of Deeds"), *"Ha-Mikhtav"* ("The Letter"), *"Iddo ve-Inam," "Ad Olam"* ("Forevermore"), and *Sefer ha-Medinah* ("The Book of the State"). The particular Yemenite milieu of Jerusalem has been dealt with by H. Hazaz.

ISRAEL PERIOD. Uri Zvi Greenberg's Jerusalem poetry belongs as much to the Mandatory period as to the period of statehood. The prophetic thunder and woeful liturgical laments are a consistent theme in his poetry. The poet, however, not only exhorts—he also dreams; and in *Mi-Sifrei Tur Malka* ("From the Books of Tur Malka") he sees the *Shekhinah* which has returned to Jerusalem and the celestial Jerusalem which comes down to the earthly city. In *Kelev Bayit* ("House Dog," 1928) Greenberg sees at the gates of Jerusalem a "miraculous horse" waiting for its rider. "Jerusalem the Dismembered," a dirge from the greater work *Yerushalayim shel Mattah,* bemoans the shame and desecration of the holy city. Despite its despair and sense of infinite loss and infinite horror, his Holocaust poetry is characterized by a leap of faith rather than a loss of faith in God. Out of the ashes he sees salvation and imagines the host of the martyred dead gathered in Jerusalem.

The theme of Jerusalem recurs less frequently in the literature of the 1950s which is concerned with the more immediate problems of the decade. At most it is a realistic landscape. Amos Elon's work *Yerushalayim Lo Nafelah* ("Jerusalem Did Not Fall," 1948) is a description of the siege of Jerusalem in 1948 written by an eye witness. Yet in the late 1950s a change occurred and the canvas of the dramatist as well as of the poet and prose writer extended.

Among the younger poets Yehuda Amichai is probably the most representative. He used the Jerusalem motif in different time settings, contexts, and even mythical landscapes. The city seems to have a strong hold on him, a hold which he wants to break but cannot. In *"Ha-Kerav ba-Givah"* ("Battle for the Hill") he says he is going to fight that battle and then "I shall never return to Jerusalem"—but he does in "Jerusalem 1967." The "sea" of Jerusalem, a symbol found already in very early Hebrew poetry, is a recurring image in "Battle for the Hill"—"the sea of Jerusalem is the most terrible sea of all." Amichai's tendency to fuse historical and mythical landscapes with the present can perhaps best be seen in "If I forget thee Jerusalem" where he uses ancient themes to create new myths. His novel *Lo mi-Kan ve-Lo me-Akhshav* ("Not of This Time, Not of This Place," 1963) contains vivid descriptions of Jerusalem.

A. B. Yehoshua's Jerusalem in *"Sheloshah Yamim ve-Yeled"* ("Three Days and a Child"; in *Tishah Sippurim*, 1970) is an impressionistic yet realistic portrait of the city marked by a note of hostility which endows it with a personality as well as a landscape. The play *Laylah be-Mai* ("A Night in May," 1969) dramatizes the effect of the tension of May 1967 on a Jerusalem family; Jerusalem however is only incidental to the play. Another writer who has made Jerusalem the setting of many of his works is David Shahar: *Moto shel ha-Elohim ha-Katan* ("Death of the Little God," 1970), *Al ha-Halomot* ("On Dreams," 1955), *Heikhal ha-Kelim ha-Shevurim* (1962), and *Maggid ha-Atidot* ("Fortune-teller," 1966), four collections of short stories.

Part Four

IN OTHER RELIGIONS

1 IN CHRISTIANITY

In the sources, Christian concern with Jerusalem involves the ancient concept of the city as a shrine of preeminent holiness, marking the physical and spiritual center of the cosmos, the spot at which history began and at which it will reach its apocalyptic consummation. The idea of an *umbilicus mundi,* a scale model, as it were, of the universe itself, at which a nation or tribe would gather periodically to renew its corporate life by the observance of the now familiar year-rites was known to many ancient peoples, and the nations converted to Christianity had no difficulty accepting the supreme eschatological significance of Jerusalem and its Temple. The city's unique status, however, raised certain questions that have never ceased to puzzle and divide Christian theologians, namely: Just how literally are Jerusalem's claims and promises to be taken? How can the prized continuity (back to Adam) of the city's long history be maintained if Christianity is a completely new, spiritualized, beginning? How can Jerusalem be the Holy City par excellence without also being the headquarters of the Church? How can the city's prestige be exploited in the interests of a particular church or nation? These issues have all come to the fore in each of the main periods of Christian preoccupation with Jerusalem, namely: the "Golden Age" of the second and third centuries; the Imperial age from Constantine to Justinian; the Carolingian revival; the Crusades; the period of intrigues and grand designs; the time of patronage by the great powers; and the rise of Israel.

IN THE SECOND AND THIRD CENTURIES. The question of literalism was paramount in the second and third centuries; 309

the early Christians had been Jews of the apocalyptic-chili-astic persuasion with lively visions of a literal New Jerusalem, while an educated and growing minority (also among the Jews) favored a more spiritual interpretation of the biblical promises and accused the old-school Christians of superstition and "Judaizing." The banning of Jews from the city by Hadrian gave an advantage to the gentile party, and the "Doctors of the Church" made the Hellenized or "spiritualized" image of Jerusalem the official one (e.g., St. Jerome). Still, the millennialist teachings survived beneath the surface, occasionally bursting out in sectarian enthusi-asm or becoming general in times of crisis, while the "Doctors" themselves repeatedly succumbed to the entice-ments of a real and earthly Holy City. Hence the ambiguities of literalism versus allegory might have been minimized were it not that the continued presence and preachings of the Jews forced the Christians in self-defense to appeal to the doctrine of a purely spiritual Jerusalem.

From Origen's time, churchmen of all sects have been one in insisting that the New Jerusalem is for Christians only, since the Jewish city can never rise again. In the absence of scriptural support for this claim, various stock arguments are used, namely, Josephus' description of the destruction of 70 C.E. with its atmosphere of gloom and finality; the argument of silence in that the New Testament throughout says nothing about a restitution of the city after Vespasian; the ominously lengthening period of time since the expul-sion of the Jews; various tortured allegorical and numer-ological demonstrations; and the appeal to history with the ringing rhetorical challenge: "Where is your city now . . .?"

A favorite argument (akin to a Jewish teaching about the Diaspora) was that Jerusalem had to be destroyed so that Jews and Christians alike might be scattered throughout the world as witnesses to the fulfillment of prophecy in the new religion. Against these were arguments that never ceased to annoy: Why did the city and Temple continue to flourish for 42 years after the final pronunciation of doom, and why during that time did the Christians show every mark of reverence and respect for both? Why did Jesus weep for the destruction if it was in every sense necessary and desirable? Why do the Doctors insist that the destruction of Jerusalem by the Romans was a great crime, and yet hail it as a blessed event, saluting its perpetrators as the builders of the New Jerusalem, even though they were the chief persecutors of the Christians? If expulsion from Jerusalem is proof of divine rejection of the Jews, does the principle not also hold good for their Christian successors? How can the antichrist sit in the Temple unless the city and Temple are built again by the Jews? The standard argument, that only a total and final dissolution would be fit punishment for the supreme crime of deicide, was frustrated by the time schedule, which suggested to many that the city was destroyed to avenge the death not of Jesus but of James the Just.

But if Jerusalem was to be permanently obliterated, the Christians could only inherit it in a spiritual sense. The Church was the New Jerusalem in which all prophecy was fulfilled, the Millennium attained, and all things became new. This raised a serious question of continuity, however: Has God chosen another people? Can one preserve the meaning of the eschatological drama while changing all the characters? Can a people (the Christians) be gathered that was never scattered? And what of the Heavenly Jerusalem? The approved school solution with its inevitable rhetorical antithesis was to depict the Heavenly and the Earthly Jerusalems as opposites in all things, the one spiritual, the other carnal. Yet none of the fathers is able to rid himself of "corporeal" complications in the picture, and the two Jerusalems remain hopelessly confused, for in the end the two are actually to meet and fuse into one. Palestine was the scene of busy theological controversy on these and related mysteries when the "Golden Age" of Christian Jerusalem came to an end with the persecutions of 250.

THE IMPERIAL AGE. After the storm had passed, Constantine the Great at Rome, Nicaea, Constantinople, and elsewhere celebrated his victories over the temporal and spiritual enemies of mankind with brilliant festivals and imposing monuments. But his greatest victory trophy was "the New Jerusalem," a sacral complex of buildings presenting the old hierocentric concepts in the Imperial pagan form, with the Holy Sepulcher as the center and chief shrine of the world. Jerusalem was treated as the legitimate spoils of Christian-Roman victory over the Jews, whose entire heritage—including the Temple—accordingly passed intact into the hands of the Christians. Henceforth, there remained no objections to giving Jerusalem its full meed of honor. Continuity back to Adam was established with suspicious ease by the rapid and miraculous discovery of every relic and artifact mentioned in the Bible, and a flood of pilgrims came to rehearse, Bible in hand (the earliest pilgrims, Silvia (383) and the Bordeaux Pilgrim (333), are markedly partial to Old Testament remains) the events of each holy place and undertake weary walks and vigils in a cult strangely preoccupied with caves and rites of the dead. The patriarch Macarius, who may have contrived the convenient discoveries of holy objects with an eye to restoring Jerusalem to its former preeminence, promoted a building boom that reached a peak of great activity in the sixth and seventh centuries.

Financed at first by Imperial bounty, the building program was later supported by wealthy individuals, and especially by a line of illustrious matrons whose concern for the Holy City goes back to Queen Helena of Adiabene and whose number includes Helena, the mother of Constantine; his mother-in-law, Eutropia; Eudocia, the wife of Theodosius II; Verina, the wife of Leo II; Sophia, the mother of St. Sabas; Paula; Flavia, Domitilla, and Melania, rich Roman ladies and friends of St. Jerome. By the end of the fourth century, Jerusalem had more than 300 religious foundations sustained by generous infusions of outside capital, until the economic decline of the fifth century forced the government to take the initiative, culminating in Justinian's ambitious but fruitless building program. The period was one of specious brilliance in which, as J. Hubert notes, everything had to be *splendens, rutilans, nitens, micans, radians, coruscans*—i.e., brilliantly surfaced, while the actual remains of the buildings show slipshod and superficial workmanship.

Spared the barbarian depredations suffered by most of the world in the fifth and sixth centuries, Jerusalem was an island of security and easy money, where the population of all ranks was free to indulge in those factional feuds that were the blight of the Late Empire. Points of doctrine furnished stimulation and pretext for violent contests involving ambitious churchmen and their congregations, hordes of desert monks, government and military officials and their forces local and national, the ever-meddling great ladies, members of the Imperial family and their followings, and the riotous and ubiquitous factions of the games in confused and shifting combinations. The Jews of Alexandria became associated with one of these factions, which in that notoriously fickle city found itself opposed to the faction of the Emperor Phocas, who ordered his general, Bonossus, to suppress the corresponding faction in Jerusalem by converting all Jews by force. While pitched battles raged in the streets, a Persian army appeared at the gates, sent by Chosroes, the pro-Christian monarch seeking vengeance on the treacherous Phocas for the murder of his friend Mauritius. The Jews regarded this as a timely deliverance by a nation that had succored them before and sided with the Persians—an act not of treachery (as Christian writers would have it) but of war, since Phocas had already called for their extermination as a people. The Christian world was stunned when Chosroes took the cross from Jerusalem in 614 and elated when the victorious Heraclius brought it back, in 628. Under the vehement urging of the monk Modestus, whom he had made patriarch and who aspired to rebuild Jerusalem as a new Macarius, Heraclius, against his better judgment, took savage reprisals on the Jews. But within ten years the city fell to Omar, who allowed the pilgrimages to continue, while making Jerusalem a great Muslim shrine by the 313 revival of the Temple complex, which the Christians, after long and studied neglect, also now claimed as their own.

Though Christians, originally as Jews and later on Church business, had always made pilgrimages to Jerusalem, the great surge of popular interest beginning in the fourth century alarmed some churchmen, who denounced the pilgrimage as wasteful of time and means, dangerous to life and morals, and a disruptive influence in the Church. Along with monasticism, with which it was closely associated, the pilgrimage to Jerusalem was an attempt to get back to the first order of the Church, retrieve the lost world of visions, martyrs, prophets, and miracles, and this implied dissatisfaction with the present order. The writings of the Church Fathers furnish abundant evidence for the basic motivation of the pilgrims, which was the desire to reassure oneself of the truth of Christianity by seeing and touching the very things the Bible told of and experiencing contact with the other world by some overt demonstration of supernatural power (healing was the most popular). Only at Jerusalem could one receive this historical and miraculous reassurance in its fullness; only there did one have a right to expect a miracle.

The earliest holy place visited was not, as might have been supposed, the Holy Sepulcher, but the footprint of Jesus on the Mount of Olives, the spot where he was last seen by men as he passed to heaven and would first be seen on his return (Cabrol and Leclercq, Dic. 7, 231). Contact was the basic idea—contact with the biblical past and with heaven itself, of which Jerusalem was believed to be a physical fragment. Tangible pieces of the Holy City, carried to distant parts of the world, gave rise to other holy centers, which in turn sent out their tangible relics like sparks from a central fire. The Christian world was soon covered by a net of holy shrines, built in imitation of the Church of the Holy Sepulcher or the Temple and often designated by the names of Jerusalem, the Temple, or the Sepulcher. Each became a pilgrimage center in its own right, and there was a graded system of holiness measured on a scale of distance in time from Jesus and in space from Jerusalem, which remained "as far above all the other cities in the world in renown and holiness as the sun is above the stars."

THE CAROLINGIAN REVIVAL. In 800, after being fought over for two centuries by Muslim dynasties, Jerusalem was placed under the protection of Charlemagne, who was doing Hārūn al-Rashīd the service of annoying his Umayyad enemies in Spain. Although Rome had come under his protection five years earlier in the same way—by the presentation of holy keys and a banner from the bishop—it was the prestige of ruling Jerusalem that warranted the change in Charlemagne's title from king to emperor. Like Constantine, Charlemagne stimulated a revival of large-scale pilgrimage to Jerusalem and a tradition of royal generosity, endowing a church, school, monastery, and library. The Jerusalem hospitals for pilgrims were a tradition going back to pre-Christian times. From Darius to Augustus and the emperors of the West, great rulers had courted the favor of heaven by pious donations to the Holy City, and this tradition of royal bounty was continued through the Middle Ages, when kings imposed Jerusalem-taxes on their subjects and monks from Jerusalem made regular fund-raising trips to Europe.

During the years of the "quasi-protectorate of the Western emperors" over Jerusalem and the revived Byzantine control (made possible by Muslim disunity), a steadily mounting stream of pilgrims even from the remotest regions of northwestern and Slavic Europe came to bathe in the Jordan, pray at the Holy Sepulcher, and endow pious foundations. Stimulated by the end-of-the-world excitement of the year 1000, this stream "multiplied tenfold" in the 11th century, culminating in great mass pilgrimages of thousands led by eminent lords and churchmen. When the Seljuks, having defeated the Byzantine army in 1071 and occupied Jerusalem in 1075, became oppressive in their fees and controls of the holy places, Christian leadership felt obliged to "take up again the part of Charlemagne," and the armed pilgrimage led by Robert le Frison (1085–90) was hailed enthusiastically throughout Europe and viewed by pope and Byzantine emperor alike as advance reconnaissance for a crusade.

THE CRUSADES. The Crusades were the expression of a popular religious revival in which Jerusalem, restored to its full apocalyptic status (the Crusading literature has a strongly Old Testament flavor), offered a welcome door of escape to all classes from economic and social conditions that had become intolerable in Europe. The Crusades have also been described as the complete feudalization of Christianity by an ancient chivalric tradition, with Jesus as a liege lord whose injuries must be avenged and whose stronghold must be liberated. The language of the Crusading literature bears this out, as does its conscious affinity with older epic literature (reflected later in Tasso), the significant exchange of embassies, and the close resemblance of Asiatic to European arms and accoutrements, suggesting an older common "Epic Milieu," and the nature of the Crusades as a *Voelkerwanderung*.

From the fourth century the Western Church had accepted, with the Roman victory cult, the concept of world polarity, dividing the human race into the blessed (Jerusalem, Church, *ager pacatus*) and the damned (Babylon, unbelievers, *ager hosticus*), reflected in the *jihad* concept of the Muslim countercrusade. Such a concept assumed papal leadership of all crusades, giving rise to baffling questions of imperial, papal, and royal prerogative. These came to a head in the Latin Kingdom of Jerusalem, whose assizes, though the most perfect expression of a model feudal society, remained but an ideal, "a lawyers' paradise," where royalty, exploiting the city's propinquity to heaven, dramatized its own claims to divine authority with pageantry of unsurpassed splendor. This motif was developed by the military religious orders of the Hospitalers (founded by the Amalfi merchants in 1048 and open only to the nobility) and the Templars, each claiming a monopoly of the unique traditional power and glory of Jerusalem and the Temple and hence displaying an independence of action that in the end was its undoing.

INTRIGUES AND GRAND DESIGNS. The Crusades challenged the infidel to a formal trial-of-arms at Jerusalem to prove which side was chosen of God. The great scandal of the Crusades is accordingly not the cynical self-interest, betrayal, and compromise with the enemy that blights them from the beginning, but simply their clear-cut and humiliating failure, which dealt a mortal blow to medieval ideas of feudal and ecclesiastical dominion. With the loss of all the East, "Operation Jerusalem" adopted a new strategy of indirection, approaching its goal variously and deviously by wars against European heretics, preaching missions (through which the Franciscans held a permanent Roman bridgehead in Jerusalem), and local crusades against Jews and Muslims as steps in grand designs of global strategy. The grandiose plans of Charles VIII, Alfonso of Castile, João II, Albuquerque, and Don Sebastian all had as their ultimate objective the liberation of the Holy Sepulcher, as indeed did all of Columbus' projects (S. Madariaga, *Christopher Columbus*). A marked kabbalistic influence has been detected in these plans, and indeed the ever-living hopes of the Jews, fired by new prophecies and new messiahs, were not without effect in Catholic and Protestant circles, as appears in the career of the humanist Guillaume Postel who, acclaimed at the court of France for his philological researches in Jerusalem, urged the transfer of the papacy to that city and finally declared himself to be the *Shekhinah*.

Christians in the post-Crusader period continued their dream of Jerusalem but those who did manage to obtain a foothold there were largely engaged in unseemly squabbles over minute rights in the Holy Places. The great reformers, while mildly condemning pilgrimages, placed strong emphasis on the purely spiritual nature of the New Jerusalem and the utter impossibility of the Jews ever returning to build an earthly city. This was necessary to counteract the tendency to apocalyptic excitement and renewed deference to the Jews attendant upon the Reformation's intensive preoccupation with the Bible, as various groups of enthusiasts took to building their own local New Jerusalems or preparing to migrate to Palestine for the task. Such groups flourished down through the 19th century. Protestant pilgrims to Jerusalem from the 16th to the 20th centuries have consistently condemned the "mummery" of the older pilgrimages while indulging in their own brand of ecstatic dramatizations. Whereas the Catholic practice has been to identify archaeological remains as the very objects mentioned in the Bible, the Protestants have been no less zealous in detecting proof for the Scriptures in every type of object observed in the Holy Land. Chateaubriand's much publicized visit to Jerusalem in 1806 combined religious, literary, and intellectual interest and established a romantic appeal of the Holy Land that lasted through the century.

When Jerusalem was thrown open to the West in the 1830s by Muhammad Ali, European and American missionaries hastened to the spot with ambitious projects of converting the Jews with an eye to the fulfillment of prophecy in the ultimate restoration of the Holy City. Even the ill-starred Anglo-Lutheran bishopric of 1841 had that in view, and Newman's denunciation of the plan as a base concession to the Jews and Protestants indicated the stand of the Roman Catholic Church, which in 1847 appointed a resident patriarch for Jerusalem. In the mounting rivalry of missions and foundations that followed, France used her offices as protector of Roman Catholics and holy places in the East (under Capitulations of Francis I, 1535, renewed in 1740) to advance her interests in the Orient, e.g., in the Damascus blood libel of 1840. When Louis Napoleon was obliged by his Catholic constituents to reactivate French claims to holy places that France had long neglected and the Russians long cherished, "the foolish affair of the Holy Places" (as he called it) led to the Crimean War and its portentous chain of consequences.

PATRONAGE BY THE POWERS. In the second half of the 19th century, the major powers and Churches were stimulated by mutual rivalry to seek commanding positions in Jerusalem through the founding of eleemosynary institutions over which they retained control. Beyond the hard facts of geography and economics, the religious significance of the city continued to exert steady pressure on the policies of all Great Powers, as when the German kaiser gratified his Catholic subjects with the gift of the "Dormition," proclaimed Protestant unity by the dedication of the great Jerusalem Church, and sought personal fulfillment in a state pilgrimage to Jerusalem and the patronage of Zionism (thwarted by his advisers). The taking of Jerusalem by Allenby in 1917 was hailed through the Christian world as the fulfillment of prophecy and deplored by the Muslims as a typical Crusade against their holy city. World War II was followed by increasing interest in Jerusalem as a center of ecumenical Christianity, though old religious and national rivalries of long standing and great variety continued to flourish. The 20th-century pilgrimages acquired a touristic air in keeping with the times, interest in Jerusalem having a more sophisticated and intellectual tone. Even the old and vexing problem of the priority of Jerusalem, "mother of Churches," over other Christian bishoprics is now approached in a spirit of mutual concession and with respect for the autonomy of the various bishoprics of Jerusalem. This liberalized attitude may be a response to what is regarded in some Christian circles as the Jewish challenge to the basic Christian thesis that only Christians can possess a New Jerusalem. While the Great Powers for over a century cautiously sought to exploit the energies of Zionism and its sympathizers, it is now openly conceded that the Jews might indeed rebuild their city—though only as potential Christians. Though some Christians are even willing to waive that proviso, the fundamental thesis is so firmly rooted that the progress of Israel is commonly viewed not as a refutation of it but as a baffling and disturbing paradox.

A NEW IMAGE OF ISRAEL. With the Israel military victories of 1948, 1956, and 1967, the Christian world was confronted by a new image of a heroic Israel. The picture was 319 agreeable or disturbing to Christians depending on which of two main positions one chose to take, and the years of tension following the Six-Day War of June 1967 were marked by an increasing tendency among Christians everywhere to choose sides. On the one hand, the tradition of the Church Fathers and Reformers, emphasized anew by Arnold Toynbee, looked upon a Jewish Jerusalem as a hopeless anachronism, and deplored any inclination to identify ancient with modern Israel. This attitude rested on the theory, developed by generations of theologians, that only Christians could be rightful heirs to the true Covenant and the Holy City. Roman Catholics continued to hold the position, propounded by Pope Pius X to Herzl in 1904, that the return of the Jews to Jerusalem was a demonstration of messianic expectations which that Church considered discredited and outmoded. Those suspicious of the progress of Israel naturally chose to minimize the moral and world-historical significance of Jerusalem, and to treat the problems of modern Israel as purely political. On the other hand were Bible-oriented Christians of all denominations in whom the successes of the Israelis inspired to a greater or lesser extent renewed hope and interest in the literal fulfillment of biblical prophecy. To such persons in varying degrees the Jewish military achievements appeared as steps toward the fulfillment of the eschatological promise to Abraham (Gen. 15:18). As interest in Jerusalem shifted from the antiquarian appeal of the 1950s to heightened eschatological allure, something of the old Christian vision of Jerusalem seemed to stir the Christian conscience.

2   IN MUSLIM THOUGHT

According to the teachings of orthodox Islam, there are three temples in the world to which special holiness is attached: the Ka'ba in Mecca, the Mosque of Muhammad in Medina, and the Temple Mount in Jerusalem, in order of their holiness to Muslims. While orientalists of past generations viewed the traditions favoring Jerusalem as originating in the period of the Umayyad caliphs who lived in Syria and had to fight against the rebels who ruled Mecca and Medina, modern orientalists deny this and maintain that the adoration of Jerusalem is found in early Islam. According to Ezekiel 5:5 and 38:12 the Temple Mount, and especially the *even ha-shetiyyah*—the rock on which the Ark stood—is the hub of the universe. Muslim scientists even found corroboration for this view in their calculations that the Temple Mount is located in the center of the fourth climatic zone, the central region north of the Equator in which man can develop civilized life.

The adoration of Jerusalem in Islam, however, is primarily based on the first verse of Sura 17 of the Koran, which describes Muhammad's Night Journey *(isrā')*. Tradition states that when the "Servant" (Muhammad) was sleeping near the Ka'ba, the angel Gabriel brought him to a winged creature *(Burāq)* and they went out to the "Outer Mosque" (al-Masjid al-Aqṣā). From there they rose to heaven *(mi'rāj)*. On their way through the heavens they met good and evil powers; on reaching their destination they saw Abraham, Moses, and Jesus. The "Servant" prayed among the prophets as a leader, i.e., he was recognized as the foremost among them. There are differences of opinion regarding the nature of the journey and its purpose. Some view it as a description of a dream, but the official opinion of Muslim theologians is that Muhammad made this journey while awake and actually traversed the ground. Some hold that the "Outer Mosque" is in heaven, but the accepted opinion is that this is the Temple Mount in Jerusalem (not the mosque which was built later and called al-Masjid al-Aqṣā). This story was probably told to Muhammad by Jews, since he was familiar with the midrashic works popular in his time, e.g., *The Book of Jubilees, The Book of Enoch,* and *Toledot Moshe* (extant in an Arabic version), which describe Moses' journey to heaven and his visits to paradise and hell. This story and its usual interpretation greatly elevated the holiness of Jerusalem in Islam. In addition to the Temple Mount, other places in Jerusalem were also regarded as holy, e.g., the tomb of Mary where the first Umayyad caliph Muzʿāwiya is known to have prayed at the time of his coronation in 661.

At the beginning of his mission, Muhammad apparently recited the prayers facing toward Jerusalem, and probably continued to do so after the *hijra* ("flight") to Medina. However, failing in his attempts to attract the Jews to his religion, Muhammad enjoined—16 or 17 months after his arrival in Medina (Rajab or Shaʿbān of 2 A.H., i.e., January or February 624)—that the *qibla* ("direction of prayer") be changed to the direction of Mecca (see Sura 2:136ff.). Omar acted in accordance with this injunction during the conquest of Jerusalem. When Kaʿb al-Aḥbār, a Jew who had converted to Islam, suggested that he build the mosque north of the former Holy of Holies, the caliph rebuked him for attributing the intention to him that the worshipers face not only the Kaʿba but also the *even ha-shetiyyah* as well.

Despite this change Jerusalem retained its special holiness among the Muslims, and Muslim tradition added numerous layers to it. There are also hadiths (sayings attributed to Muhammad which are the basic oral law of Islam) regarding the great value of prayer said in Jerusalem. Muslim tradition relates, among other things, that the holy rock (*al-ṣakhra,* i.e., *even ha-shetiyyah*) is located exactly beneath Allah's throne and above a cave which is the "well of spirits" where all the souls of the dead congregate twice weekly. Due to the rock's holiness, the angels visited it 2,000 times before the creation of the first man and Noah's ark came to rest on it. It is part of paradise and all the sweet waters on earth emanate from it. These stories, mostly taken from rabbinic *aggadah,* reached the Muslims mainly from Jews converted to Islam, as indicated by the names of the narrators recorded in the tradition itself.

Muslim legend closely connects Jerusalem with the day of judgment. According to the Muslim faith, at the eschatological end of days, the angel of death, Isrāfīl, will blow the ram's horn three times while standing on the rock, which will be done after the Ka'ba comes to visit the Temple Mount. Arabic works such as *Kitāb Aḥwāl al-Qiyāma* ("Book of the Phases of Resurrection") contain detailed descriptions of the day of judgment which will then commence. All the dead will congregate on the Mount of Olives and the angel Gabriel will move paradise to the right of Allah's throne and hell to its left. All mankind will cross a long bridge suspended from the Mount of Olives to the Temple Mount, which will be narrower than a hair, sharper than a sword, and darker than night. Along the bridge there will be seven arches and at each arch man will be asked to account for his actions. The faithful who are found innocent will receive from Āsiya, Pharaoh's wife, and Miriam, the sister of Moses, sweet water from the rivers of paradise in the shade of a palm tree which will also be beneath the rock. Most of these stories came from midrashic literature, such as *Pirkei Moshe,* and some of them from Christian works.

Jerusalem also has a special place in Muslim mysticism. There is a Muslim tradition that Jerusalem is the pit of the ascetics and servants of God and that 40 righteous men live in it, thanks to whose virtues the rains fall, plagues are averted, and the world in general exists. These righteous men are called *abdāl* ("those who are replaced") because when one dies another replaces him. Actually this tradition 323 is apparently not an early one but reflects the importance attributed to Jerusalem by the mystics from the beginnings of the mystical trend in Islam and the growing emphasis on its sanctity from generation to generation. Even the first Muslim mystics held that living in Jerusalem or elsewhere in Erez Israel purifies the soul and that eating its fruits is permitted and legal (ḥalāl). For this reason many of them came to Jerusalem to be close to its holiness. Apparently the adoration of Jerusalem on the part of the Muslim mystics was mainly influenced by the example of Christian asceticism, which flourished in Erez Israel, and especially in the vicinity of Jerusalem, during the centuries preceding its conquest by the Muslims.

Affection for Jerusalem and its sanctuaries grew as a result of its temporary loss during the Crusades. Indeed, the reaction to the wars with the crusaders in the 12th and 13th centuries was an important factor in the development of Arabic literature and travelogues on Jerusalem, Hebron (al-Khalīl), and Palestine as a whole, and their importance for Islam. Descriptions of the Muslim holy places have been preserved from that time on. Some are of great historical importance, being the principal stimulus for Muslim pilgrimages to the holy places in Jerusalem.

Part Five

IN THE ARTS

1 IN LITERATURE

Not surprisingly, an immensely rich and varied treasury of literature, art, and music has been devoted to Jerusalem by both Jews and non-Jews from early medieval times onward. Many of these treatments deal with specific events such as the Return from the Babylonian Captivity and the Roman siege and destruction of Jerusalem. Many medieval Jewish *paytanim* composed hundreds of poems on the subject (see above: Liturgy) and parallel Christian devotional works include "Jerusalem the Golden" (from *De contemptu mundi*) by Bernard of Cluny and several other hymns of the same title. Prefabricated stage settings of medieval English mystery and miracle plays often represented the Holy City; and innumerable "descriptions" were written by Crusader chroniclers, Arab historians, and travelers of various periods. The most important Renaissance treatment of the subject was the Italian poet Torquato Tasso's epic *Gerusalemme liberata* (1581; translated 1594 and again by Edward Fairfax as *Godfrey of Bulloigne*, 1600), an account of the crusaders' siege and capture of Jerusalem combining the traditions of classical and medieval romance writing. Following the Reformation, many Protestant writers evoked the image of the Holy City in verse and prose, but few works were specifically devoted to the theme.

Probably as a result of the social, political, and religious ferment of the 19th century, particularly in Britain, the "New Jerusalem" became the symbol of man's yearning for a better life and a nobler form of society. This tendency had a remarkable development in the works of the English poet

326 William Blake (e.g., in *Jerusalem, The Emanation of the*

Giant Albion, 1804), whose "Jerusalem," a poem prefacing *Milton* (1804) which was later to become a British Labor Party anthem, ends:

"I will not cease from mental fight,
Nor shall my sword sleep in my hand,
Till we have built Jerusalem,
In England's green and pleasant land."

This type of idealization also characterizes John Mason Neale's "Jerusalem the Golden," one of the best-known hymns of the Victorian era. In 19th-century works ranging in tone from pious devotion to cynicism and humor, the modern city of Jerusalem was described by writers such as the Catholic Chateaubriand and the Protestant Pierre Loti in France, the Austrian Ludwig August Frankl, and the U.S. authors Mark Twain and Herman Melville.

From the beginning of the 20th century, there was an even more pronounced literary interest in Jerusalem's present and future, especially as a result of Zionist settlement and the development of the city's new Jewish section. An outstanding Scandinavian work on the theme was Selma Lagerlöf 's two-volume *Jerusalem* (1901–02; Eng. 1915), a novel about Swedish settlers in Palestine. Her fellow-countryman, Sven Anders Hedin (who was of partly Jewish descent), described his tour of the Holy Land from Damascus to Sinai in *Jerusalem* (c. 1916; *To Jerusalem,* 1917), a travel book markedly pro-German and anti-British in tone. Hedin, who was later sympathetic to the Nazis, here made many references to Jewish biblical and later history, treating Zionism in an objective manner and illustrating his text with many of his own sketches of Jewish types. A similar approach was adopted by the English Catholic G. K. Chesterton (*The New Jerusalem,* 1920) and by the French writers Jean and Jérôme Tharaud (*L'an prochain à Jérusalem!,* 1924). In most travel literature dealing with Erez Israel the main stress has been on Jerusalem.

Much popular English and U.S. fiction dealt with the city and its daily life and development during the period of the British Mandate and later, during Jerusalem's political 327 division between Israel and Jordan (1948–67). Two books of this kind were John Brophy's novel *Julian's Way* (1949) and Muriel Spark's *The Mandelbaum Gate* (1966). However, most of the important 20th-century treatments have been the work of Jewish authors. Mainly poems, novels, and short stories, these range from evocations of bygone days in the Old City to the reunification of Jerusalem after the Six-Day War. A rare Slavonic handling of the subject was *Pesni za Erusalim* ("Songs for Jerusalem," 1924) by the Bulgarian Jewish poet Oram ben Ner (Saul Mezan, 1893–1944). Personal reflections are contained in *Das Hebraeerland* (1937), a prose work by the German poet and refugee Else Lasker-Schueler. The Jewish people's historic return to the Western Wall forms the climax of Elie Wiesel's novel, *Le mendiant de Jérusalem* (1968; *A Beggar in Jerusalem*, 1970). A modern collection of literature about the city is Dennis Silk's *Retrievements: A Jerusalem Anthology* (1968).

2   IN ART

From the strictly conceptual point of view, Jerusalem has been interpreted artistically through the ages in four different ways: realistic, imaginary, idealistic, and symbolic. Each generation, influenced by contemporary thinking, has found the most suitable way of expressing its own concept of Jerusalem; and more than one conceptual point of view is to be found at the same time in the same environment.

Historically, the oldest-known representation of Jerusalem seems to have been symbolical. The first symbol was the Temple of Jerusalem, in answer to the need to remember Jerusalem after its destruction in the year 70 C.E. The facade of the Temple was depicted on the tetradrachm, the silver coin struck by Simeon Bar Kokhba in the "Second Year of the Freedom of Israel" (133 C.E.) The representation which may be clearly seen on the obverse side of the coin is a four-column facade of a temple. This was a stereotyped symbol of a pagan temple common to Hellenistic and Roman art. On his coin, Bar Kokhba included the inscription "Jerusalem," a star on top of the architrave, and a symbolical representation of the Ark of the Covenant between the two middle columns, where usually an image of an idol would have been placed. As further symbols of the Temple, the reverse of the coin depicts the *lulav* and *etrog* used on Sukkot, the most important feast of the Temple. It appears that, by the second century C.E., the aspiration for Jewish national redemption and the reestablishment of the Jewish state were concentrated in a fervent desire to rebuild the Temple. The artistic manifestations of the Temple were therefore a way of representing the city of Jerusalem. It is possible that the "Jerusalem of Gold" which R. Akiva made for his wife (Ned. 50) was a gold medallion which had a symbolical representation of Jerusalem or of the Temple engraved upon it.

No earlier artistic representations of Jerusalem have survived, neither from the Israelite nor from the Hellenistic periods, unless the figurations of Tabernacle and Temple implements on coins and stone reliefs are to be considered. These representations include the seven-branched candelabrum *(menorah)*, the shovel, the Ark of the Covenant, the altar, the *lulav* and *etrog*, the *shofar*, and the trumpets, which may all be regarded as symbolical representations of the city.

In later times, the Temple and its implements became the most commonly used symbolical representation of Jerusalem, to be rivaled later by the rotunda of the Christian Holy Sepulcher, by the round Muslim Dome of the Rock, and by the Jewish Western ("Wailing") Wall of the Temple Esplanade. In the talmudic period, the Temple facade and the Ark of the Covenant are represented quite frequently in

The Temple façade depicted in the panel above the Torah niche in the Dura-Europos synagogue, third century C.E. From E. R. Goodenough, *Jewish Symbols in the Greco-Roman Period*, vol. II, Bolingen Foundation, New York.

a way similar to that of the Bar Kokhba coin. An example can be seen on the painted panel above the niche for the Torah in the third-century synagogue of Dura-Europos and in other panels from the same synagogue representing the Tabernacle in the desert. In all cases, a reversed conch in the tympanum of the arch signifies holiness, another Hellenistic convention. At times, the Ark of the Covenant was substituted by an open Ark of the Law, revealing Torah scrolls, but in all other ways depicted in the same manner. These can be seen in the bottoms of the unearthed gold-glass plates dating from the fourth century, and in wall paintings in the fourth-century Jewish catacombs in Villa Torlonia, Rome. During the Middle Ages, the same symbolic elements represent Jerusalem, both in Jewish and in Christian art. Part of the sixth-century floor mosaic in the synagogue of Bet Alfa is occupied by a stylized ark flanked by seven-branched

Open Ark of the Law symbolizing the Temple of Jerusalem on a wall painting in the Jewish catacombs of Villa Torlonia, Rome, fourth century c.e. From H. W. Beyer and H. Lietzmann, *Die Juedische Katakombe der Villa Torlonia in Rom,* Berlin, 1930.

candelabra and other Temple implements enclosed in a frame of curtains which are drawn back. A similarly stylized representation can be found on one of the "carpet-pages" of the first Leningrad Bible, written in Hebrew in Egypt in 929 C.E. The opening page of the illuminated Latin Ashburnham Pentateuch (dating from the seventh century) also represents what seems to be a Temple facade with the reversed conch in its tympanum and two curtains drawn back to reveal a square ark in which the names of the five books of the Pentateuch are inscribed. One of the full-page miniatures of the 14th-century Spanish *Sarajevo Haggadah* in Hebrew (fol. 32) depicts the Temple as a city-scape with the Ark of the Covenant in the center, topped by the wings of the cherubim under a reversed conch.

The rotunda of the fourth-century Holy Sepulcher in Jerusalem, which was fashioned after an accepted Roman mausoleum form for prominent families, became in early Christianity and throughout the Middle Ages an idealistic symbol of Jerusalem. The apse mosaic of the Church of St. Pudenziana in Rome (early fifth century) shows Jesus among the Apostles in "Heavenly Jerusalem." The city is located in heaven, painted above the head of Jesus, showing the round Holy Sepulcher on the left and the octagonal Church of the Ascension on the right. Many memorial churches of the fourth century such as St. Constanza in Rome (c. 350 C.E.) and San Lorenzo in Milan (c. 370 C.E.) were built in the round. The sixth-century map of the Holy Land on the floor mosaic of the church at Madaba (Transjordan) depicts Jerusalem as a walled city with the dome of the Holy Sepulcher predominant in its center.

The seventh-century Muslim Dome of the Rock was also used to represent the Temple during the Middle Ages in Jewish, Christian, and Islamic art. After the crusaders captured Jerusalem in July 1099, they turned the Dome of the Rock into a church, calling it "Templum Domini," and the Knights Templars, who had the custody
of the Temple Mount, fashioned their churches all over

Jesus arguing with the doctors in the Temple, depicted as a structure resembling the Dome of the Rock. Detail of a 13th-century crusader triptych. Sinai Peninsula. St. Catherine's Monastery, Icon. 379. Photo Richard Cleave, Jerusalem.

Europe in the round, on a plan similar to the Dome of the Rock—a round wall enclosing an inner circular colonnade. The crusaders were probably responsible for propagating the dome-shaped structure as a symbol of Jerusalem. A coin of Guy de Lusignan, crusader king of Jerusalem (1186–87), depicts the Dome of the Rock. A 13th-century crusader triptych, now at St. Catherine's Monastery, Mt. Sinai, representing the joys and sorrows of Mary, depicts the New Testament episode of Mary and Joseph finding Jesus arguing with the doctors beneath a domed structure resembling the Dome of the Rock. This structure also existed in Jewish art. In an illuminated 15th-century *Mishneh Torah* by Maimonides from Northern Italy (New York, private collection, fol. 1), a circular domed building

The Temple as a domed building in an illuminated manuscript of Maimonides' *Mishneh Torah*. N. Italy, 15th century.
New York, private collection.

stands for the Temple, at the opening of the "Book of Sacrifices."

"Heavenly Jerusalem" *(Yerushalayim shel ma'lah)* acquired an eschatological significance in mishnaic and talmudic times. It became synonymous with the ideal city governed by God Himself and would, according to Christian tradition, come down from heaven at the "end of days" (Rev. 21). In most Christian medieval representations of the "Heavenly Jerusalem," a walled city is represented, with a lamb symbolizing Jesus in its center. In some instances, John the Apostle is shown being guided by an angel who reveals the city to him. One example of this is in the 13th-century Douce Apocalypse from England (Oxford, Bodleian Library, Ms. Douce 180, fol. 89), and another is a 12th-century wall painting from the Abbey Church of Saint-Chef, where Jesus himself is depicted in the center. In Jewish art, the last page of the *Birds' Head Haggadah* (S. Germany, illuminated circa 1300) seems to depict the "Heavenly Jerusalem." Within an arch of a walled city inscribed Jerusalem stands a man, and below the structure are four other men who lift their hands in adoration, pointing to it.

Most of the 15th-century woodcuts and engravings of Jerusalem are not realistic, although they were intended to be, since they were pilgrims' impressions. The most famous view of the city, dominating the Holy Land, is in a woodcut by Erhard Reuwich, in Bernhard von Breitenbach's *Peregrinationes ad Sepulcrum Christi* (Mainz, 1486). Despite its medieval attitude, this served as an example for many later "realistic" pictures of Jerusalem, such as Hartmann Schedel's woodcut of 1492 and Sebastian Muenster's Basle woodcut of 1544. These pilgrims' woodcuts and engravings were widespread in Europe and influenced the image of Jerusalem in many paintings by famous artists. Van Scorel (1495–1562) painted a typical pilgrim-type picture of Jerusalem as part of his "Christ's Entry to Jerusalem" (Utrecht, Central Museum). Jan van Eyck (1390–1441) painted two round-domed buildings as a

"Heavenly Jerusalem," represented as a walled and turreted city. From the *Birds' Head Haggadah*, S. Germany, c. 1300. Jerusalem, Israel Museum, Ms. 180/57, fol. 23.

background to his picture "The Woman at the Tomb" (Rotterdam, Boymans Museum). In his famous "Adoration of the Kings" (Madrid, Prado), Hieronymus Bosch (1450–1516) renders similar structures as Jerusalem, though in a purely Netherlandish landscape. Italian

Renaissance artists depicted Jerusalem either as a local

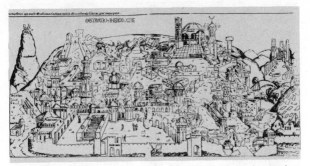

"Destruccio Iherosolime," a colored woodcut of the destruction of the Holy City by Hartmann Schedel, 1492. Haifa, Maritime Museum. Photo Sadeh, Haifa.

Colored woodcut of the Holy City in a work by Sebastian Muenster, Basle, 1544. Haifa, Maritime Museum.

Italian city, like Piero della Francesca in his fresco "The Story of the True Cross," c. 1455, in the Church of San Francesco in Arezzo, or with the symbolic round building of the Holy Sepulcher. This may be seen in "Christ Entering Jerusalem" in Duccio's "Maestà" altarpiece in the Duomo of Siena, 1308–11, and Perugino's fresco "The Delivery of the Keys," 1482, in the Sistine Chapel in the Vatican.

Even when more modern pilgrims painted Jerusalem on the spot (David Roberts in 1839, Edward Lear in 1858), 337

The Holy City, detail from the central panel of the Lochurst Altarpiece by the Flemish artist, Jan van Scorel, 1520. Utrecht, Central Museum.

Jerusalem, a detail from "The Adoration of the Magi" by Hieronymus Bosch (1450–1516). Madrid, Prado Museum.

The city of Jerusalem in a detail from the fresco, "The Story of the True Cross," by Piero della Francesca in the Church of San Francesco in Arezzo, c. 1455. Photo Alinari, Florence.

A Renaissance representation of the Temple of Jerusalem in the fresco, "The Delivery of the Keys," by Perugino, 1480–82. Rome, Sistine Chapel. Photo Alinari, Florence.

Christ entering Jerusalem, detail of Duccio's "Maestà" altar-
340 piece in the Duomo of Siena, 1308–11. Photo Alinari, Florence.

Jerusalem from the Mount of Olives, pen and watercolor
painting by Edward Lear, 1858. Jerusalem, Israel Museum.
Photo Zev Radovan, Jerusalem.

the domes and minarets of the city dominated the view
and gave it an ethereal and spiritual air.

In Jewish folk art of the 16th century, the domed
building of the Dome of the Rock dominates the
pictures and symbols of Jerusalem. Several "printers'
marks" from Venice and Prague (1551) depict the
Dome with the identification: *"Beit ha-Mikdash"* (The
Temple). The eschatological Jerusalem that the Messiah
is entering in the *Mantua Haggadah* of 1561, is represented
by a single domed building. In the same scene in the *Venice
Haggadah* of 1665, the domed building appears within
a walled city. In the imagination of the 17th century, a
new type of condensed picture of Jerusalem evolved in
Jewish folk art. To the right of the Dome of the Rock as
the Temple there now appears another dome, that
of the El-Aqṣa mosque, called "Midrash Shelomo" (i.e.,
Solomon's School). Between them is the elongated basilica
structure of the mosque, as in a *ketubbah* from Casale
Monferrato of 1671, or sometimes the Western ("Wailing") Wall. This last representation became most popular
in Jewish art of the 18th–20th centuries in *ketubbot,* Esther 341

A 17th-century Jewish folk art portrayal of Jerusalem. Detail of a *ketubbah* from Casale Monferrato, Italy, 1671. Jerusalem, J.N.U.L.

Itinerary of the holy sites of Ereẓ Israel, with Jerusalem in the center. The Temple and the "Midrash Shelomo," on the left and right of the cypress trees respectively, are fronted by the Western Wall. Lithograph by S. Litmanowitz, Turek, Poland, 1875, after a drawing by Rabbi Ḥayyim Solomon Pinie of Safed. Haifa, Maritime Museum.

Stylized Western Wall topped by cypresses on the reversed
seal of the Yeshivat Eẓ Ḥayyim in Jerusalem. Early 20th century.
Tel Aviv, Einhorn Collection. Photo David Harris, Jerusalem.

Painting of Jerusalem on the wooden walls of a collapsible
sukkah from Fischach, Germany, early 19th century.

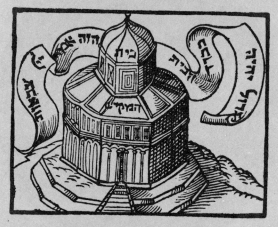

עֹל יְדֵי הָעוֹשֶׂה מְלָאכָה נְאֻם שְׁמוּאֵל בִּר רְאוּבֵן זִ״ל ׃

וְעֵצִי הַנִּקְרָא שְׁמוּאֵל דְּרֶעקְסֶלֶר ׃

A representation of the Dome of the Rock as the Temple used by the sons of Mordecai b. Gershon ha-Kohen as the motif of their printers' mark. From the colophon to Jonah b. Abraham Gerondi's *Iggeret ha-Teshuvah,* Prague, 1595. Jerusalem, J.N.U.L.

scrolls, maps of the Holy Land—either painted, printed, or embroidered, on seals, *Mizraḥ* tablets, and even in a painted 19th-century *sukkah* from Fischach. The cypress trees painted behind the "Wailing Wall" may be an allusion to Ps. 92:13–14.

Many modern artists have also painted Jerusalem. The most favored view is that from the Mount of Olives, from where the Old City blends with the New, and the main features are clearly seen. It is impossible to enumerate the Israel and foreign artists who have managed to capture the beauty and atmosphere of the city.

3   IN MUSIC

In the world of music, as in literature, there is a vast and varied body of material inspired by the theme of Jerusalem. Theoretically, the "songs of Jerusalem" include the innumerable settings of the countless biblical verses, prayers, hymns, and poems in which Jerusalem or Zion are mentioned—in art and folk music, and in Jewish and Christian culture. Such a list would also have to include the Passion compositions (since their scene is Jerusalem) and works about the Crusades (including the many compositions based on Tasso's *Jerusalem Delivered*). Until the end of the 19th century, many oratorios, operas, choral works, art songs, and symphonic works dealt with the two destructions of Jerusalem by Nebuchadnezzar and Titus (the correlation with historical events is difficult to establish in most cases). However, several English and U.S. composers have turned to the "Heavenly City" subject, stimulated by the enormous success of Ewing's hymn, "Jerusalem the Golden" (see below), and also perhaps by the medieval revival. Among notable works are Ralph Vaughan Williams' oratorio, *Sancta Civitas* (1892), based on the Apocalypse, and Horatio W. Parker's *Hora novissima* (1892), based on the Latin prototype of the hymn. Works by modern Jewish composers include Lazare Saminsky's *City of Solomon and Christ* (1932), for mixed chorus and orchestra, and Darius Milhaud's *Les deux Cités* (1937), a cantata for augmented children's chorus with text by Paul Claudel (comprising "Babylone," "Élégie," and "Jérusalem").

Israel works written before 1967 dealt with certain aspects of Jerusalem, but after the Six-Day War, there was an intense preoccupation with the subject, both spontaneously and by commission. Recha Freier organized the *Testimonium Jerusalem,* which commissioned composers in Israel and overseas to write works on the history of Jerusalem, which were played at special performances in Jerusalem. Other works composed in the years since 1967 include *Jerusalem Eternal,* a cantata by Haim Alexander; *Tyre and Jerusalem,* a ballet (based on the play by Mattityahu Shoham) by Ben-Zion Orgad; and *Jerusalem,* a symphony for mixed chorus, brass, and strings by Mordechai Seter.

Among the few Protestant chorales which apostrophize Jerusalem directly, the most famous is Melchior Franck's *Jerusalem, du hochgebaute Stadt* (first published 1663), of which there have been many English translations (e.g., *Jerusalem, thou city built on high*). The vision of the Apocalypse appears in a number of Latin hymns paraphrased again and again in the 19th century (J. Julian, *A Dictionary of Hymnology* (1892), s.v. *Coelestis O Jerusalem, Coelestis urbs Jerusalem, Urbs beata Jerusalem*). Outstanding among these was Alexander Ewing's music to John Mason Neale's text, "Jerusalem the Golden," which "conquered the world" after its publication in *Hymns Ancient and Modern* (1861). It derives from the section of Bernard of Cluny's *De contemptu mundi (Hora novissima)* beginning *Urbs Sion aurea/patria lactea/cive decora* (see Julian, op. cit., s.v. Neale) and the melody is in typical 19th-century hymn style; but the beautiful opening phrase C/DCFE/D-C goes back to the German Protestant chorale setting of *Nun ruhen alle Waelder.*

IN JEWISH FOLK SONG TRADITION. The following are some of the best-known Jewish folk songs on Jerusalem: (a) Sephardi: *"De frutas sabrosas"* (M. Athias, *Romancero Sephardi* (1961²), nos. 132, 133); *"Ir me quiero, madre, a Jerusalem"* (*ibid.,* no. 131), the latter often sung by families when saying farewell to a relative bound on a journey to the Holy Land. (b) Kurdistan Jews: *"Ha-Shem vi-Yrushalayim,"* for Shabbat *Naḥamu;* Aramaic, in the form of a dialogue between God and Jerusalem (Y. Y. Rivlin, *Shirat Yehudei ha-Targum,* 1959). (c) Eastern Ashkenazi: *"In der Shtot Yerusholayim,"* and *Zingt-zhe alle Yidelach* (Idelsohn, Melodien, 9 (1932), nos. 219, 225); *"Yerusholayim slavny gorod,"* with Russian words (*ibid.,* no. 438; the prototype for the later Hebrew *"Yerushalayim Ir ha-Kodesh,"* see below). (d) Yemenite: *"Kiryah Yefehfiyyah,"* poem by Shalom Shabbazi. The melody, already notated by A. Z. Idelsohn in his *Sefer ha-Shirim* (1911), became a Hebrew folk song, and was made famous in the interpretation of Berachah Zefirah.

Most of the Jerusalem songs in the Diaspora are lyrical and yearning in their texts and melodies, though some of the Eastern Ashkenazi tunes are more vigorous. Not all the Hebrew songs which mention Jerusalem are "Jerusalem Songs." Even in "Ha-Tikvah," the city symbolizes the whole of Erez Israel—the refrain ends, in the old version: *lashuv le-erez avoteinu/Ir bah David hanah* ("to return to the land of our fathers/the city where David abode") and in the new version: *lihyot am hofshi be-arzenu/erez Ziyyon vi-Yrushalayim* ("to be a free people in our land/ the land of Zion and Jerusalem"). Of the songs directly connected with the city, the following are the most important: (1) J. Engel and A. Hameiri, *Hoi, hoi, hoi, Na'alayim,* the climax of which is: *Halutz, beneh, beneh Yerushalayim* ("O pioneer, build Jerusalem!"); poem written by Hameiri in 1922 when the Gedud ha-Avodah was working on the road to Jerusalem; setting by Engel for the Ohel choir (1926). (2) Adapted tune of *Yerushalayim slavny gorod* (see above: Emanuel ha-Russi: *Yerushalayim Ir-ha-Kodesh* (1925). (3) M. Rapoport and A. Hameiri, *"Me-al pisgat Har ha-Zofim"* ("From the Summit of Mount Scopus," 1930), melody based on an Eastern Ashkenazi prototype. Rapoport later wrote another setting, but this was not as popular as the first. (4) S. Ferszko and H. Guri, *"Bab-el-Wad"* (1949), mourning the Jewish fighters who died during Israel's War of Independence at the "Gate of the Valley" (*Sha'ar ha-Gai,* Arabic Bab- 347 el-Wad; where the road to Jerusalem enters the mountains). (5) E. Amiran and R. Saporta, *"Mi va-rekhev, mi va-regel"* ("Some come by car and on foot") ... *Na'-aleh-na li-Yrushalayim* (1950); children's song for Independence Day, still in popular use for the Three-Day March to Jerusalem. (6) Y. Ne'eman's setting of Judah Halevi, *"Yefeh Nof Mesos Tevel"* an "orientalizing" melody, written for the Israel Song Festival. (7) N. Shemer (words and music), *"Yerushalayim shel Zahav,"* written for the 1967 Israel Song Festival; which achieved wide popularity partly because it appeared on the eve of the Six-Day War. Other Jerusalem songs written during and after the Six-Day War did not achieve the same impact.

Some Israel "Bible-verse" songs may also be considered "Jerusalem songs," e.g., Amiran's *"Al Homotayikh Yerushalayim"* (Isa. 62:6), written during the 1948 siege, *"Ki mi-Ziyyon Teze Torah"* (Isa. 2:3; c. 1942), and *"Halleluyah Kumu ve-Na'aleh Ziyyon"* and *"Uru Ahim ve-Na'-aleh Har Ziyyon"* based on Psalms (1933–36; for the Offering of the First Fruits); Y. Zarai's *"Va-Yiven Uzziyyahu"* (II Chron. 26:9; c. 1956); N. C. Melamed's *"Ve-Tehezenah Einenu"* (c. 1950); M. Ze'ira's *"Ashrei ha-Ish Yissa et Alumav/ Be-Ma'aleh Harei Ziyyon"* (c. 1942) and *"Lekhu ve-Nivneh et Homot Yerushalayim"* (Neh. 2:17/4:15); and M. Wilensky's *"Uri Ziyyon, hoi Uri, Livshi Uzzekh"* (Isa. 52:1–2).

GLOSSARY

Aggadah, name given to those sections of Talmud and Midrash containing homiletic expositions of the Bible, stories, legends, folklore, anecdotes, or maxims. In contradistinction to *halakhah.*

Akedah (lit. "binding"), the Pentateuchal narrative (Gen. 22:1–19) describing God's command to Abraham to offer Isaac as a sacrifice.

A.H., After Hijra (the Islamic era which dates from the beginning of the Arab year in which Muhammad's hijra, or emigration from Mecca to Medina took place; i.e., 622 C.E.).

Aliyah, (1) immigration to Erez Israel; (2) one of the waves of immigration to Erez Israel from the early 1880s.

Am ha-Arez, originally the masses of the people; then the common people who did not observe rabbinic law rigidly; later it meant "boorish", "ignorant."

Amidah, main prayer recited at all services; also known as *Shemoneh Esreh* and *Tefillah.*

Amora (pl. **amoraim**), title given to the Jewish scholars in Erez Israel and Babylonia in the third to sixth centuries who were responsible for the *Gemara.*

Ashkenazi (pl. **Ashkenazim**), German or West-, Central-, or East-European Jew(s), as contrasted with Sephardi(m).

Av, first month of the Jewish religious year, eleventh of the civil, approximating to July-August.

Av bet din, vice-president of the supreme court *(bet din ha-gadol)* in Jerusalem during the Second Temple period; later, title given to communal rabbis as heads of the religious courts (see *bet din*).

Baraita (pl. **beraitot**), statement of *tanna* not found in Mishnah.

Battei midrash, pl. of **Bet ha-Midrash.**

Betar, activist Zionist youth movement founded in 1923 and affiliated to the Revisionists (later to Herut).

Bet din (pl. **battei din**), rabbinic court of law.

Bet ha-midrash, school for higher rabbinic learning; often attached to or serving as a synagogue.

Capitulations, treaties signed between the Ottoman sultans and the Christian states of Europe concerning the extraterritorial rights which the subjects of one of the signatories would enjoy while staying in the state of another.

Dayyan, member of rabbinic court.

Diaspora, Jews living in the "dispersion" outside Erez Israel; area of Jewish settlement outside Erez Israel.

Erez Israel, Land of Israel; Palestine.

Etrog, citron; one of the "four species" used on Sukkot together with the *lulav, hadas,* and *aravah.*

Gaḥal, Israel party established in 1965 by two opposition parties, Ḥerut and the Liberal Party.

Gaon (pl. **geonim**), head of academy in post-talmudic period, especially in Babylonia.

Gedud ha-Avodah, first countrywide commune of Jewish workers in Palestine founded in 1920.

Gemara, traditions, discussions, and rulings of the *amoraim,* commenting on and supplementing the Mishnah, and forming part of the Babylonian and Palestinian Talmuds (see Talmud).

General Zionists, Zionist party, whose members did not join the first Zionist political parties, and who especially advocated private enterprise.

Genizah, depository for sacred books. The best known was discovered in the synagogue of Fostat (old Cairo).

Ḥabad, initials of *ḥokhmah, binah, da'at*: "wisdom, understanding, knowledge"; ḥasidic movement founded in White Russia by Shneur Zalman of Lyady.

Haganah, clandestine Jewish organization for armed self-defense in Erez Israel under the British Mandate, which eventually evolved into a people's militia and became the basis for the Israel army.

Haggadah, ritual recited in the home on Passover eve at *seder* table.

Ḥakham, title of rabbi of Sephardi congregation.

Ḥakham bashi, title in the 15th century and modern times of the chief rabbi in the Ottoman Empire, residing in Constantinople (Istanbul), also applied to principal rabbis in provincial towns.

Halakhah (pl. **halakhot**), an accepted decision in rabbinic law. Also refers to those parts of the Talmud concerned with legal matters. In contradistinction to *aggadah.*

Ḥalukkah, system of financing the maintenance of Jewish communities in the holy cities of Erez Israel by collections made abroad, mainly in the pre-Zionist era (see *kolel*).

Ḥalutz (pl. ḥalutzim), pioneer, especially in agriculture, in Erez Israel.

Ḥanukkah, eight-day celebration commemorating the victory of Judah Maccabee over the Syrian king Antiochus Epiphanes and the subsequent rededication of the Temple.

Ḥasid, adherent of Ḥasidism.

Ḥasidism, (1) religious revivalist movement of popular mysticism among Jews of Western Germany in the Middle Ages; (2) religious movement founded by Israel ben Eliezer Ba'al Shem Tov in the first half of the 18th century.

Haskalah, "Enlightenment"; movement for spreading modern European culture among Jews c. 1750–1880. An adherent was termed *maskil*.

Ḥaver, title given to scholar; group of pietists in Talmudic times; now "comrade".

Ḥazzan, precentor who intones the liturgy and leads the prayers in synagogue; in earlier times a synagogue official.

Ḥeder (lit. "room"), school for teaching children Jewish religious observance.

Heikhalot, "palaces"; tradition in Jewish mysticism centering on mystical journeys through the heavenly spheres and palaces to the Divine Chariot.

Ḥerut, movement and party in Erez Israel established 1948 as political successor to Irgun Zevai Leummi.

Ḥibbat Zion, see Ḥovevei Zion.

Histadrut (abbr. for Heb. Ha-Histadrut ha-Kelalit shel ha-Ovedim ha-Ivriyyim be-Erez Israel), Erez Israel Jewish Labor Federation, founded in 1920; subsequently renamed Histadrut ha-Ovedim be-Erez Israel.

Hoshana Rabba, the seventh day of Sukkot on which special observances are held.

Ḥovevei Zion, federation of Ḥibbat Zion, early (pre-Herzl) Zionist movement in Russia.

I.Z.L. (initials of Heb. **Irgun Zevai Le'ummi;** "National Military Organization"), underground Jewish organization in Erez Israel founded in 1931, which engaged from 1937 in retaliatory acts against Arab attacks and later against the British mandatory authorities.

Jihad (Ar.), in Muslim religious law, holy war waged against infidels.

Kabbalah, the Jewish mystical tradition.

Kabbalist, student of Kabbalah.

Karaite, member of a Jewish sect originating in the eighth century which rejected rabbinic (Rabbanite) Judaism and accepted only Scripture as authoritative.

Kavvanah, "intention"; term denoting the spiritual concentration accompanying prayer and the performance of ritual or of a commandment.

Keneset Yisrael, comprehensive communal organization of the Jews in Palestine during the British Mandate.

Keren Hayesod, the financial arm of the World Zionist Organization founded 1920.

Kibbutz (pl. **kibbutzim**), larger-size commune constituting a settlement in Erez Israel based mainly on agriculture but engaging also in industry.

Kinah (pl. **kinot**), dirge(s) for the Ninth of Av and other fast days.

Knesset, parliament of the State of Israel.

Kolel, (1) community in Erez Israel of persons from a particular country or locality, often supported by their fellow country-men in the Diaspora; (2) institution for higher Torah study.

Lehi (abbr. for Heb. **Lohamei Herut Israel,** "Fighters for the Freedom of Israel," also L.H.Y.), radically anti-British armed underground organization in Palestine, founded in 1940 by dissidents from I.Z.L.

Lulav, palm branch; one of the "four species" used on Sukkot together with the *etrog, hadas,* and *aravah.*

Mahzor (pl. **mahzorim**), festival prayer book.

Mapai, Labor Party, founded in 1930 by the union of Ahdut ha-Avodah and Ha-Po'el ha-Zair.

Maskil (pl. **maskilim**), adherent of Haskalah ("Enlightenment") movement.

Menorah, candelabrum; seven-branched oil lamp used in the Tabernacle and Temple.

Midrash, method of interpreting Scripture to elucidate legal points (*Midrash Halakhah*) or to bring out lessons by stories or homiletics (*Midrash Aggadah*). Also the name for a collection of such rabbinic interpretations.

Minhah, afternoon prayer; originally meal offering in Temple.

Minyan, group of ten male adult Jews, the minimum required for communal prayer.

Mishnah, earliest codification of Jewish Oral Law.

Mishneh Torah, halakhic work by Maimonides.

352 **Mitzvah,** biblical or rabbinic injunction; applied also to good or

charitable deeds.

Mizrachi, religious Zionist party founded in 1902 as a religious faction in the World Zionist Organization; later a political party in Israel.

Mughrebim, people originating from North Africa.

Musaf, additional service on Sabbath and festivals; originally the additional sacrifice offered in the Temple.

Mustarab, Arab-speaking, old-established Jewish communities and residents in the Middle East.

Nagid (pl. **negidim**), title applied in Muslim (and some Christian) countries in the Middle Ages to a leader recognized by the state as head of the Jewish community.

Nasi (pl. **nesi'im**), talmudic term for president of the Sanhedrin, who was also the spiritual head and, later, political representative of the Jewish people; from second century a descendant of Hillel recognized by the Roman authorities as patriarch of the Jews.

Ne'ilah, concluding service on the Day of Atonement.

Ophel, rocky protuberance north of the city of David in Jerusalem. In modern times, the name Ophel has been extended to the whole eastern hill of Old Jerusalem.

Parnas, chief synagogue functionary, originally vested with both religious and administrative functions; subsequently an elected lay leader.

Partition plan(s), proposals for dividing Erez Israel into autonomous areas.

Paytan, composer of *piyyut* (liturgical poetry).

Perushim, disciples of Elijah ben Solomon Zalman (the Gaon of Vilna), who arrived in Erez Israel during the second half of the 18th century.

Perutah, coin of minimal value.

Piyyut (pl. **piyyutim**), Hebrew liturgical poetry.

Posek (pl. **posekim**), decisor; codifier or rabbinic scholar who pronounces decisions in disputes and on questions of Jewish law.

Progressive Party, political party of the center, established 1948. Later the Independent Liberal Party.

Rabbanite, adherent of rabbinic Judaism. In contradistinction to Karaite.

Rafi, political party founded in 1965 as a result of a split in Mapai; later reunited in framework of Israel Labor Party.

Responsum (pl. **responsa**), written opinion (*teshuvah*) given to   353 question (*she'elah*) on aspects of Jewish law by qualified authorities; pl. collection of such queries and opinions in book form.

Rosh Ha-Shanah, two-day holiday (one day in biblical and early mishnaic times) at the beginning of the month of Tishri (September-October), traditionally the New Year.

Sanhedrin, the assembly of ordained scholars which functioned both as a supreme court and as a legislature before 70 C.E.

Seder, ceremony observed in the Jewish home on the first night of Passover (outside Erez Israel first two nights), when the *Haggadah* is recited.

Sefer Torah, manuscript scroll of the Pentateuch for public reading in synagogue.

Sefirot, the ten, the ten "Numbers": mystical term denoting the ten spheres or emanations through which the Divine manifests itself; elements of the world; dimensions; primordial numbers.

Selihah (pl. **selihot**), penitential prayer.

Semikhah, ordination conferring the title "rabbi" and permission to give decisions in matters of ritual and law.

Sephardi (pl. **Sephardim**), Jew(s) of Spain and Portugal and their descendants, wherever resident, as contrasted with Ashkenazi(m).

Shabbatean, adherent of the pseudo-messiah Shabbetai Zevi (17th century).

Shehitah, ritual slaughtering of animals.

Shekhinah, Divine Presence.

Shema (*Yisrael*; "hear ... (O Israel)," Deut. 6:4), Judaism's confession of faith, proclaiming the absolute unity of God.

Shofar, horn of the ram (or any other ritually clean animal except-ing the cow) sounded for the memorial blowing on Rosh Ha-Shanah, and other occasions.

Silluk, a free verse poem in Hebrew liturgical poetry.

Sitra ahra, "the other side" (of God); left side; the demoniac and satanic powers.

Six-Day War, brief war in June 1967 when Israel reacted to Arab threats and blockade by defeating the Egyptian, Jordanian, and Syrian armies.

Sukkah, booth or tabernacle erected for Sukkot when, for seven days, religious Jews "dwell" or at least eat in the *sukkah* (Lev. 23:42).

Sukkot, festival of Tabernacles; last of the three pilgrim festivals,
beginning on the 15th of Tishri.

Sūra (Ar.), chapter of the Koran.

Takkanah (pl. **takkanot**), regulation supplementing the law of the Torah; regulations governing the internal life of communities and congregations.

Talmud, "teaching"; compendium of discussions on the Mishnah by generations of scholars and jurists in many academies over a period of several centuries. The Jerusalem (or Palestinian) Talmud mainly contained the discussions of the Palestinian sages. The Babylonian Talmud incorporates the parallel discussion in the Babylonian academies.

Talmud torah, term generally applied to Jewish religious (and ultimately to talmudic) study; also to traditional Jewish religious public schools.

Tanna (pl. **tannaim**), rabbinic teacher of mishnaic period.

Tishah be-Av, Ninth of Av, fast day commemorating the destruction of the First and Second Temples.

Torah, Pentateuch or the Pentateuchal scroll for reading in synagogue; entire body of traditional Jewish teaching and literature.

Va'ad ha-Kehilah, community council.

Va'ad Le'ummi, national council of the Jewish community in Ereẓ Israel during the period of the British Mandate.

War of Independence, war of 1947–49 when the Jews of Israel fought off Arab invading armies and ensured the establishment of the new State.

White Paper(s), report(s) issued by British government, frequently statements of policy, as issued in connection with Palestine during the Mandate period.

Yeshivah, Jewish traditional academy devoted primarily to study of the Talmud and rabbinic literature: *rosh yeshivah,* head of the yeshivah.

Yishuv, settlement or popular group; more specifically, the Jewish community of Ereẓ Israel in the pre-State period. The pre-Zionist community is generally designated the "old yishuv" and the community evolving from 1880, the "new yishuv."

ABBREVIATIONS

Ag. Song	*Aggadat Shir ha-Shirim* (Schechter ed., 1896).
Ar.	*Arakhin* (talmudic tractate).
ARN[1]	*Avot de-Rabbi Nathan*, version (1) ed. Schechter, 1887.
Ashtor, Toledot	E. Ashtor (Strauss), *Toledot ha-Yehudim be-Miẓrayim ve-Suryah Taḥat Shilton ha-Mamlukim*, 3 vols. (1944–70).
Avot	*Avot* (talmudic tractate).
I Bar.	I Baruch (Apocrypha).
II Bar.	II Baruch (Pseudepigrapha).
BB	*Bava Batra* (talmudic tractate).
Ber.	*Berakhot* (talmudic tractate).
BJPES	Bulletin of the Jewish Palestine Exploration Society—English name of the Hebrew periodical known as:
	1. *Yedi'ot ha-Ḥevrah ha-Ivrit la-Ḥakirat Ereẓ Yisrael va-Attikoteha* (1933–1954);
	2. *Yedi'ot ha-Ḥevrah la-Ḥakirat Ereẓ Yisrael va-Attikoteha* (1954–1962);
	3. *Yedi'ot ba-Ḥakirat Ereẓ Yisrael va-Attikoteha* (1962 ff.).
BK	*Bava Kamma* (talmudic tractate).
BM	*Bava Meẓia* (talmudic tractate).
I (or II) Chron.	Chronicles, books I and II (Bible).
Dan.	Daniel (Bible).
Deut.	Deuteronomy (Bible).

Dinur, Golah	B. Dinur (Dinaburg), *Yisrael ba-Golah*, 2 vols. in 7 (1959–68) = vols. 5 and 6 of his *Toledot Yisrael*, second series.

Eccles.	Ecclesiastes (Bible).
Eduy.	*Eduyyot* (mishnaic tractate).
EIS	*Encyclopaedia of Islam*, 4 vols. (1913–36).
EM	*Enziklopedyah Mikra'it* (1950 ff.).
Esth.	Esther (Bible).
Ex.	Exodus (Bible).
Ex. R.	*Exodus Rabbah*.
Ezek.	Ezekiel (Bible).
Ezra	Ezra (Bible).

Galling, Reallexikon	K. Galling, *Biblisches Reallexikon* (1937).
Gen.	Genesis (Bible).
Gen. R.	*Genesis Rabbah*.
Git.	*Gittin* (talmudic tractate).

Hab.	Habakkuk (Bible).
Ḥag.	*Ḥagigah* (talmudic tractate).
Haggai	Haggai (Bible).
Hos.	Hosea (Bible).
HTR	*Harvard Theological Review* (1908ff.).
HUCA	*Hebrew Union College Annual* (1904; 1924ff.)

Isa.	Isaiah (Bible).

JAOS	*Journal of the American Oriental Society* (c. 1850ff.).
Jer.	Jeremiah (Bible).
JHSEM	Jewish Historical Society of England, *Miscellanies* (1925 ff.).
Job	Job (Bible).
Joel	Joel (Bible).
Josh.	Joshua (Bible).
JQR	*Jewish Quarterly Review* (1889 ff.).
Judg.	Judges (Bible).

Ket.	*Ketubbot* (talmudic tractate).
Kid.	*Kiddushin* (talmudic tractate).
LA	Studium Biblicum Franciscanum, *Liber Annuus* (1951 ff.).
Lam.	Lamentations (Bible).
Lam. R.	*Lamentations Rabbah.*
Lev.	Leviticus (Bible).
Ma'as.	*Ma'aserot* (talmudic tractate).
Mal.	Malachi (Bible).
Meg.	*Megillah* (talmudic tractate).
Mid. Ps.	*Midrash Tehillim* (Eng. tr. *The Midrash on Psalms* (JPS, 1959)).
MK	*Mo'ed Katan* (talmudic tractate).
Nah.	Nahum (Bible).
Naz.	*Nazir* (talmudic tractate).
Ned.	*Nedarim* (talmudic tractate).
Neg.	*Nega'im* (mishnaic tractate).
Neh.	Nehemiah (Bible).
Num.	Numbers (Bible).
Obad.	Obadiah (Bible).
PdRE	*Pirkei de-R. Eliezer* (Eng. tr. 1916, 1965²).
PdRK	*Pesikta de-Rav Kahana.*
PEFQS	*Palestine Exploration Fund Quarterly Statement* (1869–1937; since 1938—PEQ).
PEQ	*Palestine Exploration Quarterly* (until 1937 PEFQS; after 1927 includes BBSAJ).
Pes.	*Pesaḥim* (talmudic tractate).
PJB	*Palaestinajahrbuch des deutschen evangelischen Institutes fuer Altertumswissenschaft,* Jerusalem (1905–1933).
PR	*Pesikta Rabbati.*
Prawer, Ẓalbanim	J. Prawer, *Toledot Mamlekhet ha-Ẓalbanim be-Ereẓ Yisrael,* 2 vols. (1963).

Press, Ereẓ	I. Press, *Ereẓ-Yisrael, Enẓiklopedyah Topografit-Historit*, 4 vols. (1951–55).
Prov.	Proverbs (Bible).
Ps.	Psalms (Bible).
QDAP	*Quarterly of the Department of Antiquities in Palestine* (1932 ff.).
RB	*Revue biblique* (1892 ff.).
REJ	*Revue des études juives* (1880 ff.).
Ruth	Ruth (Bible).
I and II Sam.	Samuel, books I and II (Bible).
Sanh.	*Sanhedrin* (talmudic tractate).
Sem.	*Semaḥot* (post-talmudic tractate).
Shevu.	*Shevu'ot* (talmudic tractate).
Sif. Num.	*Sifrei Numbers*.
Sof.	*Soferim* (post-talmudic tractate).
Song	Song of Songs (Bible).
Song R.	*Song of Songs Rabbah*.
Sot.	*Sotah* (talmudic tractate).
Suk.	*Sukkah* (talmudic tractate).
Ta'an.	*Ta'anit* (talmudic tractate).
Tanḥ.	*Tanḥuma*.
Tanḥ. B.	*Tanḥuma*, Buber ed. (1885).
TB	Babylonian Talmud or Talmud Bavli.
TJ	Jerusalem Talmud or Talmud Yerushalmi.
Tosef.	Tosefta.
Wars	Josephus, *The Jewish Wars*.
Yad	Maimonides, *Mishneh Torah (Yad Ḥazakah)*
Yal. Mak.	*Yalkut Makhiri*.
Yoma	*Yoma* (talmudic tractate).
Zech.	Zechariah (Bible).
Zeph.	Zephaniah (Bible).

BIBLIOGRAPHY

GENERAL BIBLIOGRAPHY: M. Avi-Yonah (ed.), *Sefer Yerushalayim* (1956), incl. bibl.; idem, *Jerusalem* (1960); S. W. Baron, in: *Jerusalem. City Holy and Eternal* (1954), 11–32; M. Join-Lambert, *Jerusalem* (1958); Israel Exploration Society, *Yehudah vi-Yrushalayim* (1957); idem, *Jerusalem through the Ages* (Eng. and Heb., 1968); I. S. Horowitz, *Yerushalayim be-Sifrutenu* (1964); C. Thubron, *Jerusalem* (1969); F. Maraini, *Jerusalem. Rock of Ages* (1969); M. Harel, *Zot Yerushalayim* (1969); Z. Vilnay, *Yerushalayim,* 2 vols. (1967–69³), incl. bibl.; new ed., 1 (1970). GEOGRAPHY: L. H. Vincent, *Les Noms de Jérusalem* (1911); H. Kendall, *Jerusalem—the City Plan* (1948); *Jerusalem—the Saga of the Holy City* (1954); J. Scofield, in: *National Geographic Magazine,* 115 (1959), 492–531; E. Orni and E. Efrat, *Geography of Israel* (1971³); J. Dash and E. Efrat, *The Israel Physical Master Plan* (1964); D. Ashbel, *Ha-Aklim ha-Menonar shel Yerushalayim* (1965), with Eng. summary; E. Efrat, *Yerushalayim ve-ha-Perozedor* (1967). BIBLICAL PERIOD: G. A. Smith, *Jerusalem ... from the earliest times to A. D. 70,* 2 vols. (1907–08); Galling, Reallexikon, 297ff.; L. Mayer and M. Avi-Yonah, in: QDAP, 1 (1932), 163ff.; J. J. Simons, *Jerusalem in the Old Testament* (1952); L. H. Vincent, *Jérusalem de l'Ancien Testament,* 3 vols. in 2 (1954–56); M. Avi-Yonah, in: IEJ, 4 (1954), 239ff.; idem, in: *Erez Yisrael,* 9 (1969), 175ff.; B. Mazar, *ibid.,* 161ff.; EM, 3 (1965), 793–837, incl. bibl.; D. R. Ap-Thomas, in: D. Winston Thomas (ed.), *Archaeology and Old Testament Study* (1967), 277–95; S. Abramsky, *Yerushalayim bi-Ymei ha-Mikra* (1968); *Kadmoniyyot,* 1–2 (1968). SECOND TEMPLE: E. Bevan, *Jerusalem under the High-Priests* (1904; repr. 1948); S. Safrai, *Ha-Aliyyah le-Regel bi-Ymei Bayit Sheni* (1965); S. Abramsky, *Yerushalayim bi-Ymei Bayit Sheni* (1968); J. Jeremias, *Jerusalem in the time of Jesus* (1969); H. H. Ben-Sasson (ed.), *Toledot Am Yisrael,* 1 (1969), index (also incl. bibl.). ROMAN AND BYZANTINE PERIODS: C. W. Wilson, in: PEFQS, 37 (1905), 138–44; R. Harris, in: HTR, 19 (1926),

199–206; C. Kuhl in: PJB, 24 (1928), 113–40; idem and W. Meinhold, *ibid.*, 25 (1929), 95–124; A. Alt, *ibid.*, 124–6; S. Krauss, in: BJPES, 4 (1936), 52–60; E. L. Sukenik, in: JQR, 38 (1947), 157ff.; R. W. Hamilton, in: PEQ, 84 (1952), 83–90; J. Meyshan, *ibid.*, 90 (1958), 19–26; idem, in: IEJ, 9 (1959), 262–3; L. Kadman, *Coins of Aelia Capitolina* (1956); A. Spijkerman, in: LA, 7 (1957), 145–64; R. Beauvery, in: RB, 64 (1957), 72–101. ARAB PERIOD:M. Assaf, *Toledot ha-Shilton ha-Aravi be-Erez Yisrael* (1935); I. Lichtenstadter, in: HJ, 5 (1943), 39–45; J. Prawer, in: *Zion*, 12 (1947), 136–48; S. D. Goitein, *Mediterranean Society*, 1 (1967), index; idem, in: JAOS, 70 (1950), 104–8; idem, in: *Melilah*, 3 (1950), 156–65, idem, in: *Yerushalayim*, 4 (1953), 82–103. CRUSADES: S. Runciman, *History of the Crusades*, 2 (1952; repr. 1965), incl. bibl.; Prawer, Zalbanim, 1 (1963), 134–48, 549–61; 2 (1963), 386–405 and index (incl. bibl.); idem, *Mamlekhet Yerushalayim ha-Zalbanit* (1947); idem, in: *Zion*, 11 (1946), 38–82; S. D. Goitein, *ibid.*, 17 (1952), 47–129; Dinur, Golah, 2 pt. 1 (1965²), 1–127, 398–551; M. Benvenisti, *The Crusaders in the Holy Land* (1970), index. MAMLUK AND OTTOMAN PERIODS: Ben-Zvi, Erez Yisrael, index; idem, *She'ar Yashuv* (1965²), index; B. Lewis, *Notes and Documents from the Turkish Archives* (1952), index; D. Tamar, *Mehkarim be-Toledot ha-Yehudim be-Erez Yisrael u-ve-Italyah* (1970), index; Ashtor, Toledot, 3 (1970), index; idem, in: *Yerushalayim*, 5 (1955), 71–116; J. Prawer, *ibid.* 1 (1948), 139–59; C. Roth, in: JHSEM, 2 (1935), 99–104; M. Benayahu, in HUCA, 21 (1948), 1–28 (Heb. section); J. W. Hirschberg, in: IEJ, 2 (1952), 237–48. MODERN PERIOD TO 1948; THE NEW CITY: J. Finn, *Stirring Times*, 2 vols. (1878); Pro-Jerusalem Society, *Jerusalem 1918–20* (1921); *Jerusalem 1920–22* (1924), ed. by C.R. Ashbee; A. M. Hyamson (ed.), *The British Consulate in Jerusalem*, 2 vols. (1939–41); J. Rivlin, *Reshit ha-Yishuv mi-Huz le-Homat Yerushalayim* (1939); P. Grajewsky, *Toledot Battei ha-Defus ha-Ivrim be . . . Yerushalayim* (1939); A. Furst, *Yerushalayim ha-Hadashah* (1946); I. Shapira, *Yerushalayim mi-Huz la-Homah* (1947); J. Gelles, *Shekhunot bi-Yrushalayim* (1962); H. Luncz, *Avraham Moshe Luncz ve-Doro* (1963); E. Porush, *Zikhronot Rishonim* (1963); B.-Z. Gat, *Ha-Yishuv ha-Yehudi be-Erez Yisrael ba-Shanim 1840–1881* (1963); A. B. Rivlin, *Yerushalayim; Toledot ha-Yishuv ha-Ivri ba-Me'ah ha-19* (1966); Y. Y. Yellin, *Avoteinu* (1966); E. Cohen, *Mi-Zikhronot Ish Yerushalayim* (1967²); B.-Z. Yadler, *Be-Tuv Yerushalayim . . . Zikhronot me-Hayyei Yerushalayim u-Gedoleha ba-Me'ah ha-Aharonah* (1967); M. Eliav, *Ahavat Ziyyon* ve-Anshei Hod (1970), index; E. Samuel, *Lifetime in Jerusalem* (1970); M. Vereté, in: *English Historical Review,* 85 (1970), 316–45. MODERN PERIOD; 1948–1970: I. A. Abbady (ed.), *Jerusalem Economy* (1950); H. Levin, *I Saw the Battle of Jerusalem* (1950); D. Joseph, *The Faithful City, the Siege of Jerusalem 1948* (1960); *Mifkad ha-Ukhlusin ve-ha-Diyyur* (1961); *Mifkad … Mizrah Yerushalayim* (Heb. and Eng., 1968); G. Golani, *Urban Survey of Existing Residential Quarters in Jerusalem* (Eng. and Heb., 1966); B. J. Bell, *Besieged* (1966), 201–43; M. Roman, *Seker Kalkali-Ḥevrati al Yerushalayim ha-Shelemah* (1967); E. Lauterpacht, *Jerusalem and the Holy Places* (1968); R. Westmacott, *Jerusalem; a new era for a capital city* (1968); E. Landau, *Jerusalem the eternal; the paratroopers' battle for the City of David* (1968); M. Tokolovaski, *Shiḥrur Yerushalayim* (1968); M. Natan, *Ha-Mil-ḥamah al Yerushalayim* (1969*). OLD CITY: H. Bar-Deromah, *Yerushalayim, ha-Topografyah shel ha-Ir ha-Attikah* (1935); I. Shapira, *Yerushalayim, ha-Ir ha-Attikah* (1945); M. Avi-Yonah, *Yerushalayim ha-Attikah* (1948); S. H. Steckoll, *Gates of Jerusalem* (1968). WATER SUPPLY: M. Hecker, in: BJPES, 4 (1937), 95–98; 5 (1937), 10–14; 6 (1938), 8–15; Press, Erez, 2 (1948), 430–1; A. Comay, *Goremim ha-Mashpi'im al Bikkush ha-Mayim be-Yisrael* (1969). ARCHAEOLOGY: C. W. Wilson, *Recovery of Jerusalem* (1871); C. Warren, *Underground Jerusalem* (1876); G. Saint Clair, *The Buried City of Jerusalem* (1887); F. J. Bliss, *Excavations at Jerusalem 1894–1897* (1898); L. H. Vincent, *Jérusalem; recherches de topographie, d'archéologie et d'histoire,* 2 vols. (1912–26); Z. Vilnay, *Maẓẓevot Kodesh be-Erez Yisrael* (1963), index; K. M. Kenyon, *Jerusalem; excavating 3000 years of history* (1967), incl. bibl.; *Enẓiklopedyah la-Ḥafirot Arkhe'ologiyyot be-Erez Yisrael,* 1 (1970), 207–42; B. Mazar, in: *Ariel* (Autumn, 1970), 11–19 (Eng.). IN HALAKHAH AND AGGADAH: A. Buechler, in: JQR, 20 (1908), 798–811; idem, in: REJ, 62 (1911), 201–15; 63 (1912), 30–50; S. Krauss, *Kadmoniyyot ha-Talmud,* 1 (1924), 92–113; A. Aptowitzer, in: *Tarbiz,* 2 (1930/31), 266–72; S. Bialoblocki, in: *Alei Ayin, Minḥat Devarim li-Shelomo Zalman Schocken* (1948–52), 25–74; L. Finkelstein, in: *Sefer ha-Yovel … Alexander Marx* (1950), 351–69; B. Dinaburg, in: *Zion,* 16 (1951), 1–17; M. Ha-Kohen, in: *Mahanayim,* 58 (1961), 60–68 (Eng. summary in I. Jakobovits, *Jewish Law Faces Modern Problems* (1965), 128–31); J. Zahavi (ed.), *Midreshei Ẓiyyon vi-Yrushalayim* (1963); D. Noy, in: *Ve-li-Yrushalayim* (1968), 360–94; A. Newman, in: *Jewish Life* (Jan./Feb., 1968), 24–27. IN MODERN HEBREW LITERATURE: S. Ben-

Barukh, *Yerushalayim be-Shiratenu ha-Hadashah* (1955); B. Kurz-weil, *Massot al Sippurei S. Y. Agnon* (1962), 301–10; S. Y. Penueli and A. Ukhmani (eds.), *Anthology of Modern Hebrew Poetry*, 2 vols. (1966); I. Rabinovich, *Major Trends in Modern Hebrew Fiction* (1968); D. Silk (ed.), *Retrievements: A Jerusalem Anthology* (1968); S. Halkin, *Modern Hebrew Literature* (1970²). IN CHRISTIANITY; CHRISTIAN HOLY PLACES: L. H. Vincent and F. M. Abel, *Jerusalem*, 2 (1914–26); F. Cabrol and H. Leclercq, *Dictionnaire d'Archéologie chrétienne et de Liturgie*, 7 (1926), 2304–93; J. W. Crowfoot, *Early Churches in Palestine* (1941); *New Schaff-Herzog Encyclopedia of Religious Knowledge*, 6 (1950), 134–7; S. G. F. Brandon, *The Fall of Jerusalem and the Christian Church* (1951); D. Baldi, *Enchiridion locorum sanctorum* (1955); A. Potthast, *Wegweiser durch die Geschichtswerke des europaeischen Mittelalters*, 2 (1957), 1734; *Lexikon fuer Theologie und Kirche*, 5 (1960), 367, 905–10; E. A. Moore, *Ancient Churches of Old Jerusalem* (1961); D. Attwater, *Christian Churches of the East*, 2 vols. (1961–62); C. Kopp, *Holy Places of the Gospels* (1963); M. Ish-Shalom, *Masei Nozerim le-Erez Yisrael* (1965), index; *New Catholic Encyclopedia*, 7 (1967), 881 ff.; C. Hollis, *Holy Places* (1969); J. Gray, *History of Jerusalem* (1969). IN ISLAM: EIS, s.v. *Al-Kuds;* C. D. Matthews, *Palestine—Mohammedan Holy Land* (1949); J. W. Hirschberg, *Sources of Moslem Traditions Concerning Jerusalem* (1952); A. Guillaume, in: *Al-Andalus*, 18 (1953), 323–36; S. D. Goitein, *Studies in Islamic History and Institutions* (1966), 135–48; idem, in: *Bulletin of the Jewish Palestine Exploration Society*, 12 (1946), 120–6; idem, in: *Minhah li-Yhudah . . . Zlotnick* (1950), 62–66; E. Sivan, in: *Studia Islamica*, 27 (1967), 149–82; H. Busse, in: *Judaism*, 17 (1968), 441–68; M. J. Kister, in: *Le Museon*, 82 (1969), 173–96. IN ART AND MUSIC: L. A. Mayer, *Bibliography of Jewish Art* (1967), index; Y. Cohen, *Yerushalayim be-Shir ve-Hazon* (1938); M. S. Geshuri, *Yerushalayim Ir ha-Musikah mi-Tekufat Bayit Sheni* (1968), includes bibliography.

INDEX